DON'T  BUMP THE RECORD, KID

DON'T BUMP THE RECORD, KID

MY ADVENTURES WITH

MARK AND BRIAN

MARK THOMPSON

Don't Bump the Record, Kid
My Adventures with Mark and Brian

For more information go to:

www.myadventureswithmarkandbrian.com

The events and experiences detailed herein are all true and have been faithfully rendered as remembered by the author to the best of his abilities. If any details are incorrect, they have not been done on purpose or with any ill intent.

Grateful acknowledgement is made for permission to reprint Hose Pipe Memories from *South: What it Means to be Here in Heart or in Spirit* by Wendy Nilsen Pollitzer; published by Lydia Inglett Publishing and Starbook.biz.

All images and photographs courtesy of the author, except where noted.

This work of nonfiction was edited by *Michael Stringer*, the editor and publisher of Fat Dog Books.

Microphone art © iStock.com/Chereliss

Second Print
December 2022

ISBN # 979-8-3522024-7-0

66 Family is not an important thing. It's everything.99

—MICHAEL J. FOX

I didn't appreciate family until I had one of my own. It seems every move I made in my career was steeped in thoughts of how it would affect my family, and I feel good about the fact that I did right by them.

To Lynda, my wife, Matthew, Amy, Katie, my children, Eleni, my daughter-in-law, Bradley, my son-in-law, Milo, Onyx, my grandchildren, Walker, Ludo, and Luna, our dogs, thank you for allowing me to be a part of you. What I did was my job, but who I am is my family and all of you.

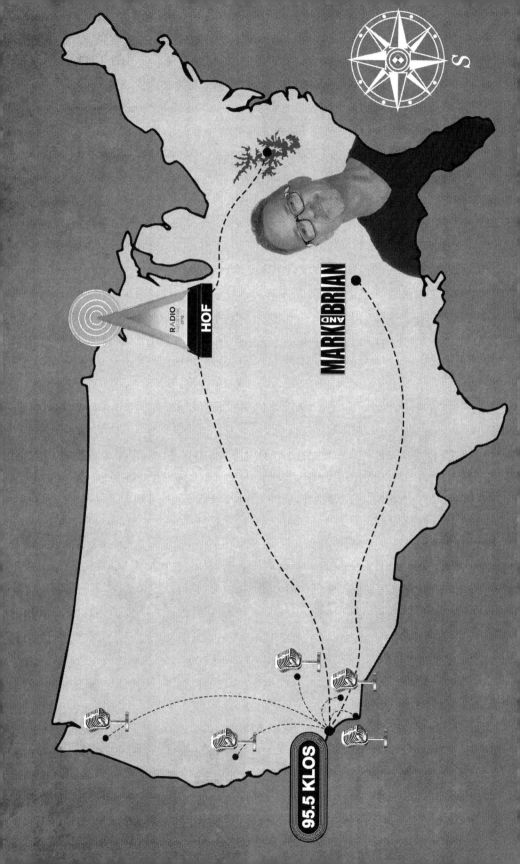

Contents

Contents

Foreword

Hello, dear reader, or listener, should you be one of smart ones who, like me, find actual reading too much of a chore. Especially, when compared to listening to the sweet, country molasses my friend Mark Thompson calls "Hey, man, that's just my voice, OK? Why you gotta . . . " followed by that seemingly involuntary laugh of his which, let's face it, may be his greatest asset. I've no doubt, though I've not been told, that Mark will, in fact, read his own book for this audio version you smarter ones are already enjoying, thanks to me so far. Oh, shit, sorry. I should introduce myself. Unlike your author, or the "feller" reading this to you right now, I am a multi-award winning actor, with a level of recognizability the world over that Mark will never know. No, not even from this book. Don't be silly. Jesus.

As I was insisting, and you should know that I chose the words "unlike your author" thoughtfully, because I mean to relay that there are a multitude of plateaus in my career that Mark thought about reaching, hell, maybe even dreamed, but failed to reach. And he failed big. I'm also an international filmmaker; that is to say, I've directed two films previous to writing this writing. One of them debuted at the world-famous Sundance Film Festival—an achievement your author is incapable of, and the second one was mostly shot in another country which, apparently, is all that needs to happen for a feller like me to be referred to as "an international filmmaker." I mention this because it is another career achievement of mine that Mark will never know. Ever. I'm tellin' ya, I don't care how many so-called good years he's got in him, it's not happening. I know this because I've appeared in both the films that he wrote, and while he turned in solid performances in both, any plan or dream he once had of being a multi-award winning actor, or international filmmaker should be taken out back and put down. I'm talkin' two in the back of the coconut. Additionally, because his historical success was in the field of delivery comedy to an audience, I need to point out that unlike myself, the author of this book was not named by Comedy Central as One of The Top 100 Comedians of All Time. Nope. That was me. Not Mark.

What the author of this book *has* accomplished, that I, and 99.999% of the population *never* will is to reign supreme for twenty-five consecutive years on a morning radio program in one of the largest and most gruesomely competitive radio markets in the world. In his chosen profession, he has, comparatively, achieved more success than almost any movie star you can name from any year or decade, because none of them had a twenty-five-year domination like my friend Mark Thompson.

When Mark called me and asked, nay, told me I was writing this foreword, I said of course I would. I knew what he knew, which was that I would not kiss his ass, but rather roast it like a pig on a spit, that is then buried for a bit before being excitedly devoured during a Hawaiian luau. But then I read his book—*this* book. Yeah, as I said, I *read* it, but only because he hadn't recorded the audio version of it yet, and as much as I hated having to read it, I just couldn't put the stupid thing down. He writes like he talks—nay, better than he talks. He writes like he thinks, which is considerably more wonderful because you don't have to listen to him talk. There's an easy, uncensored, unapologetic comfort to his relating portions of his life in this book that made me think, "Damn, man, this is what it must've been like to listen to Will Rogers talk on stage, but without all the actual knowledge, or natural genius." I also thought as I was reading this book, my friend Mark has mostly articulated in a damn hell enjoyable way a life of dreams, disappointments, and near-unparalleled success, all the while maintaining an honesty and perspective that 99.999% of the population will never come remotely close to.

I hated having to read this book. I loved this book. If you don't, lose my number; you're dead to me.

—MULTI-AWARD WINNING, LOVED THE WORLD OVER,
DEAR FRIEND OF THE AUTHOR, KEVIN POLLAK

Preface

❝ Radio is not a job, it's a way of life. You can't really ever leave it. ❞

—ART BELL

Whenever I read a book, I always skip the preface. They're normally filled with shit I don't need to know so I skip to chapter one and start reading. The preface of this book is no different. I spend these first pages telling you about radio as a business. I explain how it used to be when I started my career and how it's changed over these many years into what it is now. If that seems boring to you then please feel free to skip over to chapter one and start your adventure. I won't know that you skipped the preface and if I did know, I wouldn't care; you won't hurt my feelings. But for those of you who enjoy a little context for your reading pleasure, this may be useful to you.

For twenty-seven years, the Mark and Brian radio program entertained millions each morning, a career that was celebrated by our induction into the Radio Hall of Fame in 2020. It should be understood, however, that when we began our show together, radio was vibrant and alive, an extremely competitive medium which fought desperately for your time. Sadly, that's no longer the case.

Over the past few years, you may have noticed a change in your favorite radio station, nothing major, just a bit *off*. In order to explain that change, we need to go back and understand what it once was.

It will also help you understand more fully the exciting world Mark and Brian started in, and how it slowly changed around us during our years of doing the show.

Let's pull one kind of music out of the hat and focus on country music in say, Dallas, Texas in the 1980s. Most U.S. cities have at least two stations that play the same music format. Two country stations were fighting for the biggest number of people who like country music. Both stations combat each other fiercely as they both need *audience* ratings, which makes money; bigger ratings, bigger check. Most radio stations at that time were owned by one person, and that person normally owned only one station. Most stations back then cost more than $50 million each, so the idea of one person owning multiple stations was highly uncommon.

Both these country stations play the same songs, same promotions, same everything, so what sets them apart? The on-air personalities do. Each station was fighting to hire the best ones. How do they get them? They pay that personality more than the other is willing to pay. It is time tested and proven: Great air personalities bring great ratings, and great ratings buy a bigger house.

Back then, it was addictive listening because most all stations were interesting, fighting for your ears, and for the most part, those competitive days are over. Today's radio doesn't need high priced personalities anymore. I'll attempt to give you a layman's explanation as to why, and there's a chance you won't like it.

Somebody must have thought to themselves, "This would be easier and cheaper if I could get rid of my competition." Some would say that's not possible, but it is, because it has already been done, and I can give you the exact day.

February 8, 1996, President Bill Clinton signed the *Telecommunications Act*. The act contained tons of stuff but for this purpose, we are going to focus on two that changed the way local radio is broadcast, and why you may have noticed a difference.

The first major change was that it became legal for any company to buy almost as many radio stations as they desired. There was a limit of sorts, but that limit has been pushed of late, and continues to be challenged. The second major change is the one I believe did the damage you've noticed. It was made legal for any company to go into any city and purchase up to—but not more than—eight radio stations in the same city.

Let's say Businessman Bob goes into Dallas and buys eight radio stations, two classic rock music, two country music, two adult contemporary music, and two top 40 music. Instead of housing all eight stations in eight different buildings, he moves all of them into one large building, a highly cost-effective move.

Bob then decides to keep only one general manager (GM) to handle all eight stations and fires the other seven managers. Bob uses that same formula in all the other departments of his eight stations. Bob then tells the one employee he kept from each department that he is reducing their salary, meaning more work for less money.

Bob has now taken the staff of his eight stations, which guessing, is 800 people, and fired 750 of them, keeping only 50 employees to run all eight stations at a reduced salary. The widely used term in radio for this is "consolidation." I love the fact that it's widespread enough to have a name.

Bob then fires all his air talent with large salaries and keeps only two announcers so they can pre-record radio shows on all eight stations, and Bob only pays them an hourly wage. The air talent who pre-records the shows, on average, makes only $27 for a five-hour air shift.

Bob has essentially consumed his competition by purchasing them, meaning he doesn't need highly paid air talent to attract listeners anymore since he'll get all of them anyway, by default. Bob is now making a profit from all eight stations, he's saving massive amounts on payroll, and his big air talent salaries have been eliminated. Are the eight stations as good as they were before? Of course not, but Bob doesn't care about quality, he cares about cash flow.

But then Bob runs into a problem—his bank loan has come due. In order to buy his eight radio stations, he had to borrow millions of dollars with interest. Bob thought he would be able to make enough profit from his purchases to pay down the loan, but Bob was wrong. So, in order not to default on the loan, Bob sells his eight stations to Businessman Dan. Bob no longer owns any radio stations, but because he sold to Dan, he is able to pay off the loan and secure millions in profit for his efforts.

Businessman Dan now knows Bob's formula works, so he goes out to the top 20 markets in the country and does the exact same thing Bob did in Dallas. Dan now owns 160 radio stations and is a billionaire. With the *Telecommunications Act* in place, there is no stopping Businessman Dan. But then Dan runs into the same problem; his loan has come due, and Dan's loan was hundreds of millions of dollars larger than Bob's loan, and Dan can't pay it. So, Dan is forced to sell to one of the big corporate radio companies that consumes radio stations like you do M&Ms.

Businessman Dan no longer owns any radio stations but is billions of dollars richer, and the big corporate radio company now owns 500 radio stations. Big corporate runs all of them just like Businessman Bob did, on a shoestring budget. Everybody involved got rich, but local radio suffered greatly in the loss of quality and millions of people lost their jobs.

I know it sounds like I'm making this up, but I'm not. This has already happened in places around the country and continues to happen. Does everybody do this? Absolutely not, but the major radio chains became major by doing this kind of thing, or a variation of it, and they're getting bigger by the day.

Not convinced? Then try this: The next time you're driving along and enjoying your local radio, stop by the station and ask to see the DJ. You will be escorted into a small room where you will come face to screen with a computer. That is your DJ. You've been listening to a machine that has been programmed to play the commercials, songs, the latest weather and news, along with a pleasant, pre-recorded voice introducing the next song. That pleasant voice was recorded a month ago for minimum wage, and that same pleasant voice is used on most of the stations that company owns. By the way, that has a name too, it's called "convergence."

Why am I reminded of the *Wizard of Oz*? Dorothy pulls back the curtain and it isn't the great and powerful Oz, or even a person, it's a computer, which plays Lynyrd Skynyrd at a quarter past every hour.

The reason I fell in love with radio has been eliminated. With the exception of a few, radio is no longer hiring local personalities in your town. I can sit here and bitch about this all I want, but I get the reason why. Corporate radio companies have found a cheaper way to produce your local station at a fraction of the cost.

The scenario I've laid before you is not the norm. It hasn't happened everywhere, but it has happened. If your local radio station has live announcers sitting in the booth around the clock, then that's rare. I would be willing to say almost no one is doing that anymore.

I know we still have the Ryan Seacrest's of the world, but that's an example of what I'm talking about. Ryan's voice is heard on more than 200 stations, and it's made to sound like he's sitting right there. That means Ryan's pre-recorded radio show has replaced 200 jobs. There are still live radio personalities in some towns, but that is becoming rarer than you know, and it used to be the norm.

Look, I know I'm the old guy who spews, "I remember when radio was great!" My local radio station was the closest thing to having a friend. It made me feel like I wasn't alone.

I know everything must change, and I like change, but it should be for the better. I have a problem with greed and deception because that's what this feels like.

Just like drug companies are forced to divulge side effects on commercials, I think radio stations should have to tell you that you're listening to a pre-recorded, pre-programmed computer.

Everything I have described is legal, no one is breaking any laws. For people like me who worked tirelessly at our craft, our working world is now over. The phone no longer rings since we are no longer needed. But I feel extremely lucky, I was in it when it was great, and I have no regrets, only gratitude. *Thank you, radio, and I miss you!*

One of the things I enjoyed and hated about writing this memoir is that I did it myself. I talk in a certain way, and if I told you this story, I would tell you in my own way. I wrote every word, typed every word, so I will take all the blame, and of course, any praise that might come my direction.

I wrote this book for people who enjoyed the Mark and Brian program, and for fans of radio in general. You will know what happened on the show, and much of what happened off the show, from my perspective, and how it affected me.

But the main reason I wrote this book is for my stupid kids. They obviously know what I did for a living, but I wanted them to know in detail what I was actually doing each morning they got up and I wasn't there. And it's unfair of me to call them "my stupid kids." Only one of them is stupid.

In closing this preface that you probably didn't read, I want you to be aware that I decided to self-publish because I found out what publishers take as their percentage of the sale and realized there's no possible way I'm doing that! I want every nickel of the net profits from this book to go toward our designated animal rescue nonprofit in southern California and it will, thanks to you and the other ten or twenty people who bought this book. I thank you, and the animals whose lives will be made better by your purchase thank you, too!

" To the dreamers, who follow a path that has no known destination, driven by a reason only they understand. And they do this alone. "

—MARK THOMPSON

DON'T 🎤 BUMP THE RECORD, KID

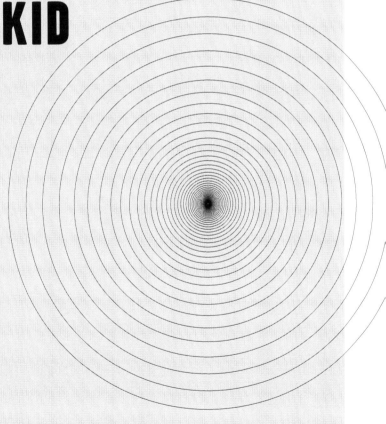

LET'S DO IT

Early 1985

66 One of my favorite things is there is no certainty. I could get a phone call that could change everything, good or bad, I never know. 99

—SAMM LEVINE

In my sixty-plus years of life, there are certain periods that are a blur, but the twenty-seven years I'm going to share with you are not. The events of these years are mostly clear, because this was the sweet spot of my existence. There was everything before them, and whatever after them, but there's no comparison, and it all began with a ringing phone.

How many phone calls in your life changed you? It's one of these monumental phone calls which began the story I'm about to share.

This particular call would become the beginning of a dream I had carried the length of my career. This moment would initiate the first step in taking me on a journey I could never have imagined, and yet there would come a time I would wish I had never picked up the receiver.

The call came one morning in February 1985. It was a call I didn't expect that presented me with a scenario I'd never considered.

I was living in Montgomery, Alabama, doing afternoons at Y-102 FM. In my many years of traveling the radio road, I lived in several beautiful cities, but Montgomery wasn't one of them. It's not that it was bad, it was just there. I remember trees and concrete. The memorable cities I lived in had a distinct beauty; Montgomery could've used a makeover.

I was in year twelve of my radio career, and by now a seasoned radio entertainer. I was #1 in afternoons, so going to the mall on weekends was dicey as teenagers who listened to me were there. Not that it was a Beatles riot, but it was enough of a thing that it made me uncomfortable, so I didn't go.

My first taste of radio fame was three years prior in Birmingham, Alabama, where I did nights at 96 WERC. I was invited to a high school pep rally, and the teacher who invited me took me into the gymnasium and told me to wait beside the rafters until they introduced me. The air was thick and stuffy, and smelled like sweaty socks. The place was packed with students, the football team, and a microphone standing center court.

Some goober stepped up to the mic, "Ladies and gentlemen, from 96 WERC, please welcome Mark Thompson." I started walking out when the roar hit, and it shocked me. I didn't realize they would even know who I was, and I admit, I was a bit uneasy. I don't remember what I said but it was basically, "Yea school." I turned to leave as the wall of screams hit again. Melodramatic as it may sound, I was never the same, but not in the way you might think. It was my first lesson in the frailty of celebrity. It feels good in the moment, but it doesn't last. Pride is something you can hold on to, fame isn't.

In Montgomery, I worked the much higher profile shift of afternoon drive, and I was on a top 40 FM, which all the teenagers listened to. I had reached peak form in my quest to be as good as I could, and without overstating it, I had achieved local celebrity status. The one thing I can say about radio fame is that it's a great training ground for learning to deal with recognizability. People, especially teenagers, need someone to look up to and cheer for. If it's not you, they'll find someone else, so I never really let it factor into who I thought I was. I was always clear about that, fame or not. Celebrity was something I would grow to distrust because fame is fickle.

A dear friend of mine, Mark St. John, and I worked together in Montgomery. He was my program director (PD), and we had known each other for years, and we talked about climbing the ladder of radio together as a team.

One day, Mark told me he had accepted the programming position at I-95 in Birmingham. He said he would get everything in shape there and then bring me in for the morning show. This was exciting since I had a large fan base in Birmingham and I wanted back on a morning show, and I-95 was FM. Music-based AM radio had died in the early 1980s.

St. John called me six months later and told me that he and Bernie Barker, the GM of I-95, were driving down the next day to listen to my show, so plan a hot one. I did exactly that, went to work, did my best possible show, and waited.

The next morning, St. John gave it to me straight, and I quote, "Bernie hated you." One of the things I've always loved about St. John is his honesty, something we have in common, but I got the feeling he enjoyed saying, "Bernie hated you." There was heavy emphasis on the word "hated" that seemed to make him joyful.

I learned early on that radio jobs appear and disappear in seconds. I swiftly removed this Birmingham possibility from my mind. I'm doing great where I am, and I'm okay for now. I had learned to move forward, while firmly believing something good was in my future. That "something good" came in the form of a life changing phone call I got several months later. It was once again from St. John who asked, "Have you ever considered working with a partner?"

Angrily, I shouted, "But your general manager hates me!"

After Bernie shared his distaste for me, St. John hired two guys for their morning show. It was to be called O'Brien and Brian, but O'Brien's wife had gotten cold feet about moving to Birmingham, so he pulled out, leaving only Brian, so it was clear this job was mine if I would take on a partner. St. John ended the call with, "I'll fly Brian down if you want to meet him. Just let me know." The Birmingham job had now changed, but so had I in those past few months. I was not in a good place.

Shortly after the Birmingham gig fell through, I got a call from Roger something, the Program Director of KRBE in Houston, Texas.

He wanted me for their morning show. He flew my wife Lynda and me out for the weekend and showed us around the station, and then took us to lunch at a Mexican restaurant where he and his wife downed three margaritas in the middle of the day. I'd never seen day drinkers before. He offered me the job on the spot at $50,000 a year. I'd never dreamed of making that kind of money, so I jumped at it.

From the time I first got into radio at sixteen, and heard air checks of major market jocks, they sounded so smooth and professional, I decided I wanted to be in major market. Houston is major market, so I had made it, and it took me only twelve years to get there. Losing the Birmingham situation seemed God-sent at this point. I turned in my notice at my apartment and began preparations to become a Texan.

The next week Roger called saying, "Listen, I'm having trouble getting the contract typed up in time, so once you get here, we'll sign it." There is no lawyer anywhere who would agree to that, but I didn't have a lawyer, so I said, "fine." Three days later Roger called again and said, "Listen, I'm having trouble getting the check cut for your move so just put it on your credit card and we'll reimburse you." There's something that happens to a person who wants something so badly that all forms of reason fly out the window, so I said, "Okay."

The following week, Roger called for the third and final time saying, "Listen, Houston locals take a little longer to warm up to a new jock, so how about we start you off at night? The audience can get to know you before we throw you into the morning gig. What do you think?"

All the warning bells were blaring loudly now. It would take an idiot not to see this was falling apart.

"Roger, this is not what you hired me for," I said.

Sometimes, silence can be so quiet that it's actually loud. Roger broke that silence.

"What do you mean?" Roger asked.

"I was hired to do the morning show," I said. "I currently have no contract, I'm paying for my own move, and now I'm doing *nights*. This isn't what I agreed to. I'm pulling out."

"But people have been fired to make room for you!" Roger shouted.

On that, I hung up the phone, and give or take a few minutes to breathe, I cried for two days.

I equated this to a devastating breakup. Your apartment isn't the same, your car drives weird, your clothes don't fit, and your current job can now suck your ass.

Once the tears stopped, I did the one thing that had to be done. I called my apartment complex to tell them I wasn't leaving. "Yes, you are," they told me. "We've already rented your apartment." A small, yet substantial turd had now landed in my pants. So now, we have to move, and we aren't leaving Montgomery.

Darkness became my favorite color. I was considering things like throwing rocks at innocent squirrels, and I was almost certain that I hated everything and everyone. I needed a change and was beginning to think this Birmingham opportunity might be my strongest possibility, but I was shaky about this partner idea. This guy they had in mind had never been on the radio in his life, but I told St. John that I would at least meet with Brian.

On the chosen day, Brian was flown in from Chicago and would meet me that night in a Birmingham hotel just off the freeway. It had been a while since I made the Montgomery to Birmingham drive, and I was thinking it was about an hour, so I made the incredibly bad decision to play a softball game after my show and then drive up.

The drive turned out to be two and a half hours, and I didn't get there until 11:30 p.m. I knocked on Brian's door and he answered, chewing. I figured we were supposed to have dinner, which I clearly missed.

Looking back, it was completely unlike me to be late for anything. Why would I choose to play a softball game knowing what my night entailed? I didn't realize it at the time, but I think I was acting out. I wasn't simply upset that Bernie had passed on me, I was seriously pissed off. But now he wants me if I'll take a partner? What I really wanted was to tell him to go fuck himself, and his job.

No matter my reasons, Brian had nothing to do with any of that, and all I'd done was disrespect him. Just so you know, Brian has never forgotten I was late and will tell you so, but he'll also tell you

I've apologized on multiple occasions. I had gone through a rough patch, but that was no excuse for my bad behavior.

I honestly didn't give much credit to this working. I'm trying to make it to major market, and the idea of taking on a partner who had never worked in radio was puzzling. How could that work? Being back in Birmingham would be a plus, and doing mornings again was a clear step up. I was definitely in need of a change, but this wasn't where I thought I was headed!

When you meet somebody you're considering working with, you notice everything; what's there, and what isn't. We talked in my room, in the two fake leather chairs with the small round table that every room comes with. I think it's funny the hotel brochure refers to this area as the "business center." I prefer to see it as two fake leather chairs with a small round table.

I found Brian to be pleasant, obviously putting his best foot forward but not awkwardly. Some comedians tend to push their humor on people, which can become tedious; Brian didn't do that. I played tapes of my air work and he told me of his comedic background. We spoke about everything that mattered.

I didn't realize how long we'd been talking until the morning sun came peeping through the rubber curtains, which were positioned perfectly next to the "business center." It was full blown morning and we both needed sleep. I came here with serious doubt as to what this meeting might bring, but I liked him. I would be back in Birmingham, back on a morning show, and a wonderful opportunity to tell Bernie to eat my balls. But there was one, singular moment in this meeting that convinced me I was going to do this.

There are two people that I put on the top shelf of comedy, and I don't think anyone will ever join them. One day in 1977, I received an album with a guy on the cover wearing bunny ears, and I soaked my shirt with tears of laughter. It was Steve Martin's *Let's Get Small*. Steve made an indelible impression, as did the next guy.

In the early 1980s I would finish each night smoking pot and watching Tom Snyder's interview show. One night, Tom had been replaced with some variety show, and I was not pleased. The host came out and said, "This being our first show, we did some research to find out what people really want to see on television, and clearly, Americans want to see two pieces of metal being welded together." And for the rest of the show, there was a welder next to him doing just that. It was ridiculous, and I couldn't take my eyes away from it. I was a fan of David Letterman from then on.

Near the end of our late-night chat, I discovered that Brian also held both of those men on the same pedestal, and I knew instantly. I looked at Brian and said words I didn't expect to come out of my mouth prior to this meeting, "This might be fun. Let's do it!"

For the record, I didn't see this situation going any further than the Birmingham gig. I thought it might be fun for a year, and then I would get myself back on track.

RADIO GOLD

1985–1986

66 It was illegal for black people and white people to play checkers together in Birmingham. **99**

—ISABEL WILKERSON

The first Mark and Brian show was set for April 17, 1985, and the wise decision was made that we would arrive in Birmingham early so we could get to know each other. The station owned an apartment, and we stayed there, two men, one bedroom, one bed. Thank the lord baby Jesus there was a couch, so we took turns with the bed.

Lynda was packing up the Montgomery house, preparing for the move. Brian had abandoned his beat-up car back in Chicago and left the keys in the ignition for anyone who might want it. The car, according to him, was in no shape to make the trip, so he drove a rental until he could buy a brand-new car with his new salary.

Birmingham is a good town, but I could be biased. Most of the television stations I watched growing up were out of Birmingham, so it was in my head that Birmingham was "big city." It's the largest city in Alabama, so it's sizable enough to be a city, yet small enough to feel like a town. Some of the best times in my life were during my first stint there.

Downtown badly needed a makeover, both physically and spiritually. Its well-documented history of racial strife is there in brick and mortar, and those ghosts roam loudly. The area of downtown where nonviolent protestors and children were attacked by police dogs and high-pressure hoses is still there to remind anyone who cares to look. As good a town as it is, it stands in its own shadows.

It was April 15, two days before our first show, and my turn on the couch. As we lay in the dark, we chatted. The apartment was so small, I could turn out the bedroom lights from the couch, so hearing each other wasn't a problem.

I made a comment about the post office being packed with people trying to get their taxes postmarked by midnight, and there might be some funny stuff we could grab.

There was a quiet pause, then Brian said, "Let's go," and up we jumped. I grabbed my professional grade cassette recorder and we drove into the midnight air to record what would officially become the first comedy bit we would do together.

These things are hit and miss. I have gone down to the county courthouse to talk with people in line to face the judge, and you would think this would be like pulling teeth, but every now and then you find a guy who's pissed off and wants to talk. I found such a person who had been arrested for "unlawful conduct with a neighbor." This guy was animated, slightly drunk, and angry as he told me, "I never intended to take a shit on my neighbors' porch." In the broadcast world we call this "radio gold." You can't make that up. This is the kind of thing listeners will quote for months after I air it.

Activity was brisk at the post office. Most people acted as though we had a passable disease when we stuck microphones in their face, but you keep going in hopes of grabbing that "shit on a porch" quote. That would not be the case on this night.

We headed to the radio station to try and edit this together, but I wasn't pleased with the raw footage we got. For two hours I cut out the bad and kept in the possible, but even with William Shatner singing "Taxman" underneath, it wasn't worthy of air.

Brian was bummed. We lost a night of sleep in our quest to set the radio world on fire, and it was not to be. I told Brian, "You'll never know if you don't go."

We got back to the apartment at eight that morning. We were

so tired we didn't stop for breakfast, and to top off what had been a wasted night, the obvious happened: The door was locked. We were in such a hurry the night before that neither of us grabbed the key. The only shot we had was the back of the building which had balconies secured to the building with steel framing, perfect for one of us to climb.

Two grown men, who the very next morning would begin the saga of a Hall of Fame radio career, and we are standing in a parking lot playing rock-paper-scissors to determine which one of us climbs, *and I won*.

The athletic prowess Brian displayed as he swung from beam to beam was impressive. He made it to our balcony, and as you would expect, both the sliding glass door and window were locked. Brian yelled, "What should I do?" I responded with only two words, "fucking break it." The couch had never slept so well.

Later that night, on the eve of our first show, I was told that a dinner was held. In attendance were Mark St. John, who brought me into this job, Randy Lane, who brought in Brian, and Bernie. This was a "what have we done?" dinner. As it was told to me, during this dinner, Bernie raised his glass and said, "I want to go on record as saying, this will never work."

I was more excited than nervous. This was my return to Birmingham, and I wondered how many of my former listeners were still around. I knew how to do a morning show because I'd done it, so I prepared the show as if I were going to be alone with little thought of Brian, and that's exactly what I should've done. I had no idea what to expect of him.

The show went about like I expected, very solid. Brian watched and listened more than he spoke, which was smart on his part; he was looking to see where he would fit in. Like driving a new car, he was getting used to the ride, a solid start I felt.

After a first show, the hallway of the station is a good indicator. I remember lots of smiles and chatter. Brian got lots of compliments; he was all teeth.

After we completed our first week, the most important factor was the buzz. Lots of people were talking about us. When you've got that, you're on your way. It's when you don't see this kind of activity that there's cause for concern.

Lynda arrived and we spent the weekend finding a house to rent. Morning radio people don't usually live far from work, as was the case here. The lady who owned the house we rented kept telling me to trim back the rose bushes, and I'm thinking, "Am I renting a chore?"

I learned about living close to work in Savannah, Georgia, where I did my first morning show, and I learned it by accident. The drive from Birmingham to Savannah was seven hours, and I was driving a used Volkswagen Jetta, a truly amazing piece of shit. I worried the car wouldn't make it, and for good reason. On the drive, my muffler developed a leak, which melted a hole in the floorboard. Exhaust fumes began to fill my car, so I drove with the windows down for the last half of the trip. I arrived in Savannah stoned, with a busted wallet and a broken car. I rented an apartment one block from the radio station so I could walk to work, and I was never late.

As beautiful as Savannah is, every morning I walked to work the air smelled like boiled cabbage. There are several large factories that function around the clock there, and one of them smells like ass!

My new job was at WSGA (AM), which was a great radio station in the 1970s, but this was 1981, and music-based AM stations were dead by then, information I wish I'd known before I took the job. As proof, one morning I had two free movie tickets to give away and promoted the fifth caller gets them, and I didn't get one single call. Most mornings, I was the only person listening, and I sometimes struggled with that myself. Other than learning the ropes of a morning show, the job was a complete bust.

A few months into the gig, a friend told me his wife oversaw the cheerleading squad at Savannah College, and she felt one of her cheerleaders was a perfect match for me. He asked if I wanted to meet her, and to be honest, I didn't. I wasn't looking to date anyone. Companionship for me would just happen for a while, and then, unhappen. I couldn't remember the last time I had an official date where you pick them up, but my friend told me this girl was a big fan, and she listened to me every day. My problem was that I strug-

gled with a serious addiction to cheerleaders, and they don't have rehab for that, and if they did, I wouldn't go.

I had an appearance that weekend at the mall, one of those embarrassing deals where the DJ is trapped inside a thousand cases of soda and can't get out until they're all sold for charity. So, I told him to have this girl drop by there.

I remembered I was meeting someone, so I wore a collared shirt. That to me was dressed up, and still is! Midway through the event, this young, beautiful girl stepped up and I could tell by her expression of "I can't believe I'm doing this," that this was the girl. "Are you Lynda?" I asked, and she nodded. We were both embarrassed and our conversation was awkwardly strained, so I quickly asked for her number and said I would call.

Putting it bluntly, Lynda wore a tight purple top that delightfully displayed she was a fully grown woman, and I knew I had to become "as one" with them, so I called.

Lynda told me years later that she would have much rather gone to the beach that day and almost didn't show at the mall. She also confessed that FM on her car radio was broken, and WSGA was the only station she could get. I was clearly deceived, and we've been married four decades.

Savannah is—without question—the most beautiful city I have ever lived in. It's one of our country's oldest cities, and they've done a remarkable job in protecting that. All the dwellings in the Historic District are kept exactly as they were hundreds of years ago. If you own one of them, you can upgrade the property provided you keep it exactly as it was. Giant oak trees line the city with their branches stretching out over the streets, with Spanish moss drooping from its limbs. Lynda and I were married in the gazebo at Whitefield Square which surrounded us with these oak trees, but we did it there because it was free.

At the start of our second week in Birmingham, I walked into the station and saw Brian sitting in the jock lounge, which is a glorified name for a storage closet. I've never seen a more sunburned, exhausted looking person.

My stare brought his response, "I flew to Chicago to get my car," he said.

"You mean the car you left for someone to steal?" I said, smiling.

He sat back. "Yes, the very same. I realized I couldn't afford a new car on my pay, so I went to get mine."

"Please tell me you flew there and your car was gone," I said hopefully.

Brian leaned in, "Oh no, it was right where I left it, because my car is such a piece of shit, nobody would steal it."

He explained that his car overheats, so his sunburn came from pacing the shoulder of the freeway while his car cooled. It took him twenty-two hours to make it to Birmingham, and he'd just pulled up. There is timing in comedy, so I stared at his swollen, burnt face and said, "Okay, have a good show," and walked out.

Several years prior, I had made a business decision that was paying off. Lynda and I were freshly married when I said to her, "I'm going to borrow $10,000 so I can build a studio here in the house." She didn't seem as overly concerned about the impending debt as I was. To take on a bank note when we're barely squeaking by was scary.

My needs for a home studio were simple. Once I got to work and attended to my production duties, there was no time left for show prep. With an in-home studio, I could write and record comedy bits when the desire struck and walk in the next day with a full show in my satchel, ready for air.

Our moving truck was about to arrive, and my studio was on it. I was anxious to set it up so Brian and I could work there. For the first few weeks we were forced to use production facilities at the station, and it's annoying to be on a roll and have someone run in and say, "Sorry, but I have to record this." One guy interrupted us one too many times and I murdered him—in cold ass blood—and then I laughed at his death.

We were a month in now and Brian was finding his footing. He quickly got a feel for my rhythm and could chime in with his shenanigans. Each day after the show, we would head to my house and work from my studio, where the rose bushes grew tall, because I never trimmed them. Getting away from the station meant no distractions, so we could focus on radio comedy and nothing else. Most days, we would toss a football in my front yard while discussing potential ideas for the show. When we hit on a good one, we headed into the studio, wrote it, and recorded it.

Brian walked in one day and handed me fifteen handwritten pages of script for his Johnny Cash character. It took me ten minutes just to read it. I told him, "There's some good jokes here. Pick the best ones and get this down to one page, two minutes tops." That was the standard length for a morning show character piece.

Brian was accustomed to going forever with a stage character, and he struggled with the two-minute radio rule. He tended to go off page and vamp, which is what made it brilliant. Truth be told, I don't think he ever made it in two minutes. However, it's a proven fact that the audience will stray if you give them a reason, and an overly long comedy bit is one of those reasons.

In my career, I've never known who my competition was. I always felt taking care of my lane gave me the best shot. I couldn't name one other show Brian and I were competing with, and there was no street talk about any of them. Our ratings were climbing, and we started making appearances to ever growing crowds.

Brian was—and still is—incredible in front of a live crowd, and I'm fairly strong. Since Brian's background was improv, he was used to working off other people, and I found it easy to work off him. He showed me the value of audience participation. There are massive amounts of humor in pulling some guy from the crowd and allowing him to be the star, and the crowd laps it up. We would do two hours and it felt like ten minutes. We got standing ovations most every time, and the majority of that was Brian, but I never once felt left out. My forté was personality radio, Brian's was live performance. He once told me, "If the other guy is struggling, you pull him out of it, and get him back in the game." I find that works in more than just improv.

One Thursday afternoon, Brian and I were working out of my studio, and fighting exhaustion from a long week. The Alabama State Fair was in town, and we were scheduled to do a live break from there that afternoon. We just weren't in the mood to drive all the way out to the fairgrounds to do one break, and I happened to have an extensive sound effects library with one track labeled, "Carnival Sounds." We called into the radio station reporting live from the fairgrounds, and as I talked up the fair, Brian was pretending he was on a ride, screaming each time the ride brought him around. Later, a sales guy complimented us on the break and how awesome he thought it was. No one knew we were a few blocks from the station sitting in my home studio, smiling as I put away my sound effects record.

With our ratings heading upward the station felt they had something that was working, so the next logical step was a billboard campaign. Neither of us had ever been on a billboard, so we were jacked.

They scheduled a photo shoot with hair and makeup, which I'd never done before, so it took a bit for me to get used to myself with makeup on, and I'm still not over it.

I was mostly known for stuff I did over the phone on the show. For example, the M&M company stopped making red M&Ms and I wanted to know why, so I called them, which explains why I'm holding a phone in the picture. Brian was known for parody songs, so he was holding a guitar.

We saw a small mock-up of the billboard, and you're so excited to see yourself on a billboard, you don't notice if it's any good. But we gave it the thumbs up, and the billboard company said we should start seeing them in about a month.

This signified a certain success for me, as Birmingham had been a part of my life from my earliest memories. Twice a year my father would load the family in the car and we would make the six-hour drive down to Tuskegee to visit my aunt Mutt, and the drive took us through Birmingham. We would start heading up this massive mountain and my father would always tell us, "Kids, this is Red Mountain, the tallest mountain in the state." Hey thanks, dad, because I had forgotten it from when you told us six months ago, and every single time we make this just-shoot-me-now drive.

Doing a morning show in Birmingham gave me a strong sense of having made it, and even though I knew the moment was coming, it hit me like lightning when I was face to face with it.

Lynda and I were out on errands and the drive took us up that very same Red Mountain, and there it was, in all its glory. It was me, smiling and holding a telephone, and a smiling Brian holding a guitar, and it was *fucking huge*. I know the size of normal billboards; this seemed twice that. I stood in its shadow as a choir of angels sang.

Lynda has always told me that I don't show excitement at things like Christmas gifts, but then again, she gets giddy when Kellogg's changes the artwork on a box of Fruit Loops.

But seeing my thirty-foot-wide face on the side of Red Mountain? I was deeply moved, and you couldn't tell. When I drove my mother to see it, she squealed, "Stop the car!" She got out and snapped off fifty clicks on her Kodak Brownie 127 while I kept telling her, "Mom, I can get you all the mock-ups you want," and she snapped back, "I don't need mock-ups, Mark! I need pictures!"

By the way, the reason M&M stopped making red ones is because of a public scare that red food dye causes cancer, and even though untrue, the company thought it best to stop making them. You're welcome!

This part doesn't mean anything, but I just remembered it. Brian and I had an appearance two hours away, so we decided to ride together. It was chilly outside, so I grabbed a tweed jacket that Lynda bought me and threw it on over my collared shirt and jeans. When Brian walked in, he surveyed what I was wearing and said, "Oh good, you're mixing in different fabrics, looks sharp!" He then went to pee, and I had no idea what the fuck he was talking about.

In early 1986, two major events took place. Mark and Brian became the number one morning show in Birmingham, and Lynda got pregnant, and neither of those are related. For the record, as wrong as Bernie clearly turned out to be, he also showed himself to be a smart GM and caring person. I just don't think personality radio is his forté.

High ratings bring attention, and attention brings vultures. It seemed everybody wanted to do a television show with us. We had lunch with one guy who spoke a strong game on the phone. He showed up at the restaurant nicely dressed and professional. As we ate, he talked about the successful things he had done in television and would do the very same for us. As lunch concluded he said, "It's meant for us to work together," and then he bolted from the restaurant. Brian and I had to pay the bill and we never heard from him again.

The second guy was Mike something. He had an actual track record of shows he had produced, so we did a thirty-minute special entitled *We've Always Wanted to Be on TV Show*, which aired to good ratings. Mike never paid us a single penny and we couldn't locate him afterward. These types of people are in every walk of life. They have no understanding of business, so they hide from it.

Somebody who was great at business was my father. He was a bank president, and a smart man. He and I didn't particularly get along, but he was proficient at sharing life lessons in a way that I could understand them. He once told me, "People will promise you anything to get you to do what they want. Write all the stuff they promised you down on paper and ask them to sign it. You'll witness how quickly bullshit walks." So, what did I learn from my experience with TV people after reviewing my father's words? We needed a great attorney! Swindlers get nervous around attorneys, because a signed document is legal tender, and they can't cheat their way around that.

We were invited to appear on a locally televised dance show. Self-promotion has always been important to me, because if you don't do it, who will, so we accepted the invite. When I arrived at the club, I was unaware that I would be on the receiving end of a major life lesson on this night, and it would define my place in the future of Mark and Brian.

Teenagers were everywhere, all hoping for their fifteen seconds on TV. The air-break with Brian and me was maybe twenty seconds, and the kids seemed buzzed we were there.

Afterward, Brian and I were hanging out chatting when a lovely teenage girl giggled up to Brian saying, "I love you on the radio, Brian, you're really funny. Can I have your autograph?"

Brian smiled, took her autograph book and as he signed, he said, "This is Mark."

The girl smiled at me and said, "Hi." She then grabbed her autograph book and ran off to her friends as they all squealed.

I sat quietly as Brian turned to me, "I am so sorry." He started making excuses as to why she asked for his autograph and not mine.

"Don't worry about it," I interrupted him.

When I got home, Lynda was asleep. I collapsed on the couch and stared at a TV that wasn't even on. I've always been honest with myself. I don't like people who play the victim, and I refuse to be one. As I processed the evening, I realized for my entire career, it had always been a one man show. If there was praise, it went to me. I wanted to be the very best at what I did, but now it was me plus one, and this strange feeling I had was brand new.

When I was a single act, I always thought that it doesn't matter who is funny as long as the show is funny. Now, I'm questioning if I really believe that. This moment at the club took me by surprise, and there was no hiding. It shook me.

As I pondered this, I came to a major realization. The tall, good-looking, funny blond guy will always pull focus, always get the spotlight, and I will be the other guy from Wham, and that's the way it is. So, I had to answer one question: Can I do this knowing this will always be the case? Because if I can't, then I need to get out. And on that note, I went to bed.

Lynda was now showing and our next-door neighbor Dee was pregnant as well, both in the same trimester. Each day, Lynda and Dee would take an afternoon walk which made me proud to see. Lynda was taking good care of herself and the baby, two swollen bellies wobbling down the road. I had never seen her in that way, and it made me realize she was about to become a mother.

Years later Lynda confessed to me that their walks took them directly to Baskin Robbins for a hot fudge sundae, every, single, day!

When you do a morning radio show, you are in constant need of good content, and something uniquely different fell into our lap. The Disney people contacted us and asked if we would like to broadcast from a Mickey Mouse hot air balloon. In the world of radio content, that would certainly be different.

I wanted to make sure listeners could see us in the balloon while we did the show, so I asked if they could fly us along the Interstate 65, which is packed with commuters. They agreed they could, so we were in.

As we took off, the pilot told us the weather was good, and we should be in for a steady flight. We glided down the interstate as car horns blared below. All was good, until the wind picked up, and we started drifting away from the interstate at a shit-your-pants pace. The pilot said we were in no danger, he just couldn't steer the thing. The inability to steer something in mid-air certainly seemed like danger to me.

The interstate was nowhere to be seen now, and all we could see below was trees. We drifted deep into the woods of God knows where, as the pilot is telling us he's looking for an open space to set down.

As I scanned the wilderness below, we passed over the only house we had seen. Chickens were roaming the yard, and it looked as though the chimney had caved in. Someone had duct taped the hole, and smoke was billowing out of a large coffee can poking through the duct tape, and we were about to set down in the area. All I could hear in my head was the banjo from *Deliverance*.

The pilot saw a clearing and began to descend, but we then heard the pilot loudly say, "Hold on." We slammed into a tree midway down the trunk and snapped it like a twig. Our basket did a bouncing, dragging landing, but we were safely on the ground.

After we had gathered ourselves, I thought it was the perfect time to smoke a joint. It was too windy to light it, so I stepped inside the half-inflated Mickey balloon, and smoked it there.

We then decided to follow a dirt road we found. After several miles, we heard talking in the distance. As we topped a ridge, there were several sheriff cars and multiple news trucks. Local stations had gone live with reports of "Mark and Brian are lost; the worst is feared." Live news cameras were quickly pointed in our direction, and *I am schmeeked*, so I simply put on my sunglasses and started talking shit.

We had been in Birmingham a year now, a clear number one in mornings, and right where we should be. We were doing a standard form morning show, meaning funny characters saying funny things, stories of weird people doing weird things, coupled with funny banter, exactly what you would find in most any city. But we were doing it better than most, and the key for us was consistency. Anybody can pull off a good show every now and then, but the great ones do it every day. And to be consistent, it helps to have a system.

Years ago, I started using a planner board. When you know what you'll be doing every second of a show, it frees you up to be spontaneous. You can't replace a morning entertainer with a great sense of humor, and if you tie yourself down with process, you have no time left to think funny. Each day, we were loose and ready to play, which brings consistent entertainment, ratings, and success.

It was late November and Lynda was near her due date. My buddy had two tickets to the Auburn vs. Alabama football game and asked me to go. Lynda bought me a beeper, so I took it to the game, which I left in the car since it was roughly the same size as the car. My buddy had a flask, so we got plowed and didn't notice or care who won.

I arrived home and discovered Lynda had been beeping me, but I was incapable of responding. She was having pains and called the doctor, who told her it wasn't time, and she should wait until morning. So, being drunk, I went to bed, woke up the next morning hung over, and Lynda had been up all night while I clearly wasn't. This is not good!

Her contractions were closer now when they discovered the umbilical cord was wrapped around the baby's neck, so an emergency C-section was ordered. All went well; Lynda was good and baby Matthew was good. However, I had an appearance with Brian that night to introduce Journey at the Birmingham arena. I'm thinking there is *no way* I go to that, but Lynda insisted there was no reason for me to stay, so I went.

Brian and I walked on stage with me in scrubs. I explained to the audience I'd just come from the birth of my son. Brian then led 20,000 Journey fans in happy birthday to Matthew while I video-taped the entire thing.

When Matt turned eighteen, I excitedly showed him the vintage video recording of this, and he had no reaction. I then realized, it's all my fault. Matthew shows no excitement because he's exactly like me. I blame myself.

Legend has it that natural born wanderers know when it's time to hit the road. I'd been an old radio dog for fifteen years now, and we get an itch. We had accomplished everything possible in Birmingham, and it was time for the next level.

My decision whether to stay with this Mark and Brian thing was made for me. After some sleep, I realized how moved I was by Brian's kind gesture of apologizing to me when the girl asked for his autograph and not mine. I think he realized how he would've felt if the roles had been reversed, and his kindness in that moment meant the world. I thought if I'm going to do this partner thing, how could I go wrong with a guy who feels compassion for me in a sensitive moment? It was revealing of his character, and I've never forgotten it.

In the world of radio, if you're soliciting for a job, you would send out an air check with résumé and hope to hear back, but this was different. What we had accomplished in Birmingham was noticed by the industry, and we were considered a hot get. Instead of us going to them, they were coming to us. We had a couple of inquiries from some medium markets, which I dismissed. I explained to Brian we weren't going from medium to another medium, our next move will be large market.

My father's words rang true, it's important to know truth from bullshit. So, the first order of business was finding a qualified negotiating attorney who specializes in radio talent. St. John recommended an attorney named Don Ephraim, based in Chicago. He represented many top radio talents and did a television deal for Oprah, so I called him. He had heard of us and was interested, so we jumped right into business and quickly agreed. I half expected Don to have a loud, gruff voice yelling, "You can't handle the truth!" But he was the most soft-spoken, quiet, polite man, who would gladly rip out your throat by its roots and eat it in front of you, if you gave him the slightest reason.

I had come into the Mark and Brian program as the senior partner, purely because of my experience. Based on Brian's performance, work ethic, and who he was as a person, I decided to make him a full partner. I didn't come to that decision easily. This would give him equal pay and equal say, but I felt if he knew he was half of the party, he would come dressed for the occasion.

Word spread that Don was our attorney, and he put us in an elite group. Mark and Brian were now in what I've always called "big boy radio." Don's phone began to ring. The first inquiry was a station from St. Louis, which was exactly the size market I had in mind. Three days later Atlanta called, which was big for me. I had spent a bit of time in Atlanta and admired the radio market there. I was excited about that possibility.

I distinctly remember the St. Louis station because their GM did one of the smartest things. While they were going after me, they also went after my wife. Every day during negotiations, a package would arrive for Lynda: T-shirts, coffee mugs, pens, pencils, calendars, all splattered with KSHE. Lynda would pass me in the hallway wearing a KSHE T-shirt. It was a brilliant move that didn't work. I wanted Atlanta all along.

Don arranged for Brian and me to fly over and meet with the Atlanta GM and see the station, which was in a high rise, and that felt classy. I once worked at a station that was in a trailer, so anything is classy after that.

We sat with the GM and some other goobers in his office, which had an incredible view of the Atlanta skyline. I had dreamed of this, but never thought I would be here.

Our conversation was pleasant, we talked about everything except the reason we were there. They were trying to get a feel for us, because we didn't ask for this visit, they did.

There was a knock as the secretary stepped in saying, "Mark and Brian, your attorney is on the phone." As we followed her out, I was thinking how odd that Don would pull us out of this meeting.

She led us to a small conference room with a speaker phone on the table. "He's on line four," she said as she exited. Fancy telephones confuse Brian so I punched in line four. Don picked up his receiver, which he never does, because he's always on speaker. There was no small talk.

"I want you to go back into the meeting and finish it out," Don said. "Be cordial, don't verbally agree to anything, and don't sign anything. Thank them and get back to Birmingham."

"Why? What's going on?" I responded, confused. This is where that silence thing was loud.

"Los Angeles has called."

WE HAD STARTED SOMETHING
First Half of 1987

66 People cut themselves off from their ties of the old life when they come to Los Angeles. They are looking for a place where they can be free, where they can do things they couldn't do anywhere else.99

—TOM BRADLEY

KLOS was a classic rock station in Los Angeles for twenty-five years before we arrived. Although I wasn't there for it, 95.5 KLOS battled their archrival, KMET, for classic rock supremacy back in the day, and as I heard it, both stations were great. KLOS had a hot morning show in the early 1980s with Frazier Smith, but he left and the station had been in comedic morning limbo for two years, and they were looking to climb back into the entertainment morning fray.

The saying goes if you win mornings, you win the day, and that's proven true. The idea is to have a hot morning show that gets people to tune their dial to your station, and most folks would leave their dial in that position the entire day. Morning radio is big business, not only for the people doing the show, but for the station. More money is made in mornings than the rest of the time slots combined. The fact that morning talent is paid big money is true, but the station itself benefits the most, if properly run.

Our negotiations with KLOS began immediately and would prove to be one, long pissing contest, as most are. We wanted as much as we could get, while the station wanted to pay as little as possible. It was January when they started, and it wouldn't be until July that the deal got done.

In most radio negotiations, money is the first thing to be agreed upon, then the smaller items take longer. Think of it this way: You're standing at the counter of a restaurant, and you're haggling over how much you'll pay for your meal. You and the manager agree right away on your entrée but take forever to agree on the sides.

KLOS felt they were taking a risk on us, and Don responded, "Then why are you trying to hire them?" Negotiations trickled along, meanwhile Brian and I continued our show in Birmingham like nothing was happening, especially not an opportunity to do mornings in the number two radio market in the country, and the chance that our lives could be changed forever; it wasn't even on my mind.

While talks continued, Bill Sommers, the GM at KLOS decided to visit Birmingham and hear us live. We had dinner with him and Charlie West, the program director. I took the opportunity to poke fun at Bill's shell hairstyle. Risky, I know, but it got a decent giggle. We did our best possible show and Bill didn't hate it since negotiations continued.

Don told us they were down to small details on the deal, and Bill requested that Brian and I come out to LA. The only thing I remember about the trip is that Bill took us to Carney's Hot Dog stand on Sunset Boulevard. We sat outside and ate this famous hotdog; keeping it real, I've had much better. Afterward, Brian went to the bathroom, which left only Bill and me. I'm not sure we were even talking at the moment, when out of Bill's mouth comes, "I've never paid over a hundred thousand dollars for a jock and I never will." In my head, I heard Don yelling, "If he tries to engage you, say nothing." I sat and gazed at Bill (I didn't stare) and said nothing. And for the record, Bill *did* pay us more!

It took seven months, but the deal was done in July. We announced on our show that we were leaving, and it took me by surprise what a big deal it turned out to be. It was the talk of Birmingham, hitting the front page of most papers.

Birmingham News—"Mark and Brian
Sign Off and Are LA Bound."

Birmingham Post Herald— "Mad Caps
Mark and Brian Say Goodbye."

Birmingham Gazette—"Mark and Brian
Are Bound for Big Time."

No matter when or why you do it, moving sucks. Plus, it was going to take every bit of our savings to pay deposits on gas, water, power, and whatever else they have in California, so this gamble had to work. The last thing Don said to me was, "The deal is done. Don't screw it up." But the truth is, no matter what the risk, I was doing it. I had gambled everything to get here, and I couldn't think of a better "bet" than this one.

Our rental house was bulging with moving boxes stacked to the ceiling. The moving van would arrive the next morning at eight. I sat on our cushion-less couch as I talked with a reporter from the *Los Angeles Times*. You could see the untrimmed rose bushes through the living room window behind me.

The reporter seemed bored as he stammered through the typical questions. Maybe he felt he was above being given the assignment to talk with another morning radio show team who thought they were coming to LA to take it over.

In the midst of his mundane query, he seemed to metaphorically put down his pen, and make a point as to how ridiculous it was to him that we would even think of coming to LA. He asked me, "Are you aware Rick Dees is here?" I paused, knowing whatever I said in response would be printed for all to read, "Yes," I hesitated, "I am." And I said it with a tone, not pissy, but a clear tone as if to say, "Of course I'm aware of that you fucking idiot." If this reporter had seen me, he would've noticed my *gaze* as I gave him my *tone*.

Lynda and six-month-old Matthew would fly to LA, and I would drive across country with our two Dachshunds, a tremendously stupid decision that clearly showed I put zero thought into how that could possibly work. The first day's drive was Birmingham to Dallas, which went well, but the second day felt like I'd lost a bet.

First off, I wouldn't recommend anyone do this drive alone. Once you head west out of Dallas, there is nothing, and I mean *nothing*, just one incredibly long stretch of black road and desert. No matter how much sleep I got, around two every afternoon I would get the kind of sleepy that kills people. It didn't matter what I tried, coffee, blasting the radio, rolling down the windows, nothing worked. I then remembered I once tried a pinch of dip at a softball game and how jacked I was, so I stopped and got me some Copenhagen, threw a wad in between lower teeth and lip, and hit the road. I was flying along singing, and talking to myself, so much so that I got annoyed, at myself, but sleepy was no longer an issue.

At one point, I passed a road sign that read, "Under no circumstances should you pick up hitchhikers." I found that odd, until five miles down the road I passed the Texas State Penitentiary, and I thought, "Good sign, good safety tip."

I finally made California on the fourth day, and I was exhausted. I stopped in San Bernardino and got a room. It wasn't until the next morning when I made the drive into LA that I realized how close I was. This was way before Google Maps, plus I was still freaked out by those windmill things I saw in Palm Springs. I didn't know what the fuck those were.

Lynda and Matt were at the hotel that sits beside the 405 and 101 freeways. That hotel still exists and is now a Courtyard by Marriott. The moment I arrived, I stepped onto the balcony of my room and watched LA traffic, and my most vivid memory is that traffic never stopped, day or night, it just kept coming. I had never seen anything like that before.

I also had to stop smoking pot because I was told there would be a drug test, only to get there and find out they no longer did them. That was a second life I gleefully took.

My decision to stay in this partnership was a huge deal for me. I moved my wife and son 3,000 miles away from everything they knew and spent our entire savings on getting here. It felt as if I had gone to a stockbroker and said, "I'm all in," then wrote a big, fat check. Everything I had or cared about was riding on this investment, and I looked at this California move as a team effort; we rise together, or we fall together.

One afternoon, Brian popped by my room and we stepped onto the balcony. As we surveyed the city, we spoke some, we were quiet some. There was, however, a moment that took place here. Brian and I were having one of those "look what we did" conversations when Brian said, "I can't wait for people to sit back and watch me cook." I paused and wondered why he didn't say *watch us* cook. His comment made me wonder if he felt the same way I did. I'm fully aware this was minor, but I've never forgotten it. I had put everything on the line for this partnership. It may have been just a slip of the tongue, but later as our challenges grew tougher, I came to realize it was the beginning of a pattern between us. I didn't say anything then, but I wish I had.

The majority of my time at the hotel, I spent on my balcony. These were reflective times filled with self-affirming moments. The entire year had been so crazy with negotiations, leaving behind our success in Birmingham, moving across the country, and now, we're here. I was pumped about what this could become, and nervous about the same thing. But mostly, I had made it to major market radio. It was a fifteen-year quest that I worked at daily, and now I'm here. The feeling of accomplishment was overwhelming. No matter how this would turn out, I had achieved my biggest and most important life goal. I remember thinking it's true that if you want something badly enough, you can achieve it, because I just had!

Our hotel room was nice, in fact for Lynda and me, it was high falootin', meaning it had a pool. The problem was Matthew. We had a portable crib which we shoved halfway into the closet so we could watch TV at night, but after two weeks of that, Matt was fed up.

We were vigilant about finding a place to live. We found a house for rent in Northridge on Kilfinan Street. It was the nicest place we'd ever lived, and it had a pool as well, which was good because someone drowned in the hotel pool. They had to drain and clean it. *Welcome to LA.*

I began to listen to KLOS religiously. My background was in top 40 radio, so I only knew a third of the songs they played, and the jocks were historians of the music. They never talked over the beginning or end of songs. They would let the music completely play out before speaking. They treated the music like gospel.

My thoughts turned to how we would possibly fit into this. And then somehow it hit me: They hired us to do what we do, not fit into their format. So, I sat with Brian and told him that when we hit the air, we're going to do our thing, not theirs, and Brian agreed. It was late July, and it had not yet been determined when our first show would be.

This part cracked me up. Brian stayed in the hotel so long that the station told him he had to get out. I discovered through the years that he loves staying in hotels. The boy loves his free room service.

We spent most of August getting to know people at the station, basically getting a feel for things. We were finally told that our first show would be Tuesday, September 8, the day after Labor Day. I asked for a test run so I could get used to the control room. I wanted to familiarize myself with all of the buttons and knobs that I would operate during the show. If you're going to fly a new plane, you want to sit in the cockpit first to get a feel, same thing here.

The weekend prior was our test run. We went on Saturday night/ Sunday early morning at two and did two hours. Their control board was an older model, so getting a feel was easy. I was actually nervous. My first words had been spoken in a major market radio station, and it turned out to be just what we both needed. We quickly fell into our rhythm. We had fun with each other and joked about our situation. It went very well, and we both left there pumped about Tuesday.

The night before our first show, I spent in my jacuzzi because my rental house had one. I sat there wondering why no one from the station had called to make sure I knew I was on the air the next day. Then I realized that this is the majors, and that I'm a pro now. Professionals don't need to be reminded, and if you do, you won't be around very long. For some reason, that relaxed me.

I didn't realize then how important our first week would be. I knew we needed to do our thing, and not try to fit into their mold of classic rock. But I didn't realize that if we failed to make a stand in this crucial first week, I don't think most of you would've ever known the radio team of Mark and Brian. We had four shows in front of us to demonstrate who we were, and more importantly, who we would be.

The moment the audience heard our voices, we would be instantly hated. People don't like change, and we were about to rearrange their house, and not apologize. The audience we inherited were fans of classic rock, and we were not what they were looking for, nor would we change. To put it more bluntly, in a kind of non-verbal way we invited every listener to leave. We made fun of all the things they loved, and *them*. Something was happening to us here that wasn't by any design. We became something else, a better version of us.

In my jock years, I always knew people don't like you on your first day, and they love to call and tell you. The idea of airing those calls never dawned on me, but that's what we did. We made the negative go away by making fun of it. We playfully were saying, "We don't care that you don't like us, we find it funny." It's the kind of attitude the blue-collar crowd loves. The core of rock and roll is "fuck you," which was the essence of what we were doing in that first week. I didn't realize we would be viewed as rebels who bucked the system. We were just having fun!

We started playing a Neil Young song, and we began yelling, "God, what is this? He sounds like he's in pain." I grabbed the needle and raked it across the record, then threw it into the wall. Brian then said, "Let's put on some good music." We played Glen Campbell's "Southern Nights" and sang along.

We then took a call from a man in tears yelling, "Neil Young doesn't sing because he wants to, he sings because he has to." We responded, "Sir, no one needs to sing like that. He sounds like a cat trapped in a barbed wire fence." The caller screamed "No!" as we faded up Southern Nights.

As we finished our first week and exited the control room, we started up the long hall of KLOS. There stood Arlo, a sales guy, at the head of the hall with his arms out yelling down to us, "Come to me my little money makers." I realized then we had started something, in the second largest media market in America.

DON'T BUMP THE RECORD, KID

Second Half of 1987

66 We're down in Muscle Shoals, Alabama, and we gotta cut some Fred McDowell stuff. If ever I'm gonna do it, it's gotta be here.99

—KEITH RICHARDS

It was Saturday morning, which meant weekend, which meant breathe in what turned out to be a strong debut. You're here, you did good, enjoy it!

I sat outside in my rented backyard, sipping a cup of coffee, when I noticed how good it was. It was hot and rich because Lynda made it for me. She poured it in my favorite cup while Matthew demanded his next handful of dry Cheerios. Morning radio people rarely get to drink their wife's coffee, we drink radio station coffee made by God knows who, at God knows when. But you don't notice because it's semi-warm black water you need to get you through the next thing.

For the first time, I noticed the California foothills that swooped down and met the back fence of our Northridge home. Our house sat on top of a sizable mountain that overlooked the entire San Fernando Valley, it seemed.

I'd been in California for three months, but most of that was spent preparing for our first shows, and I was just now seeing all of this. As a kid, I used to wonder what was beyond the confines of my hometown, and I realized I was now seeing part of it.

My hometown was small, not tiny, just small. I didn't realize what a nice place it was until I left it. I liked my town but, even at a young age, I had a strong desire to know what was outside of it. There were two places that connected me to whatever that was: the movie theater and the radio station. Both places provided me with something that wasn't from my town, and I have no other way of saying it, I was strongly attracted to "out there," without knowing what that was.

I would run home from school because I was afraid to miss something. My favorite radio station was WOWL, one of two top 40 stations in my birthplace, Muscle Shoals, Alabama. Their jocks were hellions who partied together on the weekend. They would pop in on each other's show, and it made for addictive listening, and I didn't want to miss any of it.

The only other choice in town was WLAY, who billed their jocks as, "The Good Guys," which bored me senseless. The WOWL jocks had attitude, the WLAY guys just read the card and sounded like my father. The songs on both stations were the same, commercials, promotions, all the same, except for the jocks, and that's what I listened for.

My favorite jock was Christopher J. Bellou, the afternoon guy at WOWL. He once got drunk at one of their parties and poured cement in the program director's trunk. He got suspended, but not before he told the story, killer great stuff.

I would ride my bike to the radio station and hang out in the lobby, until they kicked me out. I was hoping to meet Christopher. They had eight by ten, black and white headshots of each jock lining the lobby wall, and in the middle was Christopher, my first time to see what he looked like.

They announced that Christopher would do a live broadcast from the shopping center near my house, so I rode my bike there. This was back in the day when they would bring the portable control board, complete with microphone and two turntables, and Christopher at the helm. I didn't realize it, but I started walking toward him. Christopher turned to me and said, "Don't bump the record, kid." Little did I realize, but six years from that moment, I would become a jock at WOWL and work alongside Christopher.

When I was freshly sixteen, I went to WOWL and told the lady at the front desk I wanted to be a jock. She asked if I had any experience, "No," I told her. She told me I can't work there without it, so I called every other station in town, and got much the same response.

One day after school, I stopped at WSHF, a country station that only broadcasts during the day. I sat in the office of the GM, who told me he could give me the job of cleaning up after they signed off, then afterward, I could practice in their control room.

I also ran the station on Sundays when the hellfire and damnation preachers came in. They had to pay me $27.50, cash up front, and I was not to open the door until they paid. Some of the preachers would bring an extra guy to yell "Amen, brother," during the sermon, but the extra guy didn't cost any more.

As I practiced, it dawned on me that if I rolled tape and recorded myself, it would sound like I was on the air, so I did, and took the tape back to the lady at WOWL, who hired me to do weekends. Yes, I lied, but I got hired, so go ahead and judge me for out-thinking the chicken or the egg thing.

One afternoon, looking every bit the proud, teen jock I was, I walked into the lobby of the station, the same lobby I was kicked out of many times as a kid. I was checking the weekend schedule at the front desk when I saw it. Staring back at me from the lobby wall was my eight by ten, black and white headshot, alongside the other jocks. I was officially one of them. I didn't think there could be a prouder moment in my life than that, and thankfully I was wrong.

As we began our second week of Mark and Brian, we were both energized because we were somehow changed. In Birmingham we fit in, here we didn't, and while I didn't understand the whole of it, I liked this rebel thing. We were bucking the system, and we liked it. Nobody had told us, "Don't do it," so we kept on. This thing we were doing wasn't normal or boring, we were getting a huge reaction, and even though that reaction was negative, it felt right, it felt electric.

At 6 a.m. the phones were packed, twenty-five blinking lines, and every person on hold wanted to bitch, moan, or complain about us. With each call we never wavered, never gave in to any inkling of remorse. We were relentless as we made fun of the music and them, but not once did we come off as mean or hurtful. It was all very playful, and I believe that was the magic rabbit in the hat. There was a smile in our rudeness, and though listeners were pissed, they were entertained.

We would start playing "Black Dog" by Led Zeppelin, and then decide we didn't want to hear that crap. We would instead play Jim Nabors, "If I Had a Hammer," and sing along while Brian accompanied on bongos, which is quite rare in these parts. By the end of that week, I don't believe two men had ever been verbally attacked in so many varied and vile ways. It was truly inspired morning radio, and even though people had threatened to kill us, they knew our name.

As mentioned, the station hallway is a great indicator. The employees we met in August were friendly, but they didn't know us, or what we were capable of. Now they had heard it, and I saw a different side of them, a warmth that comes with confidence for the move the station made.

The two years prior to us, KLOS had been a straight-ahead classic rock station. Their ratings hovered around a 2.5, which isn't very sexy. KLOS was now starting the day with four hours of our shit, offering them hope of higher ratings, which in turn saves jobs, pure and simple. The bottom line was, Mark and Brian represented the possibility of a new day for them.

Being in LA held within it a new toy that we now had the opportunity to play with. Celebrities live in LA and were ripe to be picked. Our very first in-studio guest was Donny Osmond. I had always been a fan of Donny's and I was pumped about his visit, plus Donny would come to hold a major distinction in the saga of Mark and Brian.

We had a keyboard set up in the event we could talk him into singing. He couldn't have been nicer, he was open to discussing all topics, and yes, he did sing. I asked him to do "Go Away, Little Girl." He smiled, as he put his fingers on the keyboard saying, "I'm not sure I remember the chords." He then launched into a slower—and fairly

Image courtesy of Laura Stringer

meaningful—version of the song. The ladies in the switchboard swooned all the way through it. And then?

At 7:42 a.m. the Whittier earthquake hit, our first experience with a shaker. I'd never experienced the earth slamming me into a wall. As I dove for the doorway, Donny slowly got up and strolled to it, all while Brian was crawling up his back. After the rolling stopped, Donny went into the switchboard and calmed all the girls, then took pictures with each (see photo above taken that morning). *And that, my friends, is strength of character.* Then I shared something with Donny off the air that seemed to make him reflect on a happier time and see me in a different light.

Fame Recording Studios was in my hometown and the Osmonds recorded there. I told Donny that when I was a kid, I was secretly a fan of his and I would ride with my mother when she went to the mall, because Fame Studios was right across the street.

While she shopped, I would stand in front of Fame hoping to meet Donny. My dumb ten-year-old ass didn't realize they weren't even in town. A genuine grin crept up Donny's face as he said, "That was you?" We enjoyed a laugh inside a small bonding moment, and we still talk to this day.

I didn't know it at the time, but Donny was not in a good place. After *Donny and Marie* was cancelled, the entertainment business had drained every last dollar out of him, and he was figuratively put out to pasture. Donny fell into, "Self-exile behind the orange curtain," as he put it. (The "orange curtain" he refers to is Orange County, California, immediately south of Los Angeles, where many residents take pride in being different or separated from LA.)

Shortly after, Donny found out he was nearly broke. Four years of successful network television and there was no money to show for it. When asked in an interview what happened to the money, Donny claimed, "I don't know."

We had knocked on his door at the right time. Donny will tell you he credits Mark and Brian for helping to make him relevant again. I had finally met Donny, and I wasn't even ten-years old, waiting in front of Fame Studios when it happened. I would have to wait years, and travel thousands of miles for the moment.

Growing up in Muscle Shoals was interesting, in that it wasn't odd for locals to see the Osmonds, Otis Redding, or Aretha Franklin, milling about town. Being raised in it, I thought all towns had recording studios, and it was normal for major recording stars to be seen at local eating spots. Muscle Shoals was unique in the music world, and it wasn't until I lived other places that I realized that.

But a fair question is, why would major music talents choose a small town like Muscle Shoals to record in? I'll give you two reasons: The first is The Swampers, the backing band for Fame Studios. In most cases, when an artist records at a studio, they never bring their own musicians, they use the local studio players.

The reputation of the Swampers had grown throughout the 1960s, with their talents displayed on some of the biggest rhythm and blues hits on the charts, and name artists wanted to work with them. Of the numerous artists who collaborated with the Swampers, Aretha

Franklin was the most well-known—at the time—and reportedly was shocked to find four small southern white guys sitting in the studio. As legend tells it, each of the four Swampers weren't particularly good when playing alone but together, magic happened.

The Swampers played on hundreds of hits, but I will list three. Listen to "Respect" by Aretha, "I'll Take You There" by the Staple Singers, or "Kodachrome" by Paul Simon, and you'll hear the Swampers.

And second, the sound of the room at Fame was like no other. Rick Hall, who built Fame, spent quite a bit of time tweaking the room for optimal production quality, and those who recorded there reported the sound captured inside those walls had no equal. Plus, if you lived in Muscle Shoals, it was impossible not to run into a star who was there to record.

I was in an all-night eatery around 1 a.m., which was behind Fame Studios. An entourage of about fifteen people entered and caused a rolling buzz, which made me look. In the middle of it was Rod Stewart. In most places, this would have caused a scene, but for us, it was merely interesting. But this next one is my favorite because I had a close encounter of the third kind, making contact.

My first real job was being a bellhop at the Holiday Inn. Most of the recording artists stayed there since it was considered the nicest around and located just across the Tennessee river from the studios.

My jobs were varied but included room service. Normally, the front desk would tell me what the guest needed, such as a crib, blankets, but if I was told room 201 wanted to see me, that was normally one of two things: liquor or women. The women weren't a possibility—I'm sixteen—I couldn't even get one for myself. But the liquor was something I could've done. There was a local bootlegger who delivered, so I could've easily honored the request at a tidy profit, but the chances of getting caught were strong. I didn't want to be sixteen and have a police record for illegal booze. So, what have we learned? That sixteen-year-old boys can make good decisions, unless their penis is involved.

One day, I was told room 108 wanted hot tea, which confused me. I knew what iced tea was, sun tea, sweet tea, but hot tea? Never heard of it. So, I assumed they wanted tea in a glass, with no ice. There, hot tea! The door was answered by three women and an older man. The woman who ordered it looked at the tray, confused.

"No sweetie, I asked for hot tea," she said. My face must've also displayed confusion. Realizing the situation, she smiled and asked, "Do you have any hot water back in that kitchen?"

"Yes ma'am," I said.

"Do you have any individual tea bags?" she replied.

"Yes ma'am," I said, now realizing what she wanted. She was clearly tickled by my dumb ass.

"Okay, could you bring me some hot water, a few of those tea bags, and an empty coffee cup?" she said with a giggle.

"Yes ma'am."

As I headed back to the kitchen, my stupidity embraced me because I became aware of who I had just spoken to. The three women and the old man were the Staple Singers, and the lady I dealt with would go on to sing the theme song to *Christmas Vacation*. So, I can always say that Mavis Staples taught me what hot tea is. Thank you, Miss Staples, and welcome to the Holiday Inn!

It would have been major gossip in my town if I'd been arrested for bootlegging, but there is a big difference between gossip and street buzz.

One night in the late 1960s, there was a small club in England called the Bag of Nails. You could have a drink or a bite of bar food as you listened to whatever act was playing. The club allowed most anyone to perform, and the majority weren't very good. One Friday, the 1 a.m. act was late, but finally jumped on stage and plugged in his guitar. Though only three people were in the audience, he played a full set. The artist wasn't scheduled again until Tuesday at one in the morning.

By eleven that Tuesday evening, the place was standing room only with a line around the block. In the audience were Eric Clapton, Pete Townsend, and Paul McCartney. They had heard the talk and had come to see this guy named Jimi Hendrix. Never underestimate street buzz.

Mark and Brian had been on the air for two months, and Lynda and I were having dinner out. As we dined in this fairly busy restaurant, we overheard a guy at the table next to us say, "Dude, you have got to check out these two guys on KLOS, Mark and Brian. They do crazy shit." Lynda and I stopped eating, fork in midair. I thought maybe they were fucking with me, so I glanced over, but they were oblivious to me. I was witnessing genuine street buzz.

It doesn't matter how many billboards you put up, you simply can't beat the power of your best buddy telling you something he wants you to check out.

Over the coming year, I would witness the same thing a handful of times, and if I was in earshot of that many, I'm betting it was happening in other places across the city. And not once did I lean over and tell the guy who I was. He wouldn't have believed me, plus Lynda wouldn't let me.

By November, we had hit a new stride. We had only been on for two months, and we were never this good. Every day was brand new, and we had no idea what was going to come out of our mouths. I've honestly never felt that free. I remember feeling we had nothing to lose, so fuck it! It was unfiltered Mark and Brian at a level of creativity I didn't know was achievable.

Before I tell you about the very first Mark and Brian Christmas Show, let me share the origin of the show. The tradition of it began when I was in Montgomery, not realizing it would one day become something much more. I put quite a bit into my show, which paid off in great ratings, so at Christmas I wanted to do something special to say, "thank you."

The very first Christmas Show was little more than a raucous office party. Station employees were sneaking in flasks, and party central was my control room, but in attempting to do something unique, I invited Montgomery's Mayor Emory Folmar.

This guy was a local superstud, a staunch Republican who would take his deputies down to local concerts and arrest people for drinking or drugs, and the locals loved him for it. Plus, he always made the news as the top story.

I invited him to come down and read *Twas the Night Before Christmas*. This was the very first entry of the celebrity driven tradition that would continue on the Mark and Brian Christmas Shows.

His arrival was an attention-grabbing spectacle, as he intended it. Traffic was stopped on the road in front of the radio station, as several State Trooper vehicles with lights flashing, pulled into the parking lot in a straight line. In the middle of that line was a State Trooper four by four, and out from it climbed the mayor, as television cameras followed.

The mayor entered our on-air party flanked by a host of troopers dressed to the military hilt. The mayor was accompanied by two guard dogs, one on each side, and he was wearing a holster that cradled a white pearl handled pistol. It was both awesome and hysterical.

As the mayor read the Christmas poem, you could hear his pearl handled pistol rubbing against the metal frame of the chair. I was hoping it would go off; how awesome would that have been? When he finished reading, all the troopers cheered, and his visit made the local evening news. I could watch that entrance every day. Merry Christmas, Mayor Folmar!

The first Mark and Brian Christmas Show in LA was on a very small scale, much like in Montgomery but without Mayor Folmar, though he would've been welcomed. Since we had just started at KLOS, we didn't get any time off for the holidays, so our first show was Christmas Eve morning. During these meager beginnings, it was still called the Mark and Brian Christmas Party. It was held in the control room and our guests were Heather Locklear, Tommy Lee, Ray Manzarek, and Alvy Moore, who played Hank Kimball on *Green Acres*. And I don't remember a single moment from that show. Who knew a small, humble show could grow into the legendary greatness that became the Mark and Brian Christmas Show? Although I *do* remember the first KLOS Christmas party.

We were in the same building as the legendary KABC. KLOS was the unappreciated stepchild in that building. We didn't have the ratings, the respect, or the reputation that KABC enjoyed, and the station Christmas party reflected that reality. The whole party was run by KABC, and it was as though we weren't even there, but Bill Sommers had Mark and Brian in his employ. We were trending up and everybody there was aware of it.

Bill personally asked us to attend the party, so we sat at Bill's table. Bill enjoyed the evening as he sat there with us flanking his side. Did he gloat? No! But he knew certain people were looking, and Bill liked what they were seeing.

I didn't really drink, but Bill insisted, so I drank. We three had a drunken moment of a "this is going to work" kind of vibe. When KABC took the microphone to do their little Christmas "pat on the back," Bill drunkenly chatted all the way through it. KLOS wasn't even invited to speak, but Bill knew the future might change that.

So, what does one do when they get home from a party where they've been drinking? They drink more. Lynda and Matt had gone to bed, so I sat up to watch some Christmas crap on TV, and I drank. One wall of our rented living room was covered in mirrored glass, you couldn't miss yourself. I thought I'd have one more smoke and get to bed. I lit my cigarette on the candle next to me, then back to the TV.

After a moment, I started hearing a sizzling sound. I glanced over to see if the candle was acting up, and I saw my reflection in the mirrored wall, and noticed *my hair was on fire*; hairspray, I assumed, had been ignited by the candle. Being drunk is good in this situation. I simply put out my hair and calmly went back to TV.

I drunkenly sat and reminisced about what a year 1987 had been. It started with us in Birmingham, waiting seven months for a deal to get done. We were now living in LA, and no one could have wished for a better on-air debut. I felt good about being in major market. I even felt good about the divot I now had in my hair, so I went to bed.

As I stumbled up the stairs, I couldn't have known the challenge coming in two months. It would be a defining moment that would allow me to peek into the future of this morning beast we were building. Merry Christmas to all, and to all a good night!

GOD, WHAT HAVE I DONE?

1988

66 Being a child star is great. It's being a former child star that sucks.**99**

—DANNY BONADUCE

Years ago, I read Steve Martin's book, *Born Standing Up*. He talks about his beginning where he opened for the Nitty Gritty Dirt band. They attracted a certain faction of the hippie crowd, and Steve was dressing just like them, blue jeans, tie-dyed shirt, turquoise jewelry, and long hair. His act was going okay, but not as well as he had hoped. Steve, being a philosophy major, began to dissect his act. He realized the audience saw him as one of them, but he wondered what reaction he might get if the audience was watching their own father act this way. Intrigued by the idea, Steve decided to make a change. He got a conservative haircut, bought the white linen suit with skinny black tie, and went on stage. He did the exact same act he'd done every night prior, and it killed. The wild and crazy guy was born.

From our first day in Los Angeles, we had the same comedic approach as we did in Birmingham, but this time, we directed our humor at the listener, not some politician. And as a result, we were hated and adored, and I didn't fucking get it. We were the same guys, same humor, but different approach. Figuratively, we were wearing different clothes. To this day, the number one thing I still hear from listeners is, "I hated you guys when you first started," and no other comment comes close.

Sitting before us was our first full year to display what and who we were, only I wasn't clear on *what or who* that was. We changed almost daily, and we were both feeling the possibilities of bigger things, plus we had complete support from the station. As we took this new ride into territories unknown, so was KLOS, and we both were enjoying the scenery.

This new vibe we had found was addicting and I got hooked on it like a drug. There was nothing standard or stolen about this approach; it had a road of its own, and nobody was steering. We would start each day with a couple of things that were planned, but the rest we made up as we went. We were in a special zone of creativity, and I didn't understand this new place, because I'd never been here before.

Listeners were eating it like dessert they'd never tasted and couldn't get fast enough. This new heat we were feeling was coming from them. But the beautiful thing is we were being ourselves, and it was one of the purest things I've ever felt.

The cornerstone of my creative approach came from a solitary moment in Knoxville, Tennessee, in 1979. It was the single greatest bit of advice I've ever received—my lightbulb moment—and it changed everything.

The station was WRJZ. I was the music director, which had become my main focus. I did an air shift because I had to. I had become bored with air work; I read the card and played the song. My show was boring because I was bored. But I found myself surrounded by fantastic air personalities at WRJZ. Each jock was high energy and great at what they did. It was my first time to see a jock prepare for their show. I didn't know anybody did that.

The biggest star on the station was John Boy. He went on to "John Boy and Billy" fame in Charlotte, North Carolina. John Boy learned his craft here, and he was taught by our program director Bob Kaghan.

Kaghan was a master class of personality radio. Many jocks under his tutelage went on to great things. Interestingly, he was the most boring person I've ever been around. His nightmare was a social gathering. He was awkward and had nothing to say, and he had no skills on the radio himself, but he mentored his jocks into massive talents.

The greatest designer of roller coasters was terrified of them, and he'd never ridden one. Same thing here; Kaghan could teach it but couldn't do it. WRJZ was number one because of Kaghan.

I was working my air shift one Saturday afternoon, and the hottest movie at that time was *Superman*. I came out of a record and said, "I know you're either going to *Superman* or coming home from it so, on this squeaky chair, I will now perform the entire *Superman* soundtrack, all for you. Here we go." I squeaked around on the chair for ten seconds and hit the commercial.

Moments later, the control room door opened, and it was Kaghan. He stood there staring, and I'm thinking, "God, what have I done?" Kaghan then said, "From now on, every time you open the mic, I want something as entertaining and creative as that was," and walked away.

This is the kind of crap I would do for friends for a laugh, not something I would normally do on the air. But Kaghan liked it and encouraged me to do more. He was telling me to be myself. This one small, seemingly insignificant moment changed everything for me. I went to Knoxville as a music director, I left as a radio personality.

My next job was doing nights in Birmingham, and I was on a mission, nothing else seemed to matter. Instead of doing what listeners would like, I was doing shows I would like if I were listening. If I thought it was funny, I did it. Maybe you've heard the saying, "While it may seem small, the ripple effect of small things is extraordinary." I found that to be true.

This small personal change accomplished two things. First, I was having a completely new kind of fun, which was infectious to listen to, and second, you start building an audience of people who think like you do, which becomes your fan base. It changed the entire direction of my career and life.

In the early LA days of Mark and Brian, it probably seemed like we were fixated on faded stars of old television shows. In truth, those were the only guests we could get. Actors of the past were mostly forgotten and excited to have any kind of spotlight shown on them, and we became their welcome center.

One of our guests became a fan favorite because of how odd it was. We welcomed in Tina Louise, who played Ginger on *Gilligan's Island*. We were pumped since she would share fun stories from the set. Nope! *She wasn't having it.*

Apparently, Miss Louise didn't enjoy her solitude on the island, and she refused to answer questions, or talk about the show in any form. All she wanted to do was hawk her umbrella she was trying to sell, but she wouldn't allow us to call it an umbrella. She kept insisting it was a "parasol." Good lord, Tina!

We kept trying to slip in Gilligan questions, which were followed by sizable periods of awkward silence, before "parasol" would come out of her mouth. Fucking kill me now.

Well, I looked up parasol, Tina, and here's the definition: "A light umbrella used to give shade from the sun." Sorry Miss Louise, but the word "umbrella" is used in the definition, so I can call it umbrella all I want. And if you would stop calling it a parasol you might sell a few, because God knows, classic rock fans love a good parasol!

After she left, which was quickly after she arrived, we shared our frustration with her interview, which was apparently hysterical, and the audience loved it. Because we were so uncomfortable in the interview, it had become memorable for them. And I learned a valuable lesson, that people love to hear awkward shit!

One of the first lessons you learn in radio entertainment is to embrace topicality, stuff your listeners are thinking about. It could be holidays, tax time, topics in the news, anything that's top of mind.

We were approaching February and obviously people had Valentine's Day on the brain. Brian and I began throwing around themed ideas about what we might do. Our thought process was a bit different than other shows. Some might host a "Best Looking Cupid" contest. I throw up in my mouth when I think about having to do something like that. We wanted something Valentine's themed, and

Image courtesy of Shooting Stars Maui

stupid, something that had never been done. We traditionally didn't take long when discussing stupid stuff. It came to us quick, and it came to us different.

We had tossed around the idea of melting down some chocolate and dipping weird things into it, like dildos and cock rings. Brian then said, "Why don't we dip ourselves into it?" It only took me a second to get a visual before saying, rather loudly, "That's it!"

This was the first time our mutual admiration of David Letterman fell into frame. This idea was so Letterman, I could see him doing this.

The plan was simple. We had to get a giant tub the size of a kiddie pool, a large crane with harnesses, and a thousand pounds of melted chocolate. We knew this was going to cost, so we went to Bill Sommers and told him the idea.

We wanted to do it in the station parking lot and invite listeners. He had a hard time understanding why we wanted to do this and we explained, "Because it's Valentine's, and this must be done." He chuckled and said he would get some costs.

The promotions department explained that KLOS had never—in their history—invited listeners to any event on station grounds. In response we said, "Well, we're going to now!"

We were aware we were sailing into unchartered waters here, so in the kindest way possible, we might have alluded that we would do it with, or without them. When doing stupid shit, a little hardball leaves a valid impression, but you have to mean it!

Herein lies the significance of this event. This was our litmus test and I knew that. In February, we will have been on the air for six months, and this question was about to be answered: Are people buying into our thing? Are we relevant? I've seen politicians hold rallies and no one comes. This will be our first time in front of listeners; will they come? I would rather do something that was different and have no one show up, than to hold a best-looking cupid contest that was well attended. *This ain't your daddy's morning radio, bitch!* That's where I stood.

We then did something we'd never done and would repeat many times. We went on the air and announced our plan to dip ourselves in chocolate and explained we needed a giant tub to be dipped in, and asked, "Does anybody have one?"

Within twenty minutes a guy called from a company that makes heavy duty tubs that are placed underground for God knows what. He said he would handle all our needs, so we ended the call by telling him that if he let us down, we would sue him. We find that when someone offers to do a kind thing, it's always best to threaten them with court.

On Valentine's morning, cars were lined up as far back as you could see, and traffic was a snarled mess. It was a beautiful sight! We walked out into the largest crowd of listeners I'd ever witnessed. We wore boxer shorts with red hearts, red goggles, red swim caps, and red fins; the chicks love that look.

We built the crowd into a frenzy as the crane operator lowered us into a vat of ice-cold melted chocolate. We were then raised so the crowd could throw chopped nuts at our dripping bodies. They cheered as we hung there looking like wet seals. It was clearly ridiculous and enjoyed by all.

No matter from which angle you viewed this, it was a major victory. Listeners showed in droves, the event was better than promised, and it was the first of many moments where we indulged in our mutual love of dumb shit. This would also mark the first and last time I would pick chopped nuts out of my butt crack.

In six months, Mark and Brian had become representatives of something completely new, and there was clearly an audience for our kind of crap; this event proved that. The press we got was astounding, with coverage on every television channel and all the papers.

During one of our meetings with Bill Sommers, he said something he would repeat to me many times over the years. Bill was impressed with the chocolate dipping success. He had never seen this kind of attention, and he felt we might be on to something. I think Bill felt we might have great success in our future because as we stood to leave the meeting Bill said, "Always remember where you came from." This statement landed about as well as any statement that comes out of nowhere. I didn't know what the fuck he was talking about, specifically, but the day would come that I would appreciate the sentiment of his message.

While our reputation grew as the "curators of stupid crap," it was a natural progression for listeners to want to talk to us. The idea that we would answer our own phones felt so old school, well, like 1985. In Birmingham, I would answer the phones because we only had two lines, but in LA we had twenty-five lines.

If you called the show, the phone line would be answered more than likely by "Switchboarder" Laura, as she became known to listeners. Laura, now a teacher and mother of two daughters, had been with us from day one and loved our show. She saw our show as "important work," and her job was relentless. All twenty-five lines rang constantly, and Laura would go through each deciding if it was air worthy. She was checking to see if you were able to speak clearly, had a point, and were either funny or interesting. Most callers didn't meet any of those requirements.

Out of twenty-five calls, maybe two were air worthy. "Live air" was a precious commodity, and we didn't want to fill it with babbling. Laura knew if she allowed a bad call on air, she would get beheaded. If Laura said the call was good, it went on the air. And it's funny, I promoted the phone number of KLOS for twenty-five years, and I still remember it. Watch this . . . 1-800-955-5567. When I've lost all my marbles and I'm drooling on myself, I'll probably still remember that damn number.

One of the major adjustments we made around this time was doing comedy bits live instead of prerecorded, and this was a sizable game changer. There were elements of pre-recorded I had grown to dislike, and the benefits of going live were numerous.

When you're doing live broadcast, there is an energy that naturally comes to you, body and mind rise to the occasion. There's an innate danger to live, which is what makes it addictive. Recorded pieces are normally done hours after a show, when you're tired, and no matter how hard you try, you cannot match the decibels of a fresh, live broadcast.

We could be doing the show and plug in a bit recorded yesterday, and you could literally hear the energy drop, the whole show crashed. To my ears, the difference was startling, and as a listener you might not have been consciously aware but trust me, you noticed it. Radio doesn't do live broadcast much anymore, and that takes the human element out of the equation. I like to hear a jock fuck up. It lets me know there is a living soul in the mix, and that's comforting.

Brian had a character named DeLyle, a radio host who gives relationship advice. We did this live, and the bit had several moving parts that had to come together at the same time.

As we were doing it, Brian lost his place in the script and was desperately trying to recover, which got me tickled. He then started reacting to my laughter, and the bit became the kind of funny you can't plan. The wheels fell off and there was no turning back because we were live. You can't write that stuff, and you also can't pre-record it! Human error in broadcast makes you smile, because mistakes are one of the things that connects us.

Our ratings went from trickling up, to exploding up, and part of me didn't trust it. I'd never seen numbers go up like that, not in a major city. I'd seen large fluctuation in small towns, but in LA? If anyone doubted before, they weren't now. LA radio people were noticing and so were we, which simply made us scary dangerous!

The success we enjoyed at work seemed to carry over at home. Clearly, it's a big deal to move across the country, but with California being our new home, it was overwhelming. Lynda and I were entrenched in our southern life, and the LA culture shock is a very real thing, though I never grew tired of seeing palm trees. We don't have those in the south. But we took to California and we liked our new life.

When the weather was good, which was every day, we would throw Matt in his stroller and walk our neighborhood after dinner. There was a park two minutes away, and Matthew loved going since it had swings, seesaws, and room to play.

The thing he played on most was a jungle gym in the shape of a caterpillar, and Matthew was drawn to it. He gave little time to the other stuff; he always headed for the caterpillar.

One afternoon, the movie *E.T.* was on television, so Matt and I watched a bit. I wasn't paying much attention when I heard Matthew making noises and pointing to the TV. I looked up, and it was where Elliot was running from the bad guys on his bike with E.T. in the front basket, and he rode through a park with a caterpillar jungle gym. There was no mistaking it, that scene was filmed in our neighborhood park.

We had lived in LA for a year, and it takes time to absorb the fact that a major movie was filmed in your backyard. I think LA has to be culture shock central, and it's not something you can prepare for. I'll give you another example, and it's a stark reminder that you're not in Kansas anymore.

I was meeting a friend for breakfast in Santa Monica at a place called The Rose, and I couldn't find it. This was during the era of Thomas Guide map books. I saw a couple walking, so I pulled alongside and asked for directions. The man pointed to the cafe behind me saying with a smile, "It's easy to miss." I thanked him and pulled away, proud of myself for not freaking out that I had been given directions by Jackson Browne. Moments like this remind you of where you aren't. A note to the rookies: Stars don't like it when you make a scene, it embarrasses them. I learned this by making a scene on more than one occasion.

Let's move from a real star to a former star, as we make another entry into Mark and Brian's TV Star Clown Car. I give you, former *Partridge Family* star, Danny Bonaduce.

Unlike Tina "Parasol" Louise, Danny would not disappoint. He bounded in with a ton of energy. There was no story he wouldn't tell. He took calls and played along with everything. But the story I'm going to tell is about Danny off the air.

I was a fan of the *Partridge Family* and here I have the adult version of little redheaded Danny, who comedically carried that show on his twelve-year-old back. So, I invited Danny out to our house for dinner. Lynda was also a Partridge fan, so she was semi sort of, so-so excited.

Danny arrived at our house on a Moped. I thought maybe it was the hot new thing in LA, so I didn't question it. Danny sat outside with me as I grilled dinner. He hovered over the cooking meat like he hadn't eaten in days. I don't remember dinner, or the rest of that night, however I do remember the next four days, because that's how long Danny stayed. We had a guest room and Danny slept in it for four days.

It wasn't a problem, he was very pleasant, very respectful, it was just odd to come home and find Danny Partridge standing in my kitchen next to my wife and son.

One night during Danny's stay, I had an appearance, so I asked Danny if he wanted to come along. I thought it might be funny and weird for listeners to see. But he declined saying, "No thanks, Lynda is going to make popcorn and she, Matthew and I are going to watch the *Wizard of Oz*." Dear God! *What is happening here?*

One afternoon, Danny said to me, "Let's take a road trip." We loaded into my car, and I had no idea where we're going. We wound up in Burbank, per Danny's directions. We pulled up to a gated area with a guard shack and Danny told the guard, "My name is Danny Bonaduce, from the *Partridge Family*. It was because of me that Warner Brothers could afford to build this neighborhood. I'm not on your list, but I would like to show my friend around the neighborhood that I built, please." The gate was opened.

Danny took me to "The Ranch," as it's known. As we drove, Danny pointed out various houses saying, "That's the *Bewitched* house, that's *Dennis the Menace's* house, that house was in the *Twilight Zone* and, stop right here." Danny got out of the car, then leaned into the window, saying, "And this is my house." Danny proceeded to walk through the white picket fence of the Partridge family home.

It was too much for this redneck to process. I'm standing in the middle of my childhood because I watched all these shows, and Danny Partridge just walked through his own TV front door. Once home, I had to lay down.

I found out later that Danny was living on a small sailboat in Marina Del Ray, and I don't think the boat was his, which meant he rode thirty miles on California roadways to my house and back, on a Moped.

Danny's struggles with substance abuse have been well documented, an issue he eventually got a handle on, and good things came his way once again. Eighteen years after Danny's week-long stay with us, my family and I were at Disneyland for our summer visit. An area of the park had been roped off with red carpet running the length of the street. Cameras clicked away as various celebrities strolled by us, when a clean and sober Danny Bonaduce worked his way down the carpeted path, showing off his gym rat body. We stood and observed as Danny noticed me and walked over to say hello. I guided Danny's attention to a now eighteen-year-old Matthew, standing beside me. Danny shook Matt's hand and chuckled, saying, "Matt, the last time I saw you we were *both* in diapers," a great one-liner for a nice reunion moment between former roomies.

Danny and I have a long running friendship. There is no one like him, a true original. Danny is the greatest storyteller I've ever encountered. He once told me the single most vile, true story about himself, so repulsive I can't tell it here. And I don't think I've ever laughed harder, or longer, at anything. If you're ever in his presence, you will be thoroughly entertained, because that's how Danny rolls.

Have you ever had an allergic reaction to something no one else does? I understand being allergic to things, but not people. I was in the presence of a rock star and couldn't stop sneezing. We got word that Joan Jett was in the building and available for an interview. We were already done with the show, so we recorded the interview in the back studio. That studio only had one microphone, so Joan, Brian, and I had to huddle close together.

As we chatted, I began to sneeze, so I stepped out while Brian continued with Joan. I got myself back in control and went to join the interview, and it started again, and violently. Brian had to finish the interview while I hacked away in the hallway. I don't know if it was something in her hair, makeup, perfume, or maybe I'm allergic to Joan Jett, but I've avoided her ever since.

Joan is looked upon as a pioneer in rock because not many females have stood alone as the focal figure in classic rock music. But I would be willing to bet that Joan probably borrowed a few things from someone she looked up to back in the day. Most people in entertainment have at some point; actors borrow from other actors, comedians borrow from other comedians, etc. It's an accepted practice in all forms of entertainment, and radio is no different.

I noticed most high-profile radio personalities kept a varied collection of toys they used on their show. The one thing all these items have in common is they make some kind of noise. I started doing this many years ago, and still do it. But I didn't really steal the idea, I borrowed it.

On Mark and Brian, we had our own collection of wacky albums, various drums, maracas, cymbals, but there's one item we are best known for. Before I reveal it, I need to first make a confession, and to do that, I need to reintroduce John Boy, who I worked with in Knoxville.

John had an old, beat-up trumpet he kept in the control room at WRJZ, and in the middle of any song, he would open the microphone and play his trumpet loudly, and badly. I thought it was one of the funniest things I'd ever heard.

I borrowed that concept and introduced the idea that Brian and I would play the trumpet and trombone on our show. Just like

John Boy, we would play them through any classic rock song we felt needed horns. I borrowed the idea from John, but we perfected it on Mark and Brian. We accompanied Tom Jones with our brass while he sang, "Help Yourself," and Tom laughed all the way through it. Thank you, Johnny.

And for the record, I have in my possession the original trombone and trumpet we played on the show. I still play my "bone" on the Mark and Lynda Podcast periodically, and my ability for bad hasn't diminished.

Who's to say Florence Henderson didn't borrow her approach at playing Mrs. Brady from someone? We had her on the show, and I'll always remember her as one of the nicest stars I ever met. It was that side of her that started something for us that lasted years. We appeared in numerous television shows and movies as extras, and we called them "concerned onlooker roles," because of Florence.

We had a way of making guests feel comfortable. We were friendly toward them and tried to present an atmosphere that let them know we weren't out to get them. The interview was always about them, not us. Florence relaxed and felt at home, as we did with her.

During the interview we started calling her "Flo," and she welcomed it because she liked us. She told us she was in the middle of shooting *A Very Brady Christmas* and invited us to come down to be extras.

The movie was being filmed at Paramount. Our scene was where Mr. Brady had fallen down a well, and rescuers were working diligently to save him. The Brady family had gathered by the outside of the cave to look worried and sing, "Oh Come All Ye Faithful," you know, like you do.

Our job was to stand in the crowd behind the Brady's, looking concerned. Get it? They'll be a test on this shit later. We were trying to fit in somewhere in the onlooker group when Florence scanned the crowd saying, "Come here, Mark and Brian, stand by the money." She placed us directly behind her, which pissed off all the other onlookers, and I say fuck 'em!

We did the first take, when the director came over to us and said, "Less is more guys." I guess we had a little too much concern going on.

At one point during the shoot, I warmly referred to Florence as Flo. Barry Williams, who played Greg, overheard and didn't appreciate it. He shot me a look, saying, "Her name is Mrs. Henderson." Calm the fuck down, Greg!

Earlier that afternoon, I was hanging outside my dressing room, which was next to a giant soundstage. The huge doors were open slightly, so I took a peek inside. The stage was dark, except a few dim lights angled on the center of a set. I was completely alone, and aware I shouldn't be there, but I snuck over and rounded the corner.

I found myself standing in the *Brady Bunch* living room, and it was decorated for Christmas. I checked to make sure no one was around, then walked through the living room and climbed the Brady stairs. Luckily the area was lit, because the stairs go nowhere, and I would've plummeted to my death.

I was thirty-three at the time, but I watched the *Brady Bunch* as a kid, just like the rest of America, and I'm from the center of the south. Where I come from, not many people get to experience something like this. I just met Florence Henderson, I'm in a *Brady Bunch* movie, and now I'm spending a solitary moment, standing in the Brady living room at Christmas time. It was another moment that told me I'm not in Kansas anymore. I knew I would never forget it and haven't.

Something else you never forget is your first time at Dodger stadium, and your first Dodger dog. The moment I walked into the stadium and saw those jagged edges of the roof that cover the outfield seats, the hair on my neck stood up.

We had Oral Hershiser on the show, and he got us both tickets for the World Series. Seeing Kirk Gibson's historic walk-off home run, and hearing Tommy Lasorda say, "We're gonna put it on the shoulders of the bulldog," you're instantly a fan.

My series seats were behind first base, and a foul ball was coming my way. To get to it, I would have to go through an old lady who was sitting next to me, so I backed off. That old lady elbowed me in the face going for the ball, and I've always regretted not taking her out. Go Dodgers! But not everyone is a Dodgers fan.

I have a very dear friend who was born and raised in San Francisco. He's a short, Jewish, stand-up comedian, who co-starred in the film, *A Few Good Men*. To protect his anonymity, I can't tell you his name, but it rhymes with Devin Hollak, and he says, "Fuck the Dodgers!!!"

To wrap up 1988, we had our first on-location Christmas Show. It was held in some hotel ballroom out by the airport, which shouts classy, doesn't it? Everything by the airport is five stars. We had a stage, but we tried to simulate the way we do the radio show, so we sat at a table with microphones, and stayed seated the entire show. Listeners were present, and the only guest I remember is Butch Patrick, who played Eddie Munster. I remember nothing else about it, which isn't a good sign, but they let us do it again the next year so it couldn't have been that bad.

With our ratings racing up, we were no longer just "that morning show" on "that classic rock station." We were now players in the bigger game.

The top five morning shows in town were watching, and so were we. Our ratings were cutting into their profits, and I doubt seriously if any of them knew who we were at the beginning of the year, but 1988 solidified that we were here to stay. LA radio people, and a healthy chunk of listeners, had discovered who we were, and they knew our names now.

You can dream it, you can attempt it, you can taste it, but nothing compares to achieving it. The coming year would contain a moment I had never dreamed because I didn't think it was possible, yet it happened.

ARE YOU AWARE RICK DEES IS HERE?

1989

66 When someone does a small task beautifully, their whole environment is affected by it. 99

—JERRY SEINFELD

Last year felt like our warmup, and this year would be our first real workout. We had stretched, we broke a sweat, now let's see how much we can bench.

Thinking back to the night we first met in the business center of a Birmingham hotel room, I couldn't have known it would become this. I couldn't have known the creative chemistry we would develop, and the kind of unique radio we would create. But as I look at it now, the essential elements were there.

The recipe is old and proven. I could use any number of examples, but I'll go with Martin and Lewis. Dean Martin was a crooner, but not really funny. Jerry Lewis was a comedian but couldn't sing. As individuals, they were very good, but together they were *Martin and Lewis*, and they made history.

Aristotle said over six months ago that if you take a person who's good at one thing, pair them up with another person who's good at a different thing, then the whole is greater than the sum of its parts.

The one thing I couldn't predict was our ability to work together. At one point, we could finish each other's sentences when discussing ideas for the show. We were putting on the kind of morning radio people had never heard, including us. It was fresh, rebellious, hysterical, irreverent, and stupid, and we were having a blast, which is a key element. All of it together made for *must hear* radio.

Since I felt we would be around a while, Lynda and I bought our first house in Saugus. It had a pool and rose bushes. It doesn't matter who you are, buying your first house is a big deal, and the feeling of accomplishment was fairly strong. You can't explain the feeling, you have to experience it.

Every day after work, Matthew and I would swim. Afterward, we would have lunch in the gazebo, and then all three of us would nap. It was a wonderful period in our lives and satisfying knowing this move to southern California was not only the culmination of a dream, but gratifying that our gamble paid off. No, I didn't trim the roses, though I *did* trim Lynda. She was pregnant again, and the chances were skewing positive that the child was mine! Having a second child was planned, and it took a while. However, I didn't mind the work I put into it. Proper planning is an important part of a successful life, both personally and professionally.

In planning our morning show, Brian and I would prepare two major pieces each day. These would normally be scripted comedy bits and placed at key times during the show. We would then fill out the rest of the show with maybe six minor pieces, which required minimal preparation. Most mornings, we wouldn't need all minor pieces, because some topic caught fire and the phones were hot. But the major bits were a tent pole of the show and always aired.

One of our major pieces we did around this time, "Noah's Ark," is considered a classic by our listeners, and I bring it up for a reason. Throughout the sketch, Noah stood on the deck of his ark talking to God about how great everything was as he searched for land. The entire joke of the bit was that the ark had already hit land, but Noah didn't notice since he was busy talking biblical gibberish.

We did this live, with music, sound effects, and only the idea. We made up the entire thing as we went, with no script. Yet, if you ask a Mark and Brian listener about their favorite bits, many will bring up Noah's Ark.

So, what makes it classic? Well, why did people love the *Saturday*

Night Live sketch "More Cowbell," so much? The only joke was that as the band played "Don't Fear the Reaper," the producer wanted more cowbell, yet it's considered one of the greats.

Radio listeners hadn't heard this kind of *concept comedy* before. Noah's Ark certainly wasn't classic because of the jokes, there weren't any. The bit didn't even have a joke at the end to tell you it was over, we simply faded up the music.

People were used to hearing punchlines, and we threw those out, and went with a scenario that was funny, not a punchline. When you take something that's been done in only one way, and you change it by putting your spin on it, that's the beginning seed of creativity, which makes it uniquely yours. This was a minor piece of the puzzle that explains what set us apart from most others. At the very least, it was original, and originality was the main ingredient in the recipe of Mark and Brian.

When we first got to LA, there was Rick Dees and then everybody else. Rick was the master of old school morning radio, a quick paced show with lots of moving parts. He had the best joke writers, voice actors, seemingly the best of everything. It was an onslaught of top-flight morning entertainment.

The idea of unseating him never crossed my mind, until it became possible. Our ratings were climbing and his were falling. Part of the equation for our success was fringe listeners, meaning people who don't normally listen to classic rock were listening to Mark and Brian, and many of those fringe listeners came from Rick.

By the time we arrived, Rick had been on the air for eight years and his listeners may have grown weary of the same thing every day, albeit good. They were willing to check out something new, but simply being new wasn't going to impress, it had to be different.

We couldn't compete with Rick by being just like him. He was the best at old school one-liners, and we would have lost handily. Everything Rick was, we weren't. Nobody had heard what we were doing because nobody had done it, and people will change their radio for different, but it won't keep them. You have to be good to pick up a new listener, but there's one major element to anything that's good, and that's consistency.

Along with being great at what he did, Rick was consistent. You knew what you were going to get every day, and that's comforting. I learned a long time ago, it does you no good to be amazing on Tuesday and mediocre on Wednesday. You have to be good every day, or you won't be around long, and consistency is probably the single hardest thing anyone can accomplish. It's the largest dividing factor between winners and losers in any facet of business.

We had the good fortune of having a couple of consistent winners in our building with us, and I'm proud to say I got to know one of them rather well. The morning show across the hall at KABC was the legendary Ken and Bob. Ken was an old school broadcaster who always had a smile for me, and I sensed a warmth from him that said, "I was once where you are." Ken was entertained by our crap and once said to me, "Maybe we should talk," and I regret to say, I never followed up. And it's too late, because I think he's dead now and if he isn't, he should be.

Ken and Bob were the former kings of mornings in LA who had to move aside for Rick Dees. Their slogan was EGBOK, "Everything's gonna be okay." Alright Ken, let's see if *this* is gonna be okay.

It was National Farmers Day and to celebrate, a very nice farmer brought one of his cows into our control room, and it was no surprise that the cow had more teeth than the farmer. Our room wasn't very big, so the cow took up most of it. The bovine had a giant bell around his neck, so every move he made rang the bell, which was great for radio.

We had the engineering department outfit us with wireless collar mics, and the cow had one too. We walked him down the hall of the building and his ringing bell was impossible to ignore. Everyone came out of their offices to look. There's virtually no way to not smile at that unless you have a problem with livestock in the workplace.

We walked into the studio of Ken and Bob and with the cow standing between us, we sang the "Happy Farmers Day" song, which we had written just for this occasion. We then turned and exited, leaving the cow behind, and we didn't go back for him.

There was Ken, there was Bob, and now there was a cow. When Ken realized we were leaving the cow behind, he started that wheezy, cackle laugh he had. Every time I saw Ken after that, he would smile and bring up the cow, because as I said, he was entertained by our crap. For the rest of that week, the hallways smelled like cow ass.

And for the record, no cows were harmed during that celebration of National Farmers Day!

It's not that I wondered what happened to our Northridge rental house, but the evening news showed me all the disgusting, sordid details. Normally, I was playing with Matt around news time. The TV had remained on from Matt watching *Mr. Rogers*. Matt would put on his coat and tie for the start of the show, then take off the coat and put on a sweater when Mr. Rogers did. Crazy cute, I know.

The local news reported a "den of sin, wife swapping ring," had been busted at a house in Northridge, and that's when I looked up. The sin-ridden home was being used by paying customers to party and have sex with someone else's wife.

There had been reports of excessive noise, so the police investigated and found massive amounts of sluts and whores having sex with men they didn't know. The news reported that sex was taking place outdoors as well. They showed aerial footage of the backyard in question. *There was my jacuzzi, in my backyard, of my rental home.* My former residence had become a "den of sin." Matthew was shocked! My only question was, where were the sluts and whores when I lived there?

We tried to make laughter our number one commodity on the show, so we always had a warm chair for comedians, if they were good. You didn't have to be a star for us to book you, but you did need a strong reputation for being funny. The up-and-coming comedians who were still making a name for themselves would always bring the funny but the older, more established ones, didn't feel the need.

We had Jerry Seinfeld on the show, who was obviously established, and I don't remember him bringing down the house, but he was engaging. Two interesting things happened in this interview, which is why I bring it up.

A young comedian called and asked Jerry how he could get repre-sentation, and what Jerry told him is true. Jerry said, "My friend, you don't have to worry about finding a rep, because if you're any good, they'll find you." There was a sizable pause from the comedian caller, because I don't think this was what he wanted to hear. The reason this stuck with me is that Jerry meant what he said, and he's correct. If you suck at what you do, no one's going to care, but if you're any good, people will line up to get you. So, do your thing to the best of your ability and the rest will come to you.

And it's obvious why I would remember the second thing. Another caller asked Jerry if he had ever thought about doing tele-vision. Jerry told him, "Just recently, I signed a deal with NBC for four episodes of a sitcom. We've already shot them, and they should be airing soon." I asked Jerry if the show was any good and he said, "Yeah, they felt pretty good. We'll see how it goes." The four shows that *felt pretty good* to him wound up being classic comedy television.

During our tenure, we hosted numerous big events, which always came with high demand for tickets. The two obvious events were the Mark and Brian Christmas Show and our Disney events, and we always used these ticket giveaways to improve the show. The only way to get a ticket was through us, so we benefited greatly by the surprising things people would do to win the golden ticket.

Popular choices were throwing water on a sleeping family mem-ber (always good), a wife waking her husband with a blow job (even better), and the "go to" prank phone call, but it had to be good.

My favorite prank call was a guy who called his fiancé to pretend he was breaking up with her, only once he told her, she started crying and admitted she'd been having an affair with a co-worker. We were stunned and didn't know what to say, when both yelled, "We're kid-ding!" It was as well orchestrated as I'd ever heard, and we fell hard for it. But we had one particular event that fell in our lap and it was a massive golden ticket.

To put it bluntly, Warner Brothers was worried. When the an-nouncement was made that they were going to make *Batman, The Movie*, people were pumped, and then they announced Michael Keaton would play Batman. Many were outraged, and I mean pissed, because most didn't care for the choice. There were mock-ups of Beetlejuice wearing a Batman cowl, so they had a PR problem on a huge budget film, and they knew it.

As the premiere approached, haters were planning to demonstrate. Warner Brothers was nervous, so instead of going with one giant premiere, they broke it into several premiere showings, and offered one of the screenings to us. It was Willy Wonka's Golden Ticket, and we held it.

People came at us from all directions to get tickets. But my favorite was when Italian singer Jerry Vale called us. In the event you're unfamiliar, Jerry was a crooner from the '50s and '60s, with one of the smoothest voices I've heard. He told us that his three grandchildren wanted to see *Batman*, and we told him the tickets were his if he would sing the Star-Spangled Banner at the premiere, something he was well known for doing at sporting events. He said, "Gentleman, it would be my honor."

At the screening, Jerry stood at his seat with his grandkids beside him and belted out the National Anthem. "Lo ha fatto magnificamente," which means, "He did it beautifully."

Theater-goers didn't want to hear any of our crap, they came for the film, so after Jerry, we got right to the movie and the people in our screening loved it.

Michael Keaton's performance was incredibly strong. When Keaton said, "I'm Batman," you believed him. It only took him two hours to quiet all the haters and, in my estimation, his performance is still looked upon as *the* Batman by which all others are judged. In fact, I heard that Keaton is returning to play Batman on the *Flash*. I don't think they asked George Clooney to put on his nipple suit and do it. They asked Batman to do it!

When it was announced that Mark and Brian were coming to LA, there were some who scoffed and gave us little chance, just as Michael Keaton went to the set each day knowing most of the Batman fan base hated him in that role. I felt like Keaton must've felt, and I went to work each day feeling we had something to prove.

When the spring ratings came out a month later, I was in the backyard with Matthew when my phone rang. It was Bill Sommers, and he told me that Mark and Brian were now the number one morning show in Los Angeles. We had done the unthinkable, we had unseated Rick Dees. Bill ended our conversation by reminding me, "Don't forget where you came from." My mind wandered back to this question the *LA Times* reporter asked me: "Are you aware Rick Dees is here?"

Rick was good, we were good; Rick was consistent, we were consistent. What made the difference? This is something everyone should learn if you're going to get into the entertainment business. We won because people were ready for a change. Have you heard the adage, "Out with the old, in with the new?" People had heard Rick and were ready for something different.

It's the number one law of entertainment and if you understand this, it will make your life easier when you are cast aside for the next pretty thing, because it's going to happen. You don't have to like it, but you need to understand it, because you cannot change it. Your only hope is to prepare for it.

Jerry Reed had a good song in the 1970s and its innocent title was also a kind of warning: "When You're Hot, You're Hot." What Jerry was comedically saying turned out to be true. I experienced small levels of success in years past, however, being #1 in LA brought the kind of white-hot heat I didn't know existed.

When you've got some heat, people want a piece. They come from all angles, with all sorts of gimmicks, but when you peel back the layers and look inside it was always about money; money they could make if we said yes. They were all selling themselves, their pitch was about them, not us. It's interesting that the same thing happened in Birmingham and Los Angeles. The moment we became number one, television producers showed up at our door.

For two months, we would spend several hours after the show meeting with these questionable heathens. Being number one was only part of our draw. We clearly had the personality television looks for, but what helped is that we weren't ugly to look at, or at least I wasn't. We were considered a "good get."

I had learned from the fiasco of producers in Birmingham. I kept a keen watch on each producer we met. They all brought credentials, things they'd done, where they'd worked, but most made a big deal of who they knew. They understood the importance of being seen as part of the inner circle. But I learned long ago, desperation has an odor.

As I looked at each résumé, I was looking for two things: what shows had they produced, and were they currently employed? Each day I left those meetings I had to wipe, because there was a lot of shit flowing in there.

During one of these meetings, two guys walked in, our first duo. Their résumé showed they'd written the movie, *There's Something About Mary*, but what caught my eye was their development deal at NBC. I asked, "Is this development deal current?" They both said yes, then one of them said, "We called NBC and told them about our meeting with you, and they're interested." That nailed it, these two were genuine.

Keeping it real, Hollywood producers were lining up to meet with us. But not three short years before, we had locked ourselves out of our apartment and were forced to break in so I could sleep on a couch. This thought was never lost on me through these meetings.

This next story was twenty-five years in the making, and it's one of the top three things we're best remembered for, and the saga began here.

Elvis's home, Graceland, had been open to public tours for several years, and we decided we should broadcast from there. We asked permission, but Graceland said no. We disagreed with that answer and decided to do it anyway. I mean, why would they care if they didn't know?

We had the engineering department rig up small umbrellas with portable microphones concealed in the handles. That way, we could walk through Graceland talking to our umbrellas and no one would be the wiser.

Broadcasting from inside Graceland would prove tricky. We would be behind a stone brick building, which isn't great for receiving our signal, so engineer Rex had to constantly move the van to track our movement.

Once inside Graceland, we stayed close to the tour guide so the mics would pick her up. We kept spouting information about Elvis to our tour group which was horridly incorrect, and the tour guide kept correcting us. It was both funny *and* annoying!

We made it to the TV room, and that's where the Elvis police caught up to us. We found out later someone had called Graceland from LA and told them what we were up to. They took us upstairs through a door marked "No Admittance." We found ourselves in Elvis's kitchen, which wasn't on the tour then. They sat us down at the dining table where Elvis ate his meals, and we were the first ones to ever see that shit.

The Elvis cops took our earplugs but left our umbrellas on the table in front of us, so we continued broadcasting the entire time. Stupid Elvis police! They eventually told us they were kicking us out, so they walked us down Elvis's driveway as we carried our umbrellas singing "Love Me Tender" to them. We tried to get them to join in but the Elvis cop on the left seemed pissy.

The next year, we got a call from the Rose Parade people, who told us they had a ten-foot Elvis head covered in roses, and did we want it? Well duh! We decided to do the obvious by strapping the Elvis head to an 18-wheel flat-bed and driving it across the country to Memphis, giving it to Graceland as an apology gift for allegedly broadcasting from there. Graceland would clearly forgive us and embrace us, right?

We went to the Rose Parade dismantling center where they craned over the Elvis head to our truck bed. Brian and I would follow the 18-wheeler in a motorhome driven by engineer Rex. Our plan was to reach Memphis on Thursday and award Graceland our "Gift of Elvis Sorrow" on Friday's show.

I woke up one night in the motorhome and went to the front where Rex was driving. It was two in the morning and gushing rain. Rex was doing 90 mph, not two yards from the back of our 18-wheeler. Did I mention that Rex is about a hundred years old?

Fearing for my life, I sat in the passenger seat in order to witness my death. There was something about the rumbling sound coming from the huge tires of the 18-wheeler, which were two feet from my head, that lulled me back to sleep. I think when doom and peril are imminent, it tends to wear you out. The moment we arrived in Memphis, I fell into a hotel bed and didn't budge until showtime on Friday.

We started the show in our hotel parking lot and followed the flatbed over to Graceland while broadcasting. We arrived that morning at ten and parked the flatbed in front of the famous gates of Graceland. The tour vans were now shut down since they couldn't get past us or around us. Car horns were blaring and all of it, live on the air.

Brian and I are now out of the motorhome, wandering Elvis Presley Boulevard while broadcasting. Then, the Memphis police arrived and I'm 100 percent positive we're going to jail. The cops started directing traffic around us, but never once said, "Move your truck." We were allowed to stay, blocking traffic, and the tour, for almost two hours.

Finally, some executive from Graceland came out screaming at us, "If I had it my way, I would shoot you both in the head." Here's my favorite part, "And you will never be allowed to own or appreciate Elvis memorabilia ever again!" I'm not kidding, he said that. A bullet to the head would be rough, but being blocked from all Elvis memorabilia? Come on, man, *don't be cruel.*

Many years later, I took my family to "Elvis week" at Graceland, and I was worried about being kicked out, so I wore sunglasses most of the time. No one noticed me.

During our stay, we went to the first ever Elvis Impersonator contest. During intermission, I went to the bathroom and saw the same executive who yelled he wanted to shoot us, so I walked up and said, "This has been fantastic, thank you." He looked at me and said, "Well thank you, sir. Glad you're enjoying it." Since I wasn't appreciating any Elvis memorabilia at the time, I was completely invisible to him.

Maybe a decade later, I applied to participate in a trivia game on Elvis radio. As a test, I gave them my real name and was told, "You're not allowed to play."

Clearly, I'm still officially banned from Graceland, but I will always sneak in. And do you know who would've gotten the biggest kick out of this story? Elvis! He would've laughed uncontrollably and been pissed we didn't invite him. So, what have we learned? That rock and roll never forgets!

We began a series of meetings with the two producers we liked, John Strauss and Ed Dector. They brought New World Television into the mix. We sat in one of those conference rooms that smelled like Lemon Pledge, complete with a ridiculously long mahogany table, leather chairs, and fifteen people I will never care to know, while John and Ed pitched their idea for a Mark and Brian pilot. New World would make the pilot, John and Ed would write and produce. But before that could happen, the idea would be pitched to NBC to see if they liked it and most importantly, if they would fund it.

This would become the beginning moment of our jump into television. *If only I'd known.*

Everything has a beginning, and I have some history with this one. There's a particular person who played a part in a great moment in my life, so let me share his beginning moment. When he was sixteen, Barry Eugene Carter was thrown in jail for stealing tires. While in prison, Barry heard the song "It's Now or Never" by Elvis. He later said it was an awakening for him, like someone had hit him in the face with a baseball bat. Young Carter had fumbled around with music as a hobby and decided in that moment to follow his dream of becoming a musician once he was released from prison.

Barry Eugene Carter went on to become one of the biggest artists of the day. You would know him as Barry White, and many years later, Barry would create a wonderful memory for my family shortly after the birth of my second child.

Lynda and I decided not to find out the baby's gender. We carefully went through tons of boy and girl names and narrowed them down to two short lists that we both agreed to. Lynda said she would know the name the moment she saw the baby's face.

We had Barry on the show the day before our child was born, and I told him about the upcoming birth. His face lit up, as he got off his chair and gave me a huge bear hug, and said, "You are blessed, my friend." Barry had nine kids and was truly happy for me.

This would be a Cesarean birth, which is great because you make an appointment for that. I was videotaping every moment, with a camera the size of a traffic light.

The doctor said, "It's a girl." The moment the baby is born, drugs are administered to the mother. I leaned into Lynda whispering, "Sweetie, it's a girl, what's her name?" In Lynda's now drugged state, she couldn't find my face but said, "Her name is Amy," which is a wonderful name. However, it was nowhere to be found on the list of girls' names we had discussed. It's not like we talked about Amy and decided against it. The name was never brought up, not once, and I thought about saying something, but wisely chose not to because I love my life.

Here's a great rule for all new fathers: Never disagree with a drugged woman who has just given birth to your child! I turned to the nurse and said, "Her name is Amy."

When Lynda and I got home from the hospital, we found a gigantic basket that covered our dining room table. It contained anything and everything a new baby could need: toys, stuffed animals, and clothing. The card read, "Enjoy your little girl, much love, Barry White."

Events like the *Batman* premiere were a gift, because normally we had to create events like that ourselves. Some events came naturally to us; others were inspired by an existing event. We needed something for the show that screamed Thanksgiving. Our combined thinking was, if Macy's department store can put on a three-hour commercial and call it a parade, then we can do them one better, and we'll call it, "Mark and Brian's Day Before Thanksgiving Day Parade."

Here's a little-known fact: The caveman was the instigator of the first known parade, as proven by paintings found on cave walls in Spain. The cavemen would go hunting, and the tribe folks would line each side of the path and cheer the men coming home with their kill. Boom! First parade.

For Mark and Brian, our thinking was always simple. We'll let listeners submit ideas for parade entries, book the ones we like, and broadcast from a Mark and Brian listener parade.

We had a ton of great entries, so where does one have a parade when you need lots of space? The Los Angeles Coliseum, of course!

For me, the Wednesday before Thanksgiving had always been a holiday in itself. I would race home from school because I knew I had four glorious days of nothing that had anything to do with school. It would be food, football and not school. We got our first color television on the Wednesday before Thanksgiving, 1965.

After a year of begging, my father finally caved. Don't get me wrong; there's no replacing my beloved black and white TV. That's the set I watched the Beatles on the *Ed Sullivan Show*, and my first sighting of the *Three Stooges*. You can't replace an old friend like that, yet I waited patiently.

When the headlights of the delivery truck hit the back wall of my house, I leapt from my seat to hold the door.

"My god it's so big," I said as they heaved it through the door.

"Twenty-seven-inch color console," one of the men muttered, as he waddled it through the den.

"Put it there," I said, pointing to where the black and white sat.

"What should we do with the old one?" the man asked.

"Who gives a shit, this is color," I spouted.

The man adjusted the color levels and showed me how to work it. As soon as he left, I jacked the color all the way up. My father paid 468 bucks for this baby, let's have some color!

I would say the Macy's parade was glorious in color, but it's only the Macy's Thanksgiving parade, three hours I'll never get back. However, Underdog wearing a red suit and blue cape, I never knew that!

Based on the crowds that showed up at the Coliseum, the saying was true that "people love a parade," as thousands packed the Coliseum entrance.

The listener entry everybody wanted to see was a guy who had built a giant slingshot in the back of his truck. He promised it would have the power to catapult different Thanksgiving items over the top of the Coliseum wall. His first attempt was a pumpkin he placed in a leather pouch attached to giant rubber bands. His construction buddies pulled it back and let it fly. The pumpkin smashed into the Coliseum wall and shattered into bits. The guy adjusted the torque and tried again. The pumpkin cleared it by a ton this time, as the crowd cheered.

As he was loading the turkey, the crowd started chanting, "Wall . . . wall . . . wall," so he lowered the torque and shot it. I never knew a turkey could explode like that, and the crowd roared with approval.

One of the oddest Thanksgiving moments was the year Ike Turner was our grand marshal. He had just been released from prison and waved to the crowd as his float blasted "Nutbush City Limits."

After the parade, Ike asked if he could speak to me in private. We walked around the back of the grandstand where he handed me a cassette tape. He said they were his demos he had just finished, and he was looking for backers. He asked me if he could borrow $10,000. I declined, because I didn't have it on me but know this, the music on the tape was pretty good. Just sayin'!

And as an honorable mention, we had Bob Eubanks as grand marshal one year, and he rode a horse that was wearing a toupée, and I'm not sure why and don't care; it was hysterical. Happy Thanksgiving everyone!

We wrapped up the year with a bang. Our Christmas Show had graduated from a hotel by the airport to the Hollywood Palladium on Sunset Boulevard. I know, not much of an improvement, but the greatest moments we ever had on any Christmas Show were in that room. If you walk into the Palladium, the first thing you'll notice is that it smells like urine, but that screams rock and roll, doesn't it? It also screams champagne music, and I'll explain that.

Growing up, Saturday night at my house was a standing date with burgers on the grill, and *Lawrence Welk* on the television. This was the early 1960s, and charcoal with lighter fluid didn't exist yet. But my father was a thinking man. He figured if he soaked the charcoal briquettes in gasoline, they would light faster. We could always tell when he'd lit the grill by the sizable explosion as a plume of fire shot across the den window. We would then sit and watch the king of champagne music, Lawrence Welk, while eating burgers that tasted like a car engine.

My parents never played music in our house, and watching Lawrence Welk was my first exposure to live music. The dancers and singers on the show could kiss my ass, but watching the orchestra play had me glued, except that polka crap. Nothing says sexy like the accordion!

As we met with the stage manager at the Palladium, he told us the history of the venue, which included the fact that the Lawrence Welk show was broadcast from this very room.

I walked to the center of the stage where Frank Sinatra and countless others had stood. I looked out at the empty theater and realized I was now looking at what was beyond the confines of my hometown. But this was something I had seen before, through the viewing lens of my childhood. This was my first real birds-eye view of what was *out there*, and it still smelled like urine.

The Christmas Shows we held at the Palladium were pure. They were like plays you would put on in your mother's basement. We had volunteer switchboarders setting up sound equipment, and they had no idea what they were doing, but it worked. They would string Christmas lights across the public address speakers, and it looked like shit, but they put it there with love. We had no stage manager, we just winged it, and it somehow worked.

In those early days, tickets were free with no assigned seats. People would stand in line all night to get a seat close to the stage. The

Palladium had large round tables with white tablecloths, and maybe fifteen chairs, which I loved, because listeners who had never met would sit together for hours and the only thing they had in common was their love for our show.

People would sell their kids to get tickets because it was the hottest show in town. I believe we were the very first to hold a radio station Christmas Show, something that clearly caught on. The Christmas Show was our "thank you" for listening. It was free, and we did it for our listeners.

The week of the Christmas Show we found out that NBC had given the green light to our pilot. We were scheduled to shoot in the spring of the next year. Television was clearly in our future, but things never turn out exactly the way you envision them. We would board the NBC train, and it was on the *fast track to trouble town.*

I THINK I LOVE YOU

1990

> **"**Ambition is a dream with a V8 engine.**"**
>
> —ELVIS PRESLEY

This would be the purest year of our tenure together. We were riding a wave of creative energy, and nothing in my experience had ever felt that good. Something wonderful happens when you introduce something completely new to a place that had grown stale with years of the same old thing. The excitement becomes a living, breathing thing, that's reflected by every person there. This wonderful beast we had built must be fed with new and never-before heard stupidity. Whatever we tried seemed to work, and it felt effortless. We weren't so busy yet that we couldn't enjoy what we had created. There was no downside and anything seemed possible.

It was to be a year of firsts. We had the filming of a pilot with NBC in the spring, we were nominated for a major radio award, and we had a unique idea for Halloween that had never been conceived. But first would be what we did for Valentine's Day, and I wasn't comfortable with any part of what I agreed to do!

I guess there was self-imposed pressure to achieve a somewhat similar response to the chocolate dipping—something big, original, and flirting with a possible burning death in the process. We decided to skywrite. What better way to say Happy Valentine's Day than flying in two planes over the 405 freeway, and writing words in the sky with smoke? Nothing says "I love you" more!

Brian was in one plane, I was in another, broadcasting the entire time so commuters could watch us do this stupid thing. Getting up there was no major deal, but once the writing began, it became an entirely different experience.

The plan was to write M&B and encircle that in a heart. We did the M&B in no time, just a bunch of straight lines, but now comes the curvy part at the top of the heart. We flew straight up for the sides of the heart and then started drifting out to begin the curvy part. My plane took a jerky, sharp left turn, then sideways, and straight down, and that's when I saw God our lord. And just when I think it's over, I see Brian's plane headed directly for me. We had to crisscross to make the lines meet at the crest of the heart. I screamed like a naked girl in a horror film the entire sideways and down part. It was a big hit though, and it made all the news channels, but food was not my friend for two days.

As stated, I dreaded the skywriting thing, only to find out it was far worse than can be imagined, and I regretted it dearly. I found things in my pants that shouldn't have been there. But something I *don't* regret is the very stylish mullet I had for years.

I'm in my final throes of life now, and there's a cigar shop I frequent where my near-death cigar acquaintances and I light up and chat. One of their favorite things is to look up my past on their phones and laugh out loud at my mullet, to my face. These redneck bastards have had the same haircut since they were five, because they lack the balls to do anything different from fear their sister won't find it sexy.

It was the early 1990s, I lived in LA, and the mullet was mandatory fashion. I worked that hairstyle like my job. It's rightfully described as "business up front, massive party in the back!"

I would spend hours at a Beverly Hills stylist (we call that a barber in the south), and I would get highlights throughout, full perm in back, followed by the feathered haircut up top, then bring the whole thing together with proper styling.

I would then drive around Beverly Hills in my convertible Mercedes with my mullet proudly flapping in the wind, and my left ear sporting a diamond earring. Yes, it happened, and I would gladly deny all this but there are pictures.

My mullet was the glimmering style of the times, and I wore it proudly. The pricks in my cigar shop can kiss my ass! And tell your wives I'll see them soon.

As a kid, I watched all the TV shows you would imagine, *Brady Bunch, Partridge Family, All My Children*, and never once did I think the day would come where I might co-star in my own television show. But we were on the brink of that happening. I was about to enter a crazy, confusing time.

I knew the radio world better than many, yet I knew nothing about television. I liked it because it was new but making decisions out of ignorance would be unwise. I settled on knowing I wasn't the first, nor would I be the last, and I would learn.

For the pilot, John and Ed had basically taken our radio existence and built a script around it. In the script, Brian and I were hosts of a low-rated television show. Joining us in the pilot were Dan Lauria of the *Wonder Years*, Jane Leeves of *Frasier*, and Corbin Bernsen of *LA Law*, so we had all the pieces.

The executive producer of our pilot was a man named Steve Binder. He was the musical genius NBC hired to direct Elvis in the *'68 Comeback Special*. I've always believed that was the finest hour of Elvis's career, and it was Steve Binder who was the creative force behind it. I told Steve I was a fan of his work, and his reaction seemed odd. I figured he must hear this all the time, so I let it go.

The afternoon of the taping, I was sitting in my dressing room wondering how many stars had been involved in weird celebrity sex on my makeup table, you know, like all of them do. My thoughts were interrupted by a knock at my door. It was Steve Binder who said, "You got a minute?" I smiled and opened the door wider, but he stepped back saying, "Let's take a walk."

He took me down the widest hallway I'd ever seen, with giant stage doors. Steve stopped at one and looked up, "Stage eight," he mumbled. He pulled some chains and gave a sturdy push, as the massive door cracked open. It was pitch black inside, so Steve clicked on a flashlight. As we walked, our footsteps echoed through the giant, empty stage. Steve finally stopped and shined the light down on the floor.

"It was right about here," Steve said.

Confused, I asked, "What was here?"

Steve flashed the light around the room.

"This is NBC studios, stage eight. This is where we shot the *Comeback Special,* and it was about here where Elvis stood." He then shined the light back down on the floor.

I've often said, if I could go back in time, it would be to June 3, 1968, to see Elvis reclaim his crown in the '68 Special, and I'm now looking at the spot where he did that. I was moved that Steve took the time to show a fan something he knew would be deeply appreciated.

Things were clearly going well. We owned mornings and were now flirting with television. But Brian and I were still working under the same meager deal we signed on our arrival at KLOS. Bill Sommers and Don were already discussing a new agreement. It was clear we were about to get seriously paid. But I said it before it started, Bill was going to fight this, and he did. Over the years, the battles between those two men were notoriously famous, and their petty disagreements made me chuckle.

It was *Freddy Kruger* ugly from the beginning. They once fought for weeks over where Brian and I would park our cars, and I'm not kidding.

Brian and I were standing in our producer's office one day when Don called and calmly said, "I want you both to exit the building immediately, and do not return until you have heard from me. If Bill tries to stop you, simply tell him he has to talk to me. You got it?" We did as requested and didn't return for several days.

Apparently, Don and Bill had hung up on each other, but not before making assorted threats. Whatever it was got ironed out, and we were back on Monday morning. Rumors had spread that we had been fired, Brian was dead, I had left for KROQ, you name it. But the lesson here is, always listen to your attorney because they represent you!

Part of the new contract was a signing bonus. I was given a check sealed in an envelope. I drove home cautiously as the check was sitting in the passenger seat, and I thought about belting it in.

I walked into my house, laid the check on the dining room table, and motioned for Lynda to look. We both just stared at it. My first full time radio salary was $100 a week and I could've never imagined a radio jock could make the kind of money that laid before me. *The check was for $350,000.* Neither of us had ever dreamed we would be the recipients of that much money, so we did what most would: We shoved the check into Lynda's jewelry case. After several months we caved and bought a new Samsung front loading washer/dryer combo. Installation was free!

Let me say this right now so I can finally relax about it. I always felt the *Brady Bunch* was just whatever, not great, bordering on hokey. I was a fan of the *Partridge Family*. Judge if you will, but the *Brady Bunch* was trying to teach me life lessons, and I didn't give a shit about that. *The Partridge Family* was funny, and you then got a musical performance at the end. Plus, the *Brady Bunch* didn't have David Cassidy!

David was a good singer and underrated as an actor, I felt. I privately freaked when we had David on the show, and I found I wasn't the only one. This would be the first time I witnessed genuine excitement from people who worked in our building over a guest.

He looked exactly like himself and a good version of it. David had gone through some shit—as we all do—though maybe not as intense as David's. Twenty years earlier, David was the biggest teen idol in the world, and he hated being defined as a pop music idol, so he dropped out of that world and recorded his own material. Nothing came of it, so there he sat, willing to play the role of former teen idol David Cassidy again.

He was a sponge for all the attention. Many station employees came in early to get a glimpse. It was a massive dose of fan praise, which seemed to be just what he needed. He was genuinely happy while in the room with us.

We invited David to join us at the Christmas Show and sing the old songs, meaning "I Think I Love You." David's boyish joy disappeared for the moment, as he seemingly processed what that would mean. After a few seconds, his smile spread across his face before saying, "Sure, I'm in."

Once the mics were off, David confessed he hadn't done anything musically in years, he didn't even have a band. We told him our house band was comprised of the best musicians in LA, and there was a rehearsal the night before the show. That relaxed him and he smiled saying, "Well, this will be interesting," and then burst into a guttural laugh. They say never meet your idol, but one of mine was sitting in front of me and doing just fine.

Though it may seem big, the world of network television is much smaller than you might think. Each network knows who is talking to whom, and when. Don let us know that CBS had inquired about a meeting with us. Since we had a deal with NBC, Don had to clear it.

Brian and I went to CBS to meet with some executive who wanted to know our interest in a possible late-night talk show for them. We were very interested, since this seemed to fall more in our zone than a sitcom. The guy asked permission to call Don and begin discussions. Brian and I left there realizing this might happen.

During my five-hour drive home to Santa Clarita, I returned calls, and one was to my friend John Leader, one of the biggest voiceover artists of the time. He did all of Spielberg's stuff. I told John about the CBS meeting and that we would probably be doing a late-night show for them, and his response landed oddly. He said congratulations and all the stuff one should say, but his tone didn't ring true.

We never heard a single word from anyone at CBS, and John already knew that. He's a seasoned pro and knows these types of meetings go on every day in this town, and nothing ever comes of them. He knew I didn't understand that, and he left it alone. I felt like an idiot, getting my TV feet wet in front of him, but John was being my friend, and threw me a bone by saying nothing.

Why have a meeting with us when the things discussed are never going to happen? What's the point? Does it make you feel like a big man when you already know you don't have the power to actually pull this off? When I was in high school, if you couldn't make it to a date, you'd call the girl and tell her. It's called common courtesy, you shitbag! As stated, I didn't know television, but I was learning.

Mark and Brian had been nominated for *Billboard Magazine's* "Air Personality of the Year." I'd had my share of whatever awards throughout my career, but this was my first nomination for a major award, and Billboard carried weight in the industry. This nomination solidified that I was a player in my chosen game. I obviously showed no excitement, but I was deeply moved. The winner would be announced at a radio convention in Dallas, so we went. If we won this, *I wanted to be there.*

As a young radio jock, I'd been to many of these conventions, packed with radio people from all over the world. The top name air talent would attend and were the stars of the weekend. I remember how excited I was to have thirty seconds with them, maybe a picture. It meant more than they knew, and I never forgot their kindness. A few of the younger radio guys wanted time with me at this Dallas convention, and I gladly shared it, at $10 a head, and I could've easily gotten $20.

At the awards ceremony, Brian and I were named Air Personality of the Year and I was beaming, though cool about it. I only shouted, "I am a Radio Titan!" twice.

Afterward, we were hanging out by the lobby bar when some guy stepped up and said, "Would you like to meet Rick Dees?" He then gestured over to his left, so I looked. I saw Rick, hiding behind a marble column playing peek-a-boo, popping his head back and forth. The oddness of it started right about there.

Rick then walked over and started doing some character voices. I gave the obligatory laugh where it fit, and this went on for maybe three minutes, and he was gone. It then dawned on me I never actually met him; we never shook hands or were introduced.

If I'd been a listener of his, I'm sure this would've been a great moment, but I'm a radio entertainer just like he is, and the moment struck me as peculiar. I wish I could have met Rick Dees, *the man*, instead I met Rick Dees, the *radio star*. But I would meet him again and it's that meeting that I remember most fondly.

I was very aware of the position we held. We were number one, we were moving into television, we had a ton of heat, but oftentimes simply being aware doesn't show you the full scope of what is actually happening in the real world. I was about to step into a situation that held within it an example of our popularity, and it frightened me.

It was now fall and we hadn't done an in-person appearance in quite a while. Because of ratings data we knew—with pinpoint accuracy—where our listeners were, and where they weren't. Based on that, we knew we were very strong in the Santa Clarita Valley, and Lancaster has a huge fair each year, so we thought that would be a good spot to show up.

We spent lots of airtime auditioning listener talent for the live stage show, so everyone knew we were coming. Lynda and I took the kids, Matt now four, and Amy barely one.

We arrived early to walk the fair and see the sights. There's nothing I love more than a carnie who has a serious aversion to bathing, yelling at me to pick up a plastic yellow duck; *that drips Americana*.

Our event was being held on the fair's biggest stage. Once I arrived backstage, I could hear the attending crowd milling about, and could tell our event was packed.

Brian and I walked out to what the fair had estimated was 10,000 people. This was the largest gathering of people I would ever witness from a stage in my career. We were on stage for two hours and could do no wrong, the laughs were almost nonstop. We finished the show and moved off to a backstage area and took pictures with the executive staff from the fair. I thanked everybody, gathered my family, and headed out the backstage entrance.

We had stepped into an ocean of listeners who had been waiting for us. I picked up Matt and Lynda held Amy. I pulled Lynda close as we tried to move through, but there was nowhere to go. The crowd started to crush in, and we had zero security. At one point—and I'm sure they didn't mean to—someone grabbed a hand full of Matt's hair and that terrified Lynda. Without the crowd realizing it, they had become a mob, and there was no direction we could move. I tried to return to the stage area, but that was blocked. We were now surrounded.

Amy was crying as Matt clung tightly to me. At this point, a listener realized what was happening and leaned into me yelling, "Which way is your car?" With that, he grabbed my arm, his buddy grabbed Lynda's, and they started carving a path through the crowd while forming a pocket around us.

When we got to the car, I thanked each of them and offered up Lynda for an evening of "around the world." They politely declined.

On Monday morning's Mark and Brian meeting, Bill's first question was "Are Lynda and the kids okay?" That was very much Bill. He could be tough, but he was always a people person first, and he was genuinely concerned about what he had heard. Bill hired a professional team of security for every Mark and Brian event from that moment on.

Case in point: Soon after we were at a listener meet and greet, and there was a sizable crowd. Brian and I were busy signing but I noticed security had started chatting on their walkie talkies. There were normally two security guys near us, and one roaming the crowd.

Apparently, security had spotted a guy in line wearing no shirt and sweating heavily, and it wasn't that hot, so he reported that. Brian and I were clueless.

The guy got up to us and I noticed security had moved to the edge of our table. The sweaty guy reached for his back pocket, which was ill-advised, so security moved on him. As they reached him, he tossed something toward Brian and me. Security grabbed the item, and the guy, and they were gone in seconds.

The item he tossed turned out to be a wad of paper with mostly illegible scribbling. They could only make out a few words, but nothing threatening. The man was released outside the venue and told not to return until his poor penmanship greatly improved. You don't realize you need security until suddenly, you do.

I've never trusted when someone says, "I've got good news and bad news." That's just a way of softening the blow that shitty news is coming.

The results from the NBC test groups were in concerning our pilot. We had a meeting with John and Ed to discuss. For the record, I loved both these guys. They were funny, very knowledgeable about their business, and would complete each other's sentences, which entertained me. Ed was straight forward with his words, and John would come in behind to soften the blow.

The meeting began with Ed saying, "The test groups hated your show," with John right behind, "But they really liked you guys." Hysterical! And it was that way the entire time we worked with them.

What they told us was true. The test groups didn't like the pilot, but they liked Mark and Brian, and they liked us best when we were just talking. Based on those results, NBC had countered and wanted to make another pilot with us in unscripted form. It was clear to me then, NBC wanted this to work.

On the radio show, we had Thanksgiving and Christmas covered with solid Mark and Brian event crap, but Halloween beckoned. Such a fun, festive holiday, and we had nothing unique.

In my youth, summer nights were perfect for most anything since there was zero school the next day, but something we did on a semi-regular basis was go to the Joy Land Drive-In on Saturday night. It took something big to pull me away from those gasoline burgers dad made, but this would do it!

The fire department would bring their ladder truck and park it in front of the screen for the kids to play on, which was fun for about three minutes. I would then go to the concession stand with my father to get really disgusting food kept warm by a lightbulb. The taste didn't matter because we ate it out of cardboard boxes in the car, which is barbaric, and awesome when you're a kid, and I didn't even use a napkin. I wiped my mouth on my bare arm, which is clearly caveman territory.

I don't remember watching the movie, because the sound coming out of that metal speaker attached to my car window made it difficult to know if the movie had even started. But we always had a blast and couldn't wait to go back.

By the '90s, drive-ins in LA had become little more than farmers markets on weekends. Very few showed movies anymore and that seemed a shame. Plus, I've gotten laid so many times at the drive-in, I felt at home. So, we decided to bring it back with the first annual "Mark and Brian Halloween Drive-In."

Families brought their kids in costume, who would trick or treat from car to car. We told listeners to bring bags of candy for the occasion. The movie showing was the kid-friendly, *The Ghost and Mr. Chicken.* Then we'd do the listener talent show from a hydraulic crane in front of the screen, and then the original *Halloween* while the kids slept in the back seat. The place was packed, and this drive-in hadn't seen that many cars in decades. Plus, we made sure the concession stand was open serving barely edible lightbulb food.

The hard part of these events was finding usable, thirty-five-millimeter prints to show. Plus, we had to send in tech people to make sure the projectors still worked, but it was worth the trouble, for a couple of reasons. These kids came in with their parents not knowing what a drive-in was, and soon found out these places showed movies they could watch from their cars; how cool. Then, even better, they were allowed to go trick or treating at other people's cars, another eye-opening moment. Mark and Brian opened a window into the past for thousands of kids, an experience their parents fondly remembered, too, and that's kind of cool to me.

To quote Charles Dickens (sort of), "I was an Andy Griffith fan to begin with, there is no doubt whatsoever about that. This must be distinctly understood, or nothing wonderful can come from the story I'm about to convey."

Doing our show in LA turned out to be a huge perk for me. Many people in the film industry listened to us and were periodically moved to send us something they knew we would enjoy.

One such listener worked in a prop house, which stores various items used in film and television. To make room for new inventory, they would clean out the items no longer needed. This listener sent me an old, tarnished, brass lighter with an inscription on the front, "Congratulations on season six, #1 again," and below that was the logo for the *Andy Griffith Show*. This was one of many lighters given to the cast and crew at the end of that season. I cherished that lighter and sent her a thank you note. I never used it, I only showed it to friends.

My admiration for the *Andy Griffith Show* was the focus of one of my birthday shows. On the morning of my birthday, Brian had me wear a sheriff's outfit, then walked me out to the "fun zone" where hundreds of listeners were waiting in front of a perfect replica of Andy Taylor's office and jail, and he sat me behind the sheriff's desk. Whenever we had an outdoor event at the station and listeners were invited, it was always held in the fun zone, which was nothing more than big, empty section of the parking lot at KLOS.

Throughout the morning, Brian kept telling me to go check on the prisoners in the cell. Each time, I would find a star from the show: Betty Lynn, who played Thelma Lou, Aneta Corsaut, who played Helen Crump, but the big one was Don Knotts, who played Barney Fife. Don reached into his front pocket, pulled out a bullet and gave it to me. Yep, this pussy cried.

At the end of that show, five-year-old Matthew walked out wearing rolled up blue jeans and carrying a fishing pole and said, "You wanna go fishin', Pa?" Yep, this pussy cried again.

Later, Brian told me he tried to get Andy to come down for the show, but he was busy shooting *Matlock*. However, he arranged for me to visit the set and meet Andy.

On the chosen day, I was taken to the makeup room of *Matlock* and introduced to Andy. We talked as his makeup lady Brenda trimmed his eyebrows; how cool and weird is that? He was very engaging and exactly the way you would want your hero to be.

Since I knew Andy would love seeing it, I brought with me the brass lighter and showed it to him. His eyes grew large, mouth wide open, I knew then he was pleased. Andy turned to his makeup lady saying, "Brenda, look what Mark gave me."

Image courtesy of KLOS Radio, LLC

I tried not to show the shock on my face. Andy thought I was giving the lighter to him as a gift when my intention was only to show it to him. Obviously, I said nothing, as he thanked me for the lighter. It made him smile, as he had made me on so many occasions, and still does. The lighter had traveled forty years before landing in my hands, and now, it was where it belonged. I was merely its delivery boy!

This had been a strong year as we neared December, and we had a slam bang finish planned. There was always a buzz for the Christmas Show, but we'd never experienced anything like this. We had a good line-up: Glen Campbell, Donny Osmond, Eddie Money, but the only thing anyone could talk about was David Cassidy.

David had been virtually absent from public view, but now he was back and about to stand on our stage, singing his signature song, I Think I Love You. For the first time in twenty years, one of our biggest pop idols would rise again, and the demand for tickets was off the charts, almost to a distraction.

As we were building up to the show, Laura came into the studio while we were broadcasting, something she never did. She told us, "Dana Delany is on the phone. I verified it's her."

We took her call and she was great, but then got down to business. She confessed to being a huge David Cassidy fan, and wanted only one ticket to the show, and she offered to sing backup on I Think I Love You. We snapped her up on her offer, and she squealed like a teenager. I fell in love with her at that moment.

On Thursday morning before the Christmas Show, we got several calls from listeners who were already standing in line at the Palladium. These insane people had been there for hours and would wait another twenty-four.

As I arrived for rehearsal, I went around to the front of the venue and greeted listeners. Every one of them was exhausted, but excited.

Once inside, I said hello to the house band. These were the best players in LA: Steve Porcaro and Steve Lukather from Toto, Jeff Skunk Baxter from the Doobie Brothers and Steely Dan, Scott Page from Pink Floyd, the Tower of Power horns, and they were all jacked to play on the song. David was from their childhood too, and it was endearing to see some of the best players in the world get geeked for David Cassidy.

When David arrived at rehearsal, he was high energy and reserved at the same time; basically, he was nervous. He ran the song once with the house band, and whatever reservations he had disappeared instantly. A massive grin spread across his face, since he had never heard his signature song played with such *pop*. They ran it one more time, and David was like a school kid. All of his dread had been replaced with exuberance. For the first time in his career, he had real musicians behind him.

The morning of the show, you could feel a palpable heartbeat in the Palladium, and that energy coursed through every person. When the anticipated moment arrived, we introduced Dana, as she took her place behind her microphone. As soon as we said David's name, the house band went into the opening beat of the song, as David walked out to a deafening roar. The song was better than expected, and David stood proudly as a star, once again. The moment stood up to the hype and brimmed with a sweet, nostalgic glow. And, with a serious case of perfect timing, Dana Delany came up behind David, slipped her arm between his legs, grabbed a hand full of crotch, and held on firmly. The Palladium had a roof when we started.

David left the stage, just as he entered it, as a superstar remembered and justly appreciated!

Like I said, 1990 was the purest year of our tenure. It was vibrant, and electric, and we were available to be present in it. I couldn't have known it at the time, but the next year would be the single greatest year of my career, only I would be too busy to enjoy it. And the very thing that made the year great, would also stack the pieces in place for a sobering downfall.

CELEBRATE ME HOME

1991

❝ The road to success and the road to failure are almost exactly the same.**❞**

—COLIN R. DAVIS

In early February, I was driving home after a particularly good show and I remember thinking, "It can't be this easy." We seemed to be in that Beatles phase when they released that piece of shit, *Revolution #9*, and people thought it was genius. Well, it wasn't genius and still ain't. But everything we tried seemed to work, and I knew that it couldn't last. Before this year would end, the stones would be laid in the path to our downfall, and I had no clue it was happening. It was a silent, unseen, undetectable force, which couldn't be combatted.

I'd been in radio for eighteen years, and experience had shown me the facade of ratings, up and down on a mere whim. The radio world was dictated by them; if you've got them, you're king, if you don't, you're shit, and that was an unchangeable reality. Our high ratings were both exhilarating and frightening. I embraced them, and yet I didn't trust them.

Common sense warned me this reign had to end, but we showed no signs of slowing. We had been on top for a while and our ratings were still going up, so much so that Johnny Carson told a joke in his monologue with us as the punchline. It was something like,

"They dug up a car that had been buried for a long time and found that Mark and Brian were on the radio." Yeah, I never understood it either, but it got a laugh.

Every morning I drove to work, I would listen to the latest air personality some station had added to try and compete with us, but not one of them posed any threat. But truly, hindsight is 20/20. I realize now I wasn't looking in the right direction. I didn't see that the problem wasn't in the form of any competition; *we* were the problem. We would unknowingly orchestrate and participate in our own demise. The enemy was us!

It was no secret that NBC wanted Mark and Brian on their network. They wanted to make a second pilot with us, and nobody gets that opportunity, but we did. NBC pulled out all the stops to secure the grandest stunt possible for the next pilot.

We would hitch a ride on NASA's KC-135, best known as the "Vomit Comet." It's a large airplane used to train astronauts by flying up to the edge of the atmosphere, then shutting off the engines and plummeting toward earth, causing weightlessness. I cannot express the level of fear I carried, and to think I was worried about skywriting!

Most of the show had to be shot at NASA, where all training was done. The premise of this

new show was to attempt a difficult stunt each week, and have the audience watch us training for it.

Filming was done in either Texas, Alabama, or Florida, where the NASA facilities are located. Since we had the radio show on week-days, we had to fly out on weekends to shoot. It was an unbeliev-able opportunity to train with actual astronauts and find out what drives them. My nervousness turned from fear to excitement because I knew I was privileged.

On the day of our flight in Houston, we were outfitted in green jumpsuits. Hanging from each front pocket were plastic bags to puke in. I hugged Lynda and the kids and boarded. We rose to the proper altitude in minutes, it seemed. The astronaut in charge told us if we felt nauseous, to look at the big red circle on the wall and focus on it. I'm thinking, "How many of you Harvard doctorates did it take to figure *that* out? Eight years of college and you come up with a big, red circle?" *How about let's just not go?* One year of city college taught me that.

I could feel the engines shut down as we began to fall. Obviously, everything became weightless, even the dust lifted off the floor. Brian was doing flips and somersaults. I chose to go with the often-maligned floating method, which is not as much fun, but less puke.

Lights would flash when they were about to crank the engines and climb out, meaning, put your feet on the floor and hang on. Pulling out of free fall was seriously intense, and that's usually when the puking begins.

One weightless session is called a parabola, and each flight does forty of those, as did we. The flight and filming went well, so once again, the show would be screened for test audiences as we waited for word.

Allow me to pose a question that will require you to think, but it'll be fun, I promise. I further promise you'll get it wrong. We had a certain actor as an in-studio guest around this time, and his appear-ance caused a sizable uproar. We never had this kind of reaction from any other guest in our history. A large crowd of women formed at the front gate of KLOS in hopes of a single glimpse of this man. He signed a piece of memorabilia for me that's now worth big money.

So, the question I pose is this. What actor would cause this type of reaction? I'll let that simmer for a bit.

While doing the show one morning, we got word from security that John and Ed were there to see us, and they didn't have an appointment, so this could only mean one thing. John and Ed told us on the air that *The Adventures of Mark and Brian* would be part of the fall schedule for NBC. We were officially the proud hosts of our own television show.

This opportunity was something I never dared to dream because it never seemed possible, and I'm not sure it ever really sunk in. I remember thinking back to when I would lay on my living room floor as a kid and watch my favorite shows. The thought passed through me that maybe some kid in some town might do the same while watching me, and that made me smile, but only for a second since we had to start shooting the show!

The first thing to be done was to find a showrunner, the person who literally runs the show. NBC brought in Don Mischer. You might not know his name, but you know his work. Did you see Michael Jackson's Super Bowl halftime show? Did you see Prince's halftime show? Don produced and directed both. This man is an icon and agreed to do our show.

The show would be free of a script, so we made stuff up as we went. This had never been done at that time, and we've now been referred to as the first reality TV show. Since we already did this on the radio, it seemed like a breeze.

The difficult part of this would be the balance of time. A lot of focus would now be on the TV show, but we had to make sure the radio program wasn't the forgotten child; it's the reason we were here. I knew my time would be strained, and I wasn't sure I knew how to manage it. Turns out, I didn't.

Due to our shooting schedule, we couldn't attend the ceremony, but we were once again named *Billboard Magazine's* Air Personality of the Year. I don't think there are many who win this award consecutively. You've heard the saying, "If it sounds too good to be true, it probably is." I've never been that person who feels the bottom's going to fall out when things are good, but this was off the charts good. Let's just say, my spider senses were tingling!

Alright, earlier I asked, what actor did we have on the show that caused a hoard of women to wait outside our gate for just a glimpse? I'll give you two hints. In LA, this actor reigned supreme in the early 1990s. Tickets to see him perform were sold out years in advance. Any woman would swoon to have this guy sing into her ear, "You alone can make my song take flight." Yes, it was the *Phantom of the Opera* himself, Michael Crawford. He got word these women were waiting for him, and Michael smiled saying, "My angels." Michael signed his Phantom mask to me, which hangs on my studio wall.

As mentioned, *The Adventures of Mark and Brian* is now referred to as the first reality TV show, and shooting it was mass confusion for the crew.

We were about to shoot a scene where a van pulls up, Mark and Brian jump out and start doing whatever the moment called for. The lighting guys expressed concern because they needed to light the exact spot we would be standing. Don Mischer told them, "It doesn't matter about lights, just shoot it."

One of the camera guys was worried about getting the other camera guy in his shot, and Don again said, "It doesn't matter if he is, we want to see that. Just shoot it!" The crew stared at Don as if he were speaking Himalayan. They didn't understand this type of gorilla production, since they'd never worked this way before. It would have to be a work in progress. It was on this show that I learned to appreciate how hard crew people work. They're the hardest working bunch on any set.

Of all the NBC episodes, my favorite was with The Temptations. We became the sixth and seventh Temptation for one show. Like some of you, I grew up on their music, and what a crazy bitchin' moment being fitted for my Temptations tuxedo. These are custom fit perfection, and I still have it, but doubt it still fits.

The single best moment was standing in the wings about to go on, the seven of us in our tuxes. I'm a redneck from Alabama and

I performed with the Temptations. Thanks to the magic of editing, my dancing was flawless, just like a whore's face in bright sunlight.

There was a massive poster hanging outside the theater that read, *The Temptations, One Night Only, with special guests Mark and Brian*, and that poster takes up most of my studio wall today.

With this ridiculous schedule, there was no time for sleep, and our lack of availability had become a problem. Things were tense at KLOS because we were no longer available to them. As soon as the radio show ended, we were whisked away in a TV production van. They were right to be angry, and I never blamed them. And my private life wasn't any better.

I would get home when everyone was asleep. I would fall in bed, sometimes clothed, then up each morning at 3:30, and I'd do it again. We traveled on weekends for shooting, and Lynda would bring the kids when possible, which was the only time I would see them. There was no time left to be a husband or father, and Lynda and I became very good at arguing. It's very frustrating when you both have a valid point, yet you clearly understand the other side. In those times, you simply hang on, with hope for a better day.

It was a back breaking, gut wrenching, insane time, which left all of us exhausted and frustrated. *Be careful what you wish for, right?*

Whenever I was summoned for anything connected with NBC, a town car was sent to pick me up, and I always had the same driver. I don't remember his name, so I'll refer to him as "my driver." The town car he drove was always immaculate. I never found any evidence that another person had ever ridden in that car but me.

My driver was dressed in a form fitting black suit, black tie, sharply pressed white-collar shirt, and shoes that had been polished that day, and he was dressed like that every time. He was maybe 225 lbs. with a stocky build. When he picked me up, he always came to the door of my home and escorted me to the car. The moment he got behind the wheel, he locked all the doors. He never said a word unless spoken to, and he only answered the question I had asked. The car was quiet unless I broke the silence. The radio was never on unless I asked for it. If I allowed it, we would sit in silence the entire ride, and he wouldn't so much as sniffle, and he never broke the speed limit, I watched.

This went on for the better part of a year, until I saw something that surprised me. I had come from some bullshit meeting in the NBC building and approached limo row that had maybe ten town cars lined up. I could see my driver's stocky build sitting behind the wheel, and his head was down. I thought to myself, "Mr. Roboto is asleep . . . he's human!" As I approached the car, he saw me coming and quickly set aside what he was reading and opened my door. We started the trek to Santa Clarita and rode in silence for maybe fifteen minutes. Because I was interested, I asked, "What were you reading?" Without looking back and his head forward, he hesitated before saying, "*The Bible.*"

After that, we talked a bit about his faith, family, marriage, but nothing about him changed. He would still only answer my question and then stop talking. I did learn that he was a trained bodyguard with a license to carry. I realized then, his job had nothing to do with driving.

One night I asked him to stop at a mini mart. As he pulled up, I went to open my door and it was locked. My driver opened my door and started to follow me inside. I told him he didn't need to come in, and he informed me it was his job. He stood just inside the door with his hands clasped below his waist and that walkie talkie thing in his ear. As he scanned the store, all he saw was the clerk and me searching for a tube of Crest toothpaste, because nobody else was in the store. I was worried the clerk might do something shifty and my driver would be forced to kill him, which I kind of wanted to see.

After my alliance with NBC came to a close, I never saw or heard from my driver again. To the eye, my driver and I had nothing in common, with one exception. We both had a system we followed. We each had our own personal way of approaching what we do, and we implicitly followed our individual methodology, every day. This approach brings professionalism on a consistent basis. I barely knew my driver, yet my respect for him remains to this day.

And for the record, now that you know my association with this man, do you actually think I wouldn't remember his name? I clearly do, and I'm not telling it to you, because that would break protocol. Plus, he's *my* driver, not *yours*.

Our work continued on the NBC show. One of the episodes was mostly memorable for what you *didn't* see. It was the sportscasting episode with us doing live play by play of an NFL game. We worked with announcers Dick Enberg, and former NFL head coach, Bill Walsh to prepare us.

The selected game for our magic in the booth was Raiders vs. Chargers. When our moment came, Dick and Bill slid out and we slid in. We did four or five plays without issue, until Raiders quarterback Jay Schroeder went under center to take the snap and the center jumped, to which Brian said, "I'd jump too if someone stuck their hand up my butt." Brian had barely finished his joke before the door flew open as Dick and Bill were ushered in, and we were quickly ushered out.

It was clear NBC didn't appreciate the humor. Brian was devastated, thinking he had ruined the episode. Later, I told him, "I understand the network responding as they did, but don't ever be upset over a line as funny as that one." This moment also signified some trouble ahead, but you don't see it if you're not looking.

We finally completed the original NBC order of nine episodes, so we could now take a break and breathe a bit. I was completely drained and getting extra sleep didn't help. This was mental exhaustion. I did all the things one should; I played with the kids, had dinners with Lynda. But what helped the most was sitting in a chair and processing everything I'd been through. While clearly there were many things that were good, there were just as many that troubled me. I was absent from my children's lives, and my wife had no husband. I wondered if this was the road to success. It was taking a toll, and with things being what they were, I could see no easy fix. But one thing became clear: *I didn't want to live this way for the rest of my life.*

The break from NBC came just in time to hop on a plane for Boston, and the Marconi awards ceremony. The Marconi is rather prestigious, in that it's the only award given by the National Associa-

tion of Broadcasters, and they don't give out very many. It's considered the Academy Award of radio. Not only were we nominated, but KLOS was as well. Bill asked if we would attend because this was important to him.

Mark and Brian were announced as "NAB Air Personality of the Year," and KLOS was awarded "Station of the Year." Finally, Bill wasn't forced to sit in the shadows of KABC. When KABC flashed their Marconi, Bill could now flash his. Bill is the one who made my dream of major market a reality, and it isn't a matter of liking him, I respected him, and now I was proud of him.

It was announced *The Adventures of Mark and Brian* would debut on September 9, in a special airing right after *Cheers*. The NBC promotional machine was now cranking in full force.

We'd been scheduled for a photo opportunity with the president of NBC, Warren Littlefield, in his office. What does one wear to a network president's office? Honestly, I think NBC was worried about what I might walk in wearing and arranged for wardrobe to outfit me. I've never been what one might call a *sharp dressed man*. I'm a big fan of free T-shirts with someone's logo on them. My driver and I sat in silence on the drive down. The quiet was killing me, but I wanted to see if he would break, and he never did.

Warren was the most powerful man at NBC, and it didn't show on him, and I mean that as a compliment. We took pictures all over his office, but the one that stood out is of the three of us leaning against the front of his desk. Brian picked up a pair of scissors and cut off Warren's tie mid-way down. For a moment I thought, "Oh fuck," but Warren burst into laughter and the picture was taken mid-giggle. Turned out to be the best of the bunch. Fun dude.

From the moment we joined NBC, it was nonstop activity, but there was a clear destination in front of me. I never stopped to realize what all this meant, and when I faced it, it shook me.

Most networks do a big unveiling of their fall schedule for the advertising community. The network brings in all their stars and parades them across a stage, trying to convince advertisers they should buy time on their network. We received word we had to be in New York for that reason. The NBC event would be held at Carnegie Hall.

Brian and I did our radio show on the streets of New York that morning. Afterward, we were helicoptered over to a building next to Carnegie Hall and escorted into the side entrance of the venue. There was a crowd waiting for autographs, so I started signing, when an NBC rep pulled me aside saying, "These are professional autograph collectors. They don't know who you are, but hope you become a star so they can sell your autograph." That was a hardcore TV lesson!

We were ushered upstairs and escorted into a small room with maybe twenty people, and I began to notice some of them. Johnny Carson was talking to Jay Leno, James Garner was talking to Ted Danson, and for a moment, I thought, "We're not supposed to be here." And then it hit me: These are the stars of NBC, and *now so are we*. It was only a split second, but the room started spinning. I was floored by it, but in a good way, I guess.

We were then escorted to a large opera box and seated next to James Garner. A livestream of President Bush was playing on the screen, and it was clear Mr. Garner didn't approve, so Brian acted like he was fast forwarding a remote control. It may have been the funniest thing James ever saw, and he began doing the same for anyone who would watch. Brian sat back, pleased with himself, so I gave him a thumbs up with the head nod. I don't normally give out both "thumb and nod," but this was the *Rockford Files* dude.

Brian and I went on stage with Warren and I don't remember much, except we got a sizable laugh, and we were gone. I guess you could say we did Carnegie Hall, because we semi, kind of did.

Blindsided would be the proper description for when I was told, "You're going to be on *The Tonight Show*." We were at the Beverly Hilton Hotel, shooting footage for the whitewater rafting episode in their pool. I was toweling off when John and Ed walked up and said those words.

This was back when that really meant something. This was Johnny Carson; this signifies you've made it. Careers have been made on those words. Friends don't believe you when you tell them, and you don't believe it when you say it.

The Tonight Show does a pre-call on the day of the show. They ask you questions with the goal of digging up good stories for the interview. The pre-caller said, "We understand Brian doesn't like onions. Jay, who was the guest host that night, was thinking of having one brought out and getting Brian to eat it." I told them, "You can bring one out if you want, but I can promise you, he won't eat it." They wisely chose not to.

I arrived at my dressing room and my name was on the door. I did what all first timers do, I took it off and kept it. Jay popped by to say hello before the show, which was nice. He also asked if I could stand a little ribbing, and I told him, "Bring it."

We stood on the special spot behind the curtain, waiting. Jay introduced us as the music began, and out we came. Brian and I did as we always do when a big decision had to be made, such as who sits in the chair next to Jay. We played rock-paper-scissors, in front of everybody, and again I won.

During the interview Jay said, "You know, there have been a couple of bad reviews for your show," as he pulled out a huge stack of magazines and plopped them down on his desk with a hefty *thud*, which brought a hearty laugh. The bad reviews thing was apparently true, something I didn't know at the time.

Jay thanked us for coming and started to take a break, when I said out loud, "Wait, is it over?" I guess two guys most people don't know only get two minutes. This is one of those moments where the journey is better than the destination.

John and Ed suggested we go to Telly Savalas's restaurant, which was nearby. They said he had a satellite television, and we could watch the east coast feed of the *Tonight Show* at 8:30 p.m. This was the first time I had heard of anything like that, which left me befuddled, and verklempt.

We ate dinner and had drinks, celebrating our first *Tonight Show* appearance and a grand moment in our lives. The television was huge and there we were, in full color, with Jay on the *Tonight Show*. Just then, Telly Savalas walked by our table. He stopped and saw us on TV, then turned smiling and said, "That's you," then walked on.

Kind of a great way to cap off an incredible life moment, and how many people can tell that story and know it's true?

The next week, Brian and I were doing the radio show from the Mark and Brian mobile. We were driving through Beverly Hills when we stopped at a red light and noticed Ed McMahon sitting in the car next to us. We had bonded with Ed while on the *Tonight Show*, so we yelled at him to pull over. Ed parked his car and did the rest of the show with us while we drove around LA. Imagine pulling up and seeing that?

The week after the *Tonight Show*, I got an email from a friend I hadn't heard from in a decade. The only thing the email said was, "You were right." So, I emailed back and asked, "Right about what?"

As soon as he responded, I remembered. I can't tell you his real name, since he's still a big-name weather dude, and I don't want his viewers to know that he is a massive pothead, so let's call him "Bob."

When I was working in the same town as Bob, we would get together periodically and partake of the smoke. One night, we were watching the *Tonight Show*, and out of my stoned mouth came, "Someday, I'm going to be on the *Tonight Show*." Who would have thought there was even the slightest chance that could ever happen? I was fried, and talking complete and utter shit, but as luck would have it, it happened twice, and Bob remembered.

So, the next time you're stoned, make a prediction. You have nothing to lose, and everything to "gange." See what I did there?

NBC ordered another six episodes, which I found odd. We haven't even debuted yet, and they want fifteen shows in the can. However, this showed me how much they believed in the possibilities, so we started TV work again.

One day, John and Ed ran in my trailer with a rough cut of the Temptations show. I was excited to watch, because Brian and I were very funny in that show, getting some outrageous confessions from the guys about female companionship on the road.

As I watched, I noticed our funniest stuff wasn't used, in fact, none of the confession stuff was in there. They only used G-rated humor, and not much of that, either. Most of it was our scripted voice over, with very little funny from us. I thought there's no way it keeps going like this, but it did, all the way through the show.

After it ended, they both asked what I thought and I said, "Good." They both knew I wasn't pleased, but I said nothing. I wondered, for the first time, why they even needed us. We were barely used. My only thought was, why have I been working this hard for lame, G-rated milk toast?

As we neared September, NBC was heavily promoting the show's debut. In fact, future Superman, Dean Cain, had one of his first acting jobs doing a promo for our show on a motorcycle.

With our appearance on the *Tonight Show*, coupled with NBC's heavy promotion, our radio ratings for September were like I've never seen anywhere. We had a 12, and our nearest competitor had a 4.

But it was inevitable, the radio show's quality had greatly deteriorated. There simply weren't enough hours left in the day to do anything about it. The show was still good, but not as inventive, and I was spent. We gave it everything we had, and the average listener probably didn't notice, but we were coasting. I always said, the best way to deal with white noise that comes at you from outside is to make sure what comes out of the speakers is the best it can be, and the noise will take care of itself. I hadn't followed my own advice. We had allowed the single, most important reason for our success to suffer.

On the day of our debut, we were everywhere. We did a ton of promotion, including a live interview with Katie Couric on the *Today Show*, and she cut us off mid-sentence because our time had run out. I wondered then if that was a karmic warning.

I didn't see our debut because we were shooting. In fact, I never saw the show live because I was flying some place from somewhere. But the ratings were out the next morning and we hit the top 10. How could we not with a lead in like *Cheers*? But everybody was pumped—NBC, John and Ed, even our listeners called to say they enjoyed the show. Everything was right in our world, wasn't it?

When we were told our regular time slot would be Sunday nights at 7 p.m., I asked rather loudly, "We're up against *60 Minutes*?" It was explained that NBC needed to put a dent in the crazy high ratings *60 Minutes* was getting, and their plan was to see if the kids could control the TV by getting the remote out of dad's hand, and NBC felt our show could be the answer.

Everything in my brain froze at that moment, and their plan was immediately clear! That's why the editor didn't use any of our best stuff, because all of it was PG-13. They couldn't use it because NBC was targeting children with our show. This was the first time I'd heard this, and I couldn't help it, I was overwhelmed with a numbing, empty feeling that washed over me. We had been busting our asses to make a *kid's show?* Without overstating it, the soul of this entire endeavor left me in that moment. I was honestly without words.

From the moment we hit LA, everything had been so positive. Our horizon seemed so bright, but the sun just went down. And to be honest, I felt I'd been misled. If someone had told me up front this was a children's show, I would've said, "That's not who we are!"

Clearly this was a bleak moment, but sometimes a sliver of light shines through the dark clouds. David Cassidy publicly credited Mark and Brian with pulling him out of obscurity and back into the mainstream. Enigma Records signed him and released his album, *David Cassidy*, which contained his comeback song, "Lyin' to Myself," his first charting song in eighteen years. David appeared on the *Steve Edwards* television show and asked if we would join him. We stood beside David and threw copies of his new album to the crowd, and that would be the last time I would see him.

To think I had any part in helping David find himself made me proud, and still does. David was a good man who fought many demons. The only side I ever saw of him was his smile, and that's the way I will remember him. Rest, my friend, you were cherished!

So, what do you do when you've had the busiest year of your life? You add something else to it. I had successfully transferred my love and admiration of the *Andy Griffith Show* to Brian. We talked about how the show was never topical, which is why the jokes still play today. The only concession was their Christmas episode, where they perfectly hit what Christmas means to people. We decided that everyone needed to see this special episode, and we would host it.

We hooked up with the local Fox affiliate and shot it in one afternoon. We displayed that special stupidity which was our superpower, and no one edited out any of our stuff. The Fox station promoted the hell out of it, and we won our time slot, and an Emmy award for our efforts. Not bad for one afternoon.

So then, we went from Emmy winning TV to heavy disappointment. After our top 10 debut, we moved to our regular time slot at 7 p.m., against *60 Minutes*. NBC opened with the NASA show.

When the ratings came out, *60 Minutes* was predictably #1, and *The Adventures of Mark and Brian* was in the bottom five. Out of 105 shows that aired that week, we were #103. Mark and Brian had done nothing but win since we became a team and losing felt really shitty.

The Day Before Thanksgiving Day Parade was the biggest it would ever be. Thousands attended, all in a joyous mood, except me. After our abysmal ratings, NBC was considering moving us to Monday night, but I was no longer invested in that. I just wanted to go home and enjoy the four-day Thanksgiving break with my people.

The very last thing we would do in this year was a testament to how I felt, and the Christmas Show was the setting. Our friend, Donny Osmond, came and sang "Go Away, Little Girl," Burton Cummings sang "These Eyes," but the surprise of the show was

Image courtesy of KLOS Radio, LLC

Kenny Loggins. We asked each guest to sing one Christmas song, and Kenny chose "Celebrate Me Home." None of us were prepared for what we witnessed that morning.

It lasted nine minutes. At one point Kenny was up on a table singing, while his sax player stood next to him, and they went back and forth bringing the song to its incredible crescendo.

I've never witnessed any musical performance have that kind of impact. The Palladium exploded, in tears and applause. It was the perfect Christmas sentiment for that moment, and for me; I just wanted to go home. Both my kids grew a year older, and I didn't see it happen. Lynda and I were barely speaking, and I had a failed television show to blame for it. But I told you, I'm not a victim. I don't blame anything or anyone, except me. I walked into this with eyes wide open.

George Carlin once said, "Everybody needs time to lay on the floor and stare at the ceiling." I now know what he meant, and I'll give you another quote, and this one's mine: "Nothing is free, you pay for everything, in one way or another."

Image courtesy of KLOS Radio, LLC

I knew the NBC show was dead on arrival and I clearly didn't care. What I didn't know was the dark storm approaching on the horizon, and no umbrella in the world could've protected any of us from this rain, not even a Tina Louise parasol. But just for now, just for this moment, I simply wanted to go home.

WE KNEW HE WAS COMING

1992

> **"** It was the best of times, it was the worst of times, it was the spring of hope, it was the winter of despair. **"**

—CHARLES DICKENS

Humpty Dumpty sat on a wall, Humpty Dumpty had a great fall. All the king's horses and all the king's men, couldn't put Humpty together again.

It's oddly ironic how true that felt. I would go from the best year of my career, into my worst, in the span of a few months. It felt like I was standing on solid ground when the earth fell out from under me. This wonderful beast we'd built was about to breathe its last breath.

So, what initiated our great fall? I didn't see it then, but it seems clear to me now. We unknowingly did ourselves in, our great collapse was of our own doing. Howard Stern simply collected the spoils.

We knew he was coming. He was the very best at what he did, and we knew we were about to face a worthy opponent. This was the only time in our history where I felt we needed to raise the drawbridge, light the torches, and man our posts; I was concerned. No one in LA had been our equal, but the game had changed because we were no longer perceived as we once were. I believe we were ripe to be picked!

Earlier, I talked about that rebel image we had. We were looked on as two guys who refused proper protocol, we did things the way we wanted, and didn't care about the outcome. We weren't supposed to dig a hole in the parking lot with a jackhammer. We weren't supposed to throw Christmas trees off the roof into traffic. We weren't supposed to rip the sink out of the men's room, but we did, and our rebellious image had taken a debilitating hit.

An image is a delicate thing, and we unknowingly did one of the things that can destroy that. The "Bad Boys of Radio," the same who were kicked out of Graceland, decided to host a nationally televised children's show. Although that wasn't our intention, that's what happened. Before that show, we were James Dean, and now we were Captain Kangaroo, and I believe the transformation equally matched that comparison in the minds of our listeners.

NBC cancelled *The Adventures of Mark and Brian* shortly after the first of the year. One week, we were dead last in ratings. The NBC show was an embarrassing, humiliating failure, and we paid the price.

Stern was coming to LA in syndication. He took over Philadelphia's #1 morning show in a brutal verbal attack on the host. The guy's wife came on Howard's show and bad-mouthed her own husband.

We knew his scheme. He would start by attacking us, calling us losers, morons, and claim we stole his act, just as he had done in every town. He would have his listeners call our show and yell Howard's name.

Howard debuted in LA and did exactly as we expected he would. But what we didn't understand is that Howard's attack was psychological warfare. People were listening, and believing his boasts, and he convinced people we weren't who they thought we were. James Dean could've withstood this attack, Captain Kangaroo didn't stand a chance.

I started to notice personal friends looking at me differently, and people I worked with held their glance in a judgmental stare. People would yell at me in public that we stole Howard's act. It didn't matter how prepared we thought we were, it all took a toll in numerous and lasting ways.

I later thought, maybe we should've told people Howard was

coming, let them know what he would do. Now, I believe it wouldn't have mattered. People decided we weren't who they thought, and they wanted something new. It's one thing to understand your day will come, but it doesn't make it any easier when it's your turn at the slaughtering table.

Howard predicted he would be #1 in a year, and he did it in seven months. Lynda and I were in bed watching the news as they did a full story on Howard's new dominance, which is where I learned Mark and Brian were no longer #1.

Lynda didn't move or speak, the bedspread was beige and pink, and *A Christmas Carol* by Dickens rested on my lap. I distinctly remember these things because my senses were heightened, as if my brain snapped a picture. As Scrooge discovered, the ghost of Christmas future meant it when he warned of a bleak future. I should've listened.

When Howard held our mock funeral, thousands of our former listeners attended and cheered as he lowered us into the ground, and morning news was covering it. Brian and I didn't speak of it that morning. It was business as usual, doing the show for whoever was left, trying to keep it moving. It was one of the hardest things I've ever had to go through, trying to put on an entertaining morning show while stepping over chunks of my career, laying at my feet.

Howard's funeral was symbolic in ways. Gone were the days where everything we did worked. The curtain came down on our glory period without a final bow. It was a special time when we dominated LA mornings and were revered for our brazen antics that entertained millions. It seemed all of it was flushed and forgotten in seconds. Those five years of dominance were more than I'd ever dreamed, and the innocence and pure joy of that rested in those coffins Howard lowered. What I couldn't have known was that the effects of this moment would linger long after this day. I'm like most people, when life slaps you, it'll sting for a bit, but eventually you put it away. This was clearly a painful back-hand, but I couldn't have imagined it would haunt me for the rest of my life.

In August 2021, I was in California for the birth of my first grandchild when I noticed I had a voicemail. I don't get many of those since my outgoing message is somewhat rude. It was from one of my buddies at the cigar shop, and as he started talking, I could tell he was drunk since the guys like to sip bourbon while they smoke. As his message began, I could hear snickering in the background. "Mark, we heard you're out in California and just wondering if you've gone to visit your grave, the one Howard Stern made when he buried you," which was accompanied by louder snickering. He ended the call with, "Love you, man."

The memory of my embarrassing mock burial had been out of mind for quite some time, but this supposed friendly phone call rushed it back, front and center. I was deeply hurt by the call and thought about it for days. How could the wound still be there? After some thought, there were two possible explanations. One, that my friends are so insensitive to think I would find this funny, or two, it's been thirty years since this event, and I'm still deeply affected by it. Either I need to get better friends, or I need to just get over it! But I thought I was over it until this call. Okay, third possible answer, *I need therapy.*

I want to say this, however, because it bothers me as well: Mark and Brian didn't steal anything from anyone. All the shit we did came from us, and we take the credit or blame for all of it. Before Howard came to LA, I had heard of him, but I had never *heard* him. You can't find one thing we did on our show that Howard did before us. The claim we stole his act is a blatant lie, and Howard knows it.

Besides, what does he do on his show that anyone could steal? *Nothing!* Howard is the best morning entertainer I've ever heard, but he didn't need his vicious verbal attacks. All he had to do was be himself. I can admire his talents without having a single ounce of respect for his tactics, and I don't. He didn't have to be the bully to succeed, but I think he enjoyed it.

To go from the ultimate high to the darkness of the bottom in what felt like minutes would be unthinkable, yet it happened. It was so extreme on the human spectrum, and it unfolded so quickly. It's human to ask, "Why is this happening to me?" The simple answer is, it didn't happen to me, it simply happened, but I fully accept my role in it.

Let me share a different set of extremes, in a different place, different time, and I was only an observer who was being given a life lesson before I needed it.

In the fall of 1983, I was in Montgomery, Alabama, doing afternoons at Y-102. Though I was successful, I didn't make much money. So, in order to make life financially stronger, I would jock dances, which I dearly fucking hated. I could make more money in a weekend than I could on my weekly salary.

I had a gig at South County Academy one Saturday night. We're talking the deep, backwoods of southern Alabama. Lynda went with me, as she often did.

As we were nearing the high school my car headlights began to dim, and my car slowed, so I pulled off the road. A pickup truck pulled over in front of me and a guy climbed out with his two sons. He asked where I was headed, so I told him about the dance. He said he would drop us off at the school while he and his sons looked at my car.

While I was doing the dance, a guy sitting in the rafters of the gymnasium got up and approached me. "Play some Alabama," he barked. I promised I would as he returned to his friends. I played the next song, which wasn't Alabama, so the guy got up again. "I thought I told you to play some God damn Alabama," he screamed as the smell of cheap whiskey enveloped my head.

His girlfriend came down and tried to calm him. He angrily turned and knocked her to the hardwood floor with his fist, blood gushed from her mouth and nose. Her friends rushed down and helped her up as his buddies corralled Mr. Fantastic back up to their seats. The next song was obviously Alabama, and as I looked to confirm this made the guy happy, I saw him tongue kissing his girlfriend's bloody face.

At the end of the dance, the man picked us up as he promised. We pulled up to his farm while his two sons were closing the hood of my car. The farmer told me my alternator was dead, but that his sons had charged my battery and that it would get us home, just get the alternator replaced as soon as possible. He then told me his wife had fixed us something to eat in case we were hungry. I waved to her through the kitchen window and smiled, explaining it was late, and we needed to get back as I tried to hand him some money. He refused with a smile and said, "Happy to do it."

Two distinct examples of the extremes of humankind. Both happened on the same night, within an hour of each other, within a mile of each other, put on display as a glimpse of real life. I had nothing really to do with either, I only observed, then drove home and went to bed. But now, I can't merely walk away from this. I had been handed the best and worst periods of my career, back-to-back. So, what had I learned from these extremes? I learned if you're going to accept the good, then you must also be prepared to deal with the bad, because both are out there in full force, and you're defined by how you handle each. You can give up or learn from these lessons and move on. But it's also beneficial to take some time and gather yourself.

When you're standing inside a tornado, it's hard to realize that there's sunshine less than a mile outside of it, but there is. Our show didn't stop because of this, it changed in ways, but also flourished in others. It was business as usual when we welcomed Anthony Hopkins to the show.

His movie *Silence of the Lambs* had been released the year before in February, and the fear was that it would be forgotten by Academy voters. So, Anthony was making the rounds to remind people, and our show was one of his few stops.

Anthony had done a film many years prior called *Magic*. It was one of his early starring roles, but I felt his work in that film showed us great things were to come from him, and his sheer scene-stealing presence in *Silence* was a tour de force, considered to be the performance of the year.

We got a call during his visit from a listener who asked Anthony if he would record his voice message for his answering machine. Mr. Hopkins didn't skip a beat, asking for the caller's first name, which was David. Anthony leaned into the mic, and in character as Hannibal Lector, he said, "Hello, and thank you for calling David. He can't come to the phone right now, he's having someone over for dinner." Anthony leaned closer to the mic adding, *"He's having me."*

It was so creepy and so cool, we exploded in applause, and Anthony giggled like a schoolboy. It's sincerely heartwarming to meet one of the greats and discover how down to earth and human they are. Great dude.

By the way, *Silence* won the big five that year: best movie, actor, actress, screenplay, and director. Clearly, no one forgot it and Mr. Hopkins received his much-deserved Oscar.

As admitted, 1992 was a seriously fucked up year, and I was understandably pissed off at everything. I used to enjoy when the alarm went off, because it meant I got to talk on the radio. Now, the alarm could blow me. This particular shitty morning, I dragged myself through my shower and simmered as I drove into work. I'm thinking, I've had it, I hate this, I hate that, and I hate you, clearly having a monstrously bad morning.

I was sitting at the red light on La Cienega Boulevard, minutes from the station, continuing to fuck the world in my head, when a bus pulled up next to me. I saw my reflection in the bus windows, sitting in my convertible Mercedes, bitching at anything I chose to. At that moment, my focus changed from my reflection to what was behind the windows. The bus was standing room only, and people were sharing the hand straps. It's five in the morning and you couldn't fit another person on that bus.

I was being taught a lesson, and it's amazing how embarrassed I felt. While I'd been seething about how bad things were for me, the universe showed me what the real world looks like. I felt like the bus was Cher and she just slapped me yelling, "Snap out of it!" Humbled, I drove my Mercedes to work and had a great show.

When we first arrived at KLOS, it wasn't the nicest building I had ever worked in. It looked like it was built in the 1960s and had seen its best day. It was a bit like the Munster's house, complete with the dragon under the stairs, which was Bill Sommers. A new building was called for, and that's exactly what we got. The radio station was located on a giant lot, with most of it empty, plenty of room for new facilities.

Construction began in 1990 and seemed to go rather smoothly for a building of that magnitude. After a couple of years, we received word the new facilities were ready for us to inhabit. Meetings were held as to how we wanted to do that. We asked if we could start our show in the old building, then walk the few hundred feet over and let the new studio take over, with all of it live. Testing went on for days to make sure all the equipment was functioning.

On the day of transfer, we started the show in the old building and spent the first hour demolishing parts of the control room with sledgehammers, since we would be the last humans to occupy that building. It's shocking how much fun it is to tear up shit with a sledgehammer, especially after the year we had. It's like cocaine, you don't want to stop once you start.

Then, we got the "all go" from engineering and we started to walk while broadcasting. As we entered the new building, you could hear the echo of larger rooms, uninhabited by people, furniture, or ratings apparently. We entered our brand-new studio and sat in our brand-new seats behind our brand-new microphones, still broadcasting from our remote unit.

When we gave the word, head engineer Norm Avery flipped the switch, and the new building came alive. This won't mean anything to you, but when new broadcasting equipment is turned on, there is a certain smell to it, and I got a little horny.

Many people referred to this as "the building that Mark and Brian built." Being honest, that was mostly true. The profits made from our first years made this building possible, so I wore that moniker proudly. It was my new home and I was proud to be in it.

Here's the fun part: When the bulldozers tore into the old building for demolition, the number of chubby rats that scampered across La Cienega was in the thousands. It was both awesome and disgusting. Many of the rats didn't survive the traffic, I watched it!

A few weeks later, I was at our very first Mark and Brian event in the parking lot of the new building. I was busy signing autographs as listeners encircled me, and I see a hand reaching over the crowd clutching a videotape. "This is what I do, Mark," said the voice connected to the hand. I never saw his face.

I ran the tape when I got home and it was a clown show named, *T-Bone's World of Clowning.* I assumed the dude who gave it to me was the clown.

Now, I'm not afraid of clowns like Johnny Depp, I just think they're creepy. Even as a kid, I could never understand the desire for a grown man to put on makeup and brightly colored suits with giant shoes and do weird shit. But T-Bone loved it so much that he spent his own money to make this video showing kids all about clowning.

The show was bad, production was bad, editing, music, acting, jokes, just not good, so I tossed it in the drawer with the other family videos.

Six-year-old Matthew found the tape and wanted to see it. I told him he wouldn't like it, but he insisted. Matt loved it so much that he watched it multiple times, every day, *for years.* Then when Amy was of age, she did the same thing, as did Katie, and they all remember it fondly to this day. They should've gotten T-Bone to host the NBC show. He would've done better than we did!

T-Bone, my sincerest apologies my friend, I know nothing about clowns, except that I don't like being around them. But thank you for the video, because you gave my kids something to do for most of their childhood.

And I mean nothing personal T-Bone, but I can't believe a gig like that works with the ladies. I could be completely off base, banging a clown might be exactly what some people want. However, I'm not one of them. I get kind of weird when one stares at me for longer than he should.

I looked in my journal to see what I wrote about in 1992, and there was nothing. I made an entry in the fall of '91, and then nothing for two years. It doesn't take a scholar to understand why; I didn't have anything to say. I would normally make entries about something positive, or exciting; '92 had none of that! The year was a blur, I think numb says it best. I know I needed to get on some sort of gung-ho thing yelling, "Let's go get 'em," but I just didn't feel like it. I felt like part of me had been consumed, and I had a giant hole in me.

What do you do when you're not what you were? I went to work each day and did my job, and I don't remember doing it. However, I *do* remember how we ended the year. It was the first smile I'd had in a while, because one of the biggest musical stars of the '70s and '80s approached us about the Christmas Show.

One of the best concerts I've ever seen was Barry Manilow. Judge if you must, but Barry was a huge "get" at the time. He had just released his first Christmas album, and it was number one, and his people reached out about Barry doing our Christmas Show.

Barry agreed to do a couple of his big hits, and one song from the Christmas album, which I listened to, and requested that he do the duet, "Baby, It's Cold Outside." I asked if we could find a girl to duet with him, and they loved the idea, but with reservation. They wanted to be confident that the chosen girl was capable of the moment. I promised if we couldn't find the right talent, they could bring in a pro.

We spent a week auditioning singers, and some were very good, some just needed to stop, but the winner was clear. Pamela Holt was our winner, and she confided that she'd never heard the song before, but she got to work learning it. My concern was the song has lots of moving parts, and Pamela was having trouble remembering her lines and where they go. I reminded her that she'll be standing on the Palladium stage with Barry Manilow, and not knowing her next line would *not* be a good thing. She smiled saying, "I'll get it." I admit, any pressure I was feeling was self-imposed, but I was starting to sweat it.

Barry has a massive fan base that blew out our phones to snag tickets. Many of them had no clue who we were, which was hysterical. The usual frenzy for tickets was always there, but friends I hadn't talked to in years wanted tickets. I told most of them to go fuck themselves.

We had rehearsal the night before and Barry came straight from his appearance on the *Tonight Show*. We always provided a house band, but the moment Barry saw the band he said, "I'm going to need strings." His people jumped on the phone and the string players were there within the hour, and Barry was the one who paid them.

There are rumors that Barry is difficult to work with, but I didn't see that. Once the string players arrived, Barry worked with the house band for two hours. I didn't witness difficult, I saw a professional working diligently to get it right, which is what the great ones do.

Pamela arrived that morning looking understandably nervous. She said she ran the song nonstop and felt like she had it down. I introduced her to Barry, which didn't help, because the enormity of the moment seemed to hit her. I was genuinely worried now; this girl was a deer in the headlights.

Barry came out and did three of his biggest songs: "Mandy," "Could It Be Magic," and, "Weekend in New England." Then, the band vamped as we set up what they were about to hear, and we introduced Pamela.

The song begins with speaking parts, and then slides into the duet. Everything went well until the middle when Pamela sang the wrong line, in the wrong place. Barry stared at her, and said, "Oh really," which is not a line anywhere in the song. They both stood there, as the band kept vamping. Barry then simply led her back in with his next line as the band fell back in, and Pamela smiled, realizing where she was. They finished up great, and most people didn't realize there was ever a flub.

This is one of the things that made us unique. We worked on a classic rock radio station, but we always reflected the tastes of all people, and Barry Manilow joining us for the Christmas Show was a shining example of that. Everybody loved it and Barry got two standing ovations.

Holy fuck, what a year! I needed the two-week Christmas break to reassemble. I had no idea what our future was, but I felt like anything drastic was the wrong approach.

We needed to regroup and find our natural footing, establish a new base to work from, and see where that takes us. This was new territory for us, but I was sure the next year would be different, unlike anything we had known. But it relaxed me knowing that we had faced new ground before, and that went fairly well.

The new year would offer us a significant moment, and that would come in the form of a guest. We had our share of huge names on the program, but what do you do when you find out that the biggest star of them all is doing your show? In our case, we lied to him, but the joke would be on us.

WHEN YOU'RE NOT, YOU'RE NOT

1993–1994

66 The suspense is terrible. I hope it'll last.**99**

—WILLY WONKA

It was like the aftermath of an earthquake. You sweep and pick up the overturned furniture, and though everything is back like it was, it isn't quite the same as before. The memories of the shaking, and that horrible waiting until it stops, are flashes that come back to you without invitation.

Howard took the top spot the previous year, so the wound was still tender as we started 1993. We did the show as always, and they were good shows, but at a moment's turn, the reality of what is, versus what was, came back to me uninvited. Having never been through one, I can only imagine it was like a divorce; everything became different, and not as good.

As stated, I'd been #1 a couple of times, but I'd never lost the position. This uneasy feeling was new to me. My only thought was to keep it moving. We were still being paid handsomely to do a job. *We* hadn't changed, only *our ratings* had, or so I thought.

If your favorite TV show loses a few ratings points, you never know it. Their ratings dwindle privately until their show is cancelled, but our loss was very public and humiliating. Everyone listened as we were ridiculed and degraded. Clearly put, it was devastating to go through.

Brian and I seemed to handle it differently. He was quiet on the matter and didn't speak to me about it. There was an intensity that came out in him, while his playful side became more removed.

I could process some of what happened in a rational way because the fluctuation in ratings I'd seen over the years had prepared me. There were many moments I wanted to sit and speak openly with Brian, but the right time never seemed to present itself. We would go through each day as we always had, but there was no fun in it, no spark, only the pretense of it all. The on-air shows were fine, but our off-air chatter was minimal, and to the point. Gone were our communications where we would finish each other's sentences, and that was our superpower. Our ability to cook up something stupid and new within seconds was unlike anything I'd known. Without that, we were nothing special, just another radio show.

Brian finally spoke briefly on the matter one day while we were walking down the hall. He turned to me saying, "We're going to be number one again. Our best radio is still in front of us." I admired his confident attitude, but I disagreed with him on both counts, so I smiled and said nothing. That wasn't the conversation we desperately needed to have; that was him releasing frustration and anger. In the seven stages of grief, anger is number two on the list, depression is next. This was going to be a process, so it was best to let it play out. A conversation at this point would only make things worse.

Losing that special spark between us wasn't good, and my fear was that the worst of it was yet to come.

I've referred to Jerry Reed's song, "When You're Hot, You're Hot," and the statement of that title has proven to be true, but that's not the full song title. The last part is, "When You're Not, You're Not," and that has also proven to be true. People love a winner and have distaste for a loser. I've mentioned how fame is fickle, and that I would one day grow to distrust it. This would become that day. Our faithful had turned on us, and they felt it was time to demonstrate that point.

I've always been big on making appearances where our listeners are, and one of those places was the Mickey Thompson Off-Road Championships. These were always held in stadiums and featured a ton of dirt with big vehicles that had massive engines.

Classic rock fans love that shit. Blue collar working guys and their families attended for an evening of beer, the smell of gasoline, hot-dogs, and really loud engines. Mark and Brian were always a welcomed addition to the evening's festivities. We had a standing date with this event every year.

We were retiring our old Mark and Brian mobile for a newer replacement, and the monster trucks at Mickey Thompson were going to crush it, with us hosting.

As usual, we were driven out to mid-dirt and told to wait for our introduction. "Ladies and gentlemen, please welcome Mark," the announcer got about that far when the booing began, and it grew louder with each passing second. I started talking loudly as though that would block it out, but there was no drowning this; it sounded like most of the 60,000 were booing. Brian and I had planned a little funny, but we quickly abandoned that and got right to the flattening. We just wanted this over so we could crawl out. Crushing our car now felt more like a metaphor.

In the midst of the booing, some guy jumped over the railing onto the dirt field and started running full speed toward us. Security quickly closed in and led him away. In that moment, I felt like all our listeners were gone. I guess this crowd was without sin because their boos felt like stones.

We slunk into the vehicle that brought us and quickly vacated the area. The guy driving us didn't say a word as he dropped us in the parking lot. Brian and I parted without speaking while we walked to our cars.

Driving home, I felt hated by the people of Los Angeles. What did we do to deserve that treatment? I understand listeners move on but why would you want to embarrass us? Howard had done his job, he successfully turned millions of people against us. It was the most demoralizing moment of my life, and for the next few days, I didn't care if we ever spoke into a microphone again.

With the exception of station events, this would be the last public appearance we would make for several years. *I was ready to give up, but I didn't . . . I couldn't.*

Have you ever had moments in your life where things seemingly aren't going your way? I personally have no knowledge of this sort of thing; my life is going super great, really fucking awesome, and thank you for asking! However, you're challenged, you're down, maybe depressed, but you wake up each day to the bright morning sun in a sky of deep blue, and those happy, cheery, fucking birds are singing, and you're reminded that everything is just as it was? You might've expected the sky to be jet black and dripping blood, because your world is collapsing around you but nope, it's that sunny, cheery, bird thing.

There's been an infinitesimal blip in your super great life, but you'll work it out, just as you have so many times because life, as you know, goes on. For example, the Monday morning after the Mickey Thompson event, we had a crew working at the house doing some needed painting on this bright blue, cheery, perfect day. We had used these guys many times because they did great work, were super nice, and were big Mark and Brian fans.

They were painting around the front porch and as many work crews do, they had a radio blaring. The problem was that it was Howard Stern they were blasting, not Mark and Brian. Maybe they thought it was funny to be at Mark's house while listening to Howard. Maybe they were making some sort of statement, who knows? But what they didn't know was that Lynda was about to make a statement of her own.

Lynda clearly heard their radio, which based on its raised volume, seemed to be their plan. Lynda stepped out onto the porch and glared at the five of them. I was at work and didn't witness this, but I have lived with this woman long enough to know exactly what these five poor men saw glaring back at them. I've seen it, and it's terrifying.

Lynda had to raise her voice over the volume, "Every single one of you are fully aware who lives here, so let me make this real simple so you can understand it. Either shut that shit off, or get the fuck out of here, and whichever one you choose, do it immediately." She went back inside and slammed the door. The radio was silenced in seconds, and Lynda never hired them again. *If you mess with the bull, you get the horns.* If you're ever around Lynda, everything will be fine unless you piss her off, then it's best to vacate the area and batten down the hatches.

Bad things will always happen, but if you lay down, you lose, and bad wins. I didn't work this long or this hard to quit. I lost a lot of games in my sporting days, but I always played the next game. Let me tell you about a game I played, and I was pretty good! It's called the "shooting tequila while playing darts and winding up on the bathroom floor" game. Have you played it? Lynda's really good at it, too!

We had a neighborhood bar that served decent food and drinks. Lynda and I would frequent the place, enough for the staff to know our names. One night, we ran into friends who were playing darts, so just to be neighborly, we jumped in for a game, which led to tequila shots and multiple games.

Once we got home, Matt and Amy were both busy in their rooms, and that tequila scent coming off Lynda started acting like perfume, so we gave that bathroom carpet a pretty decent workout. Tequila should be thought of as an aphrodisiac, not a drug; I suppose it could be both. Not once did the idea of grabbing a condom cross my liquor-laden brain, and I might've been going through a rough patch, but I was able to raise the flag! So, things were looking up, if you know what I mean.

Obviously, Lynda was late for her monthly visitor, so we decided to do a pregnancy test on the air. With Lynda on the phone, we discovered she was in fact, pregnant. That entire segment is on our charity CD, *All of Me*. Our third and final child was born into the world as Katie. She became the voice of our house, and it won't fucking stop.

Monday, January 17, 1994, southern California was awakened at 4:30 a.m. by a massive 6.7 magnitude earthquake, with its epicenter in Northridge, mere miles from my home. I was showering for work when I suddenly found myself airborne, having been thrown from the shower. The power went out before I hit the floor. Lynda and I assembled the family and moved outside, knowing the aftershocks were coming. I received word that large portions of the 14 freeway had collapsed, making it literally impossible for me to get to work by car. I phoned in my part of the show as we tried to navigate through this nightmare. It would be months before the 14 could be repaired, so the question was, how would I get to work?

Brian and I were always under enormous pressure to make it to work, even when sick. Once I called in with the flu and was asked, "Have you been to the doctor for meds? Have you tried echinacea? Just come to work, we'll take care of you, but we need you on the air." We could only take vacation at certain times of the year because of the ratings period. The simple reason is money! When we weren't on the air, commercial rates fell sharply. Having us on the air, though ill, meant full commercial rates, which meant money.

So, it was arranged for Skylord to pick me up, via helicopter, each morning at the Antelope airport. The problem was the airport was closed, meaning no lights were on. I was told to park in a designated area and when I saw Skylord coming, I was instructed to flash my headlights off and on to vector him in. Skylord told me later how terrified he was because he couldn't see the power lines. We would land in the station parking lot and I went to work, and this went on for months. I got up every morning at three to meet Skylord, but I was on the air, which is all that mattered.

Once things were back to normal, Bill sat down with us and proposed a business opportunity. He had a good friend who was the GM at KCLB in Palm Springs, who reached out to Bill about syndicating Mark and Brian on his station. Bill asked if we had interest in opening a small company for syndicating the show. He said it wouldn't be much money but might be an interesting opportunity. So, we became Mark and Brian Incorporated.

We quickly became the talk of Palm Springs and we agreed to make appearances there, because who doesn't love Palm Springs? I was proud of the fact that through all the shit, the show remained solid, and Palm Springs loved us. They didn't know, or care, about

Howard Stern, and were oblivious to what we had been through. This was new territory for us, untainted by false claims. It felt like LA had mostly abandoned us, and this new love we were getting felt good. We no longer had to cower to the hatred and boos. We had a fresh start, and it began in Palm Springs. I knew then, we had a new future in syndication.

Disney then bought ABC/Cap Cities, the company we worked for. Mark and Brian had a great working relationship with Disney, so this made sense. Little did we know that Roy Disney was a huge Mark and Brian fan. His buddy owned KGON in Portland, Oregon, and they were looking for a morning show. Roy convinced his friend that he should put us on, and so it was done. That following Monday morning we hit Portland, and not that I'm counting, but that's two stations now—Mark and Brian Even *More* Incorporated!

The listeners in Portland took to us much like Palm Springs, but with more vigor and enthusiasm. It was odd how much we were embraced, and so quickly. If I had to guess, I don't think there was much morning entertainment in Portland prior to us, so we really stood out to them. Our success in Portland was immediate.

Alright, I feel like I need to confess something here. I mean it's not like we're dating or anything, but it bothers me. I talked earlier about how syndication is part of what became a problem for local radio. Obviously, we were a syndicated program, but this was 1994, the very beginning of syndication. I was unaware that it would become what it has. I would never do anything to purposely hurt radio. I knew we were relegated to the west coast only, so I didn't see the harm. But I admit I was aware that we were replacing paid radio jobs, and I felt bad about that, but it was never a ton of stations. There, I just needed to say that. And this is where we would kiss and then watch *Grey's Anatomy*.

Being syndicated was beneficial in several ways, one being it made us more attractive to big stars who could reach multiple cities with one appearance. We were in three markets now and growing.

It may have had an immediate effect because we were informed that Tom Cruise was going to do our show. There was no debate, Tom was the biggest star in the world at the time. Everyone wanted

Tom to do their show, so how did we get him? I was told that Tom's sister was a big Mark and Brian fan, and she told Tom he had to do it.

He was coming in to promote *Interview With a Vampire*, a starring role that caused an uproar from Anne Rice, the author. She wasn't pleased with Tom being cast, so Tom may have felt a little damage control was in order.

Most big stars we had on the show would come in with a ton of people in tow (managers, publicity people), but we never allowed anyone in the room except the star. All others were banished to another room. Tom showed up with only his sister, whom we allowed to stay beside her brother.

Tom couldn't have been more engaging. I was a fan of Tom's before he came in, and I was even more impressed with the man I met. He was very present in the moment, not distracted by anything; serious, funny, entertaining, thoughtful, and all very connected.

When I think of this interview, I think of three things. I've always felt I was a good interviewer, so I tried not to ask the same questions Tom heard all the time, and questions I genuinely wanted to know the answer to.

One question I asked him covered both areas.

"You have worked with some of the greatest actors of our time, Dustin Hoffman, Paul Newman, Jack Nicholson, to name a few. Was there anything that each of them did in their work that stuck out to you?"

Tom looked away and paused in thought, and I knew then I had asked something that no one else had. After a beat, he turned saying, "Yes, I was pleased to see that they're still working it out. It doesn't magically come to them. They still work at it, like I do." A great answer and revealing of Tom's observational skills.

Another thing Tom did is a moment I'll always cherish. During a commercial break, his sister laid out a bunch of pictures of Tom in front of him. He scanned them as I watched. At one point, Tom looked at me saying, "What do you think?" as he gestured toward the pictures. I walked over and perused them before picking the one of Tom standing on the edge of a cliff while the wind blew back his shirt. Tom looked at his sister saying, "That's the one."

Tom was going to be on the cover of some magazine, *Vanity Fair*, I believe, and he was the one who chose the cover shot. A month later, I saw my chosen picture on the magazine cover in Barnes and Noble.

But hands down, the best moment of Tom's visit came when we told him that Gene Wilder had called to say hello to him. To our shock, not only did Tom buy into it, but he was a huge Gene Wilder fan. He truly believed he was talking to Gene. So, our problem was how to tell Tom that he wasn't speaking with Gene, but an imposter, and not have him explode in anger and drink our blood. It was with great relief that Tom threw his head back and laughed hysterically, telling us, "You guys are toast."

For mega-stars like Tom, folks from the building would gather to sneak a peek. As Tom was leaving, he signed every autograph and took every picture.

When things change at the top, there is a domino effect down the line. Without number one ratings, revenue drops, which brings unwanted changes. First casualty, the Day Before Thanksgiving Day Parade was cancelled. Attendance was half what it once was, but it was one of our holiday traditions, and those are hard to say goodbye to. The first Wednesday without the parade was odd, since we didn't have anything to do. So, instead of hosting a parade, we hosted a family reunion, sort of.

We took off in the Mark and Brian mobile and headed over to Christopher Knight's house, who played Peter on *The Brady Bunch*. Why we went over there in the first place is a mystery. *Idle hands are the devil's workshop; idle lips are his mouthpiece.* While we chatted in Christopher's living room, we discovered that he and Eve Plumb—who played Jan—were very close, but that they hadn't seen each other since *A Very Brady Christmas*. So, we loaded Christopher in the car, found out where she lived and drove him over there.

Peter and Jan back together again, what a glorious sight, and truly amazing how boring they both were. They weren't even accidentally interesting, much like that morning's show. You tend to forget, they aren't best friends, they're actors playing a part. So, I don't blame them, they were nice to do it.

Everything about this period was weird, with very few things being the same. Thanksgiving on the show that year felt like having the big Thanksgiving celebration at your house, but nobody shows up, and your biggest concern is how it all looks to the neighbors.

This next thing was unfortunate, and hysterical. Brian and I went to a charity Christmas tree sale across from the Hollywood Bowl. The station had agreed to offer some help, and all tree sales went to charity; let me say that again, *charity*.

So, I'm talking with listeners when I look over at the sleigh where Santa is chatting with the kids, and I notice a sign sticking up from Santa's hat. I walked closer to read it and it said, "Tips for Santa," written clearly in bold letters.

I went to the head guy of the event, who was oblivious to Santa's hat message. He went over and told Santa to remove the note and stop taking tips. Santa not only refused to remove the sign but refused to stop accepting tips.

Another fun part, no one knew who Santa was, or how he got there, because he wasn't invited. As far as they knew, he just walked up and sat down in the sleigh, but he arrived dressed as Santa, so this was a premeditated act.

People are now openly complaining about the tip thing. Santa was told to leave, which he again refused. The dilemma now was, how do we remove Santa from the sleigh and the property without terrorizing the children? You don't want to drag him out of the sleigh screaming, while beating the shit out of him; that sort of thing tends to scare the kids.

Get this, Santa had to be paid to leave, $20 if I recall. So, I take my hat off to Santa's plan. He put in one hour's work, made a hundred bucks at a charity event, and he wasn't even invited. Good work, Santa! And Merry Christmas, *you fuck-wad*.

I'm going to throw in something here that has nothing to do with Mark and Brian, or even radio for that matter. It clearly doesn't belong in this book, but I find it uniquely interesting, and I may have stumbled onto something. It has to do with guys who would like to be more attractive to women. I observed something years ago by accident, and it continues to happen, which both befuddles and entertains me.

I've had a beard in some form for two-thirds of my life, so I never needed shaving gear. But in the early 1980s, I did a play where I had to shave. I went out and for the first time in years, I bought all the shaving crap I needed, including aftershave lotion, which is the focus of this brief story. Stay with me please because I'm starting to nod off myself.

I didn't know anything about shaving lotion, so I grabbed one of the popular brands. I splashed it on and could barely breathe. It smelled like shit, was super strong, and it came in a tiny bottle for thirty fucking dollars. I became that guy where people get off the elevator when I got on. There's a point here, and I'm about to make it, promise.

So, the shaving lotion thing was problematic. I was out thirty bucks and cats wouldn't come near me. So, I went to the drug store on the corner, and looked at what they had, which was all old school stuff, the very same crap my father used when he showed me how to shave. I was shocked they still made them: Old Spice, Aqua Velva, Mennen Skin Bracer, you name it, but there they were and cheap, too!

When my father taught me to shave, he told me when you rake a razor across your skin, it opens the pores, and shaving lotion closes the pores and prevents dirt build-up. It sounded important to me, so I grabbed the Old Spice, Aqua Velva, and Mennen Skin Bracer. Each was $5 and came in a gallon sized drum. The next day I shaved and splashed on the Aqua Velva, taken by the familiarity of it, since there's nothing like an Aqua Velva man.

As the years rolled on, I experienced a noticeable uptick in women who would openly speak to me, complete strangers who would start a conversation. I've never had any problem meeting women, but this was different. These women had a warmth to them and were comfortable in approaching; there was no fear or shyness. This happened to me more than you would think. I've spent time thinking about this, and I feel I've landed on a solid reason, and I'm not going to tell you what it is, because if I'm correct, then it's super creepy.

Case in point: During the spring of 2021, I met with my friend Kevin Pollak at his favorite eatery in Santa Monica. As Kevin and I chatted, a beautiful waitress approached and set down our plates. She then looked at us and asked, "Which one of you smells so good?" Kevin pointed at me. The server asked, "What are you wearing?" I told her, "Mennen Skin Bracer." She then launched into a two-minute explanation of something, and I didn't hear a word of it. I sat there, my mind blown that this was still happening. If you don't believe me, ask Kevin. He was there. His phone number is . . . .

So, my point being is, you have nothing to lose. But if you decide to try this, make sure it's old school and a name brand you've heard of from back in the day. If nothing happens, you're only out five bucks. Good luck, my friends and embrace the creepy!

On the Christmas Show that year we experienced something that wasn't creepy, but more in the "kind of cool" category. We had both KISS and the Gap Band on the bill. The Palladium has almost zero dressing room space, so we provided a large motorhome for each to use as a dressing room. We figured they would only need it for a few minutes, so we just got one motorhome.

As soon as the Gap Band arrived, they climbed in the motorhome and started partying, then their party simply poured out onto the stage at the Palladium. No matter—drunk or high—they were incredible. They had one guy whose only job was to prance around the stage blowing a whistle. How do you get a job like that?

The problem came *after* their performance. The Gap Band must've figured it was their personal motorhome, because they went back to it and resumed their party. When KISS arrived, they couldn't get in the motorhome because the Gap Band wouldn't leave. So, KISS simply walked into the motorhome and shared it with the Gap Band, and apparently the two groups bonded.

There is another KISS story that is now considered the stuff of rock legend, but the question looms, is it true? I can now confirm the answer to that, but first let me share the story in the event you haven't heard it.

KISS did a sold out show one Halloween night at Dodger Stadium. After the show, KISS climbed in their limo for the ride to their hotel on Sunset Boulevard. I don't have to tell you what kind of crazy gridlock that Sunset became on Halloween night. After not moving, the band decided to abandon their limo and proceeded to walk a few miles down Sunset to their hotel, in full makeup and boots, with zero security. No one made a fuss, no riots, and KISS arrived safely without incident at their destination. Did it happen?

After I heard that story, I waited a year for Gene and Paul to return to the show, as they had been many times before. I told that story and asked them if it was true. Not only did they confirm it to be absolutely factual, they said they were stopped many times by people who wanted pictures, and every one of them told the boys how great their costumes were, and that they really looked authentic. None of these people were aware that their photo was not with guys simply dressed like KISS, but with the real band itself, and they were oblivious to it.

Brian and I never shied away from dressing up in makeup and costumes, as evidenced by the shot at right, decked out as Elvis and Priscilla during one Halloween Show night.

It's well known that KISS sells everything imaginable including numerous books, but apparently not every rock star wants to tell their story. I read an article where Mick Jagger said he was approached by a publisher who offered him a ton of money to write his memoir, which Mick accepted and started writing. After two weeks, Mick stopped and returned the money, saying that dredging up old, bad memories was too painful, and he didn't want to live his current moments remembering bad shit from days gone by.

I can relate to Mick's words. After dredging up some of my worst memories, I seriously thought about not giving my dog fresh water. Kidding aside, some of my joggled memories from these last two chapters alone have upset me so deeply that I found it difficult to sleep, and this shit happened thirty years ago. I had no idea that

Image courtesy of KLOS Radio, LLC

much anger still lived in me, and that's a terrible truth I learned from as well.

The thing about writing your memoir is that you must pull up *all* the memories, and relive them as they were, and nobody paid me shit! In doing this, I've found moments where I can not only see the place, but I experienced fragrances in forgotten rooms. Memory is a powerful tool and if rattled, it may show you things you prefer not to see.

I've also enjoyed many of the better memories and learned things about myself I didn't know. You dust it off and live it again, only to learn of mistakes made and choices challenged.

As I wrote this book I wondered, would I still do this all over again knowing what I know now? The answer is yes, but I would've made some different choices at times, and this is one of the big ones.

In 1995, I would make a spontaneous decision that was really stupid. It was completely my fault, and it was the lead story on the local news, which is never a good thing. Lynda was so upset I had to beg her to come to bed that night. Unlike some people, I learned from my mistake, which is never, ever help a friend in need.

I RUN A CLEAN CAMPAIGN

1995–1997

> **"**A bank is a place that will lend you money if you can prove that you don't need it.**"**
>
> —BOB HOPE

This period in our tenure would be a reality check for us. If we were going to return to form and reclaim the crown, it would have happened by now, and it hadn't. Howard still held a firm grasp on his dominance, and now Kevin and Bean were recognized as having skin in the game. Though I never got to hear their show, their ratings were rivaling ours. By what people told me, Kevin and Bean were a better version of us than we were at this point. Pure and simple, we were trending down with nothing promising in sight. I realize you probably don't know what ratings numbers mean (I barely do), but this should give you some perspective. In 1991, Mark and Brian had a 12, and now we were hovering around a 4.5. That's clearly down, and clearly shitty.

The temperature inside the building Mark and Brian built had a chill to it. That glorious buzz of our heyday was a distant memory. We were treading water, and that loud silence between me and Brian wasn't helping. "We're getting no place fast," as the *Three Stooges* used to say. There was very little to be happy about; it was slowly becoming a job, not a joy for me.

These next three years would show themselves as the very beginning of the distant end. Bill Sommers would retire, and we would suffer through a series of general managers who seemed to offer little to no guidance. We would become rudderless as a show and a station. Looking back, it was a massive mess, station-wide, and when you don't have someone clearly in charge who can navigate rough seas, peril is imminent.

However, things were great in our syndicated cities. We were kings in that world. So, there was a ray of sunshine peeking through the unwanted weeds. But I wondered where all of this might lead.

I've always had a sense of wonder from as far back as I can remember, and that got me into trouble as a kid. Innocent things like wondering how much of my neighborhood I could see if I climbed that tree. However, to do that, I ignored the fact I was supposed to clean my room, crap like that. Even if I knew I would get into trouble, I still did it. I learned early on that living my life based on a set of rules handed down by someone else was simply not my bag, and I always faced the consequences. I wasn't allowed to venture beyond two streets from my house, but there was adventure on the other side, and my bicycle was made for peddling. The trouble I would face was simply the price I paid for the experience.

I was raised in the deep south, where whippings with a belt were commonplace, and my mother administered those. She adored me, so an ass-beating from her was a mere formality; I had to pretend it hurt. And though she tried, she simply couldn't force herself to bring the leather.

When I got into trouble, I was always oddly surprised, because I didn't realize I was doing something wrong. Like the time I got a chemistry set for Christmas. I mixed up a batch of stuff and poured it in my mother's gas tank. As warped as my adolescent thinking clearly was, I honestly thought it would help her car run better, and I was super shocked when it didn't. I simply didn't have that voice in me that said, "Don't do this, it's stupid," and that character flaw has never left me. I tell you this because it will help you understand why

I made this decision when probably no one else would even consider it. I'm flawed and can't help myself!

Skip to the afternoon of May 13, 1995, a date that now lives in Mark and Brian infamy, although Brian had no part in it. I went to a showing of the new Nicholas Cage film *Kiss of Death*, clearly something I shouldn't have done. As I watched this listless display of David Caruso trying to be a movie star, a buddy had tracked me down to inform me that a mutual friend of ours was in jail and asking for me. As I rose from my seat, I waved goodbye to that movie and David Caruso's career.

I was led back to see my friend, who was in a holding cell at the sheriff's department. He had been arrested for DUI, some sort of pills. He signed over his briefcase to me, which was brought out and placed on the table next to me.

As I exited the jail area into the lobby, I realized I had left his briefcase behind. I attempted going back, but the gate locked behind me. I tried for ten minutes to get someone's attention, but no one showed up.

The only thing between me and that briefcase was a three-foot-tall banister with a gate. My thinking was, since I had just been there, I could simply step over the banister, grab the briefcase, and slide back out. This is where my brain should have yelled, *don't do this*. My brain failed me in that moment, so I stepped over the gate.

I think I then heard the word, "freeze." Two or three of them yelled it, so I'm pretty sure that's what I heard. I looked and saw five deputies with guns drawn and pointed at me. With my heightened spider senses, I could clearly see bullets inside the gun cylinders; lots of guns, lots of bullets, lots of deputies. I was then pinned against the wall and cuffed, all while trying to explain, but they didn't seem interested.

Now, I'm sitting in the exact same holding cell once occupied by my friend. The briefcase I left behind was three feet from me on the table, only I still couldn't reach it, because *I'm now in jail*.

Luckily for me, I was just in time for dinner. They brought me a plate covered with some sort of beans, and a hot dog smushed down in the middle. I was just about to send my plate back to the chef, since I wished to have my wiener grilled a tad more on the left side, when they came and took me to an interrogation room. I had seen these in movies, but this was my first time entering one. They kept it nice; there were comfortable cushions on the chairs, a nicely placed throw rug, and a lava lamp.

The sheriff himself was waiting for me, which I took as a bad sign, since being in a jail cell hadn't already alerted me that this could end badly. He had been briefed on my situation, meaning he knew who I was.

"Unfortunately, you've been processed," the sheriff said.

I stared at him, like I'm supposed to know what that means.

"Meaning what?" I asked.

"You've been booked."

"Meaning what?" I repeated, holding my stare.

"The press is going to see that you've been arrested," he said.

I could tell he didn't like that truth any more than I did.

So, May 13, 1995, I was booked and processed. They did the mug shot, fingerprints, checked my butt for x-ray vision goggles, bail was posted, and I was driven home to tell Lynda where I had spent the afternoon. I would've frankly rather stayed in jail and faced that under-cooked weenie.

She was surprisingly okay with everything until the evening news hit. It was the lead story on all the stations. They reported, "He leapt over the front counter." In truth, I stepped over a gate, that's not exactly leaping, but it was clearly my fault. And none of this would've happened if David Caruso had simply stayed with *NYPD Blue*.

Obviously, I just told you a story, and storytelling is the oldest form of entertainment we have. If you're watching TV, a movie, or reading a book, those are nothing more than different forms of telling you a story.

Whenever I would meet certain listeners, they would act as if we were best friends, though we had never met. They knew quite a bit about me through the stories I had shared on the show. They would repeat to me some dumb-ass thing I had done, and then crack up. I shared these stories because I wanted to relate to a specific listener.

Every radio station caters to a certain type of person. All classic rock stations seek male listeners, ages 25 to 54. So, I created a target listener by going right in the middle, making him 40 and married with kids. Whenever I told a story, I pictured this guy, and told it to him. For example, if I did a really dumb thing involving one of my kids, and I tried to hide it from my wife because I'm afraid of her, then that story was perfect for telling.

All my stories were around two minutes, and I practiced telling the story in the car, which helped me hone it down to the best possible version. My main goal with these stories was to allow my target audience to relate to me. I wanted him to know that I'm just like him, married with kids, and an idiot. If he could relate to me, he would stay with me.

Since you now realize I'm just like you, I'm going to give you some advice, and you should heed my words! If you're ever invited to throw out the first pitch at a professional baseball game, stand tall on the mound, and throw the ball with some *serious stank*. The number one mistake you can make is to bounce it, because you'll be booed, laughed at, and ridiculed. I've seen baseball fans boo old women for bouncing it.

We had the honor of throwing out the first pitch at games for both the Dodgers and Angels. At one of them, Brian brought his friend's son. The boy stood at home plate with a bat, and Brian lobbed the ball to give the child a chance to hit it, meaning, Brian bounced it. Baseball fans don't care that a child was involved, they booed loudly, with hate and venom.

Baseball fans are purists, and they want things done the way they've always been done. And if you deviate from that, you will face their wrath.

The only perk of throwing out the first pitch is you get to keep the ball. My ball reads, "Ceremonial first pitch, Dodger Stadium," embossed in gold, and my ball has no dirt smudges on it, because I didn't bounce it.

And while I'm doling out advice, here's a big one: Never host an Easter egg hunt on your radio show. While we honored most holi-

Image courtesy of KLOS Radio, LLC

days on our program, Easter was the forgotten child. Compared to other holidays, Easter was a tough one. The thought of coloring eggs on the air was tempting, however dipping eggs in colored water is a completely silent act, so that might've royally sucked. In a weak moment, we decided to host an egg hunt in the parking lot of the station, and I murdered a listener, my kill count now at three.

As a parent, you would think I would've learned from our family egg hunts. Every year, when we dyed the eggs, we would dip one egg in all the colors, and that would be the golden egg. If found, the golden egg was worth twenty bucks, and all my kids are whores for money, so they were pumped. By the way, after dipping the egg in every color, it comes out shit brown.

I took extra care to hide the egg in an almost impossible-to-find area. Amy is extremely competitive, and she was always the one to find the turd-colored egg. So, every Easter, Amy was $20 richer, Matt was pissed, Katie was crying, and I learned nothing from any of that.

Mark and Brian's version of the golden egg was $1,000. There were ten eggs hidden that contained $100, and the golden egg held the extra zero. The only rule was *kids only, no parents allowed*.

On the morning of the hunt, a sizable crowd was held behind the large gate of the parking lot. As we had stated, once the gate opens, only kids are allowed in.

Everything went well for about a minute, until a little girl was leaning down to grab an egg, when some other kid ran up and grabbed it, which made the little girl start to cry. The girl's father then crossed through the gate to console her, and that was all she wrote. Every adult then rushed the egg hunt seeking money. Little kids were being pushed aside by cash-hungry parents. I was yelling into the microphone, "NO ADULTS, NO ADULTS," which was not my proudest moment. I was fuming, when one parent almost knocked me to the ground going for an egg. If I had been in possession of the necessary means, I would've gladly taken his life. It was an Easter nightmare, complete with yelling and crying, and we never again so much as uttered the word *Easter* on the show. Egg hunts should be banned around the world, unless you enjoy seeing small children cry. Happy Easter, everyone! Hippity- hoppity up my ass!

It was one thing for Los Angeles to hear that colored egg crap, but all our syndicated stations heard it as well. We were in twelve cities at this point, none more important than KGON in Portland, Oregon. KGON was a healthy radio station when they put us on. It was well-managed, well-staffed, and they cared about their product, which made it much easier for us to succeed. It's nice to hit the air on a station that already has a ton of listeners. Our most important job was to not run them off.

We were an immediate hit, even faster than when we first came to LA. When we traveled to Portland, it was like Elvis had landed. Listeners would greet us at the airport. When we rode in the limo to the hotel, KGON would announce we had landed, and would play, "The Boys Are Back in Town," every visit.

There was always a welcome basket in my room, packed with my favorite candies, and ample stock of my favorite wine and scotch, plus a handwritten note saying how glad they were to have us back. It was impossible not to feel at ease there.

I had built into my deal two airline seats, in case I wanted to bring Lynda, or one of the kids. The biggest event of the year in Portland is the Rose Festival, a massive celebration of the blooming season. Mark and Brian went every year, usually as grand marshals of the Rose Parade, and then we would host a rock concert. After hearing me rave about what a great time it was, every member of my family wanted to go, and it was Matt's turn.

I ended each Rose Festival the same way. I would pour a glass of wine and sit on my balcony to watch the fireworks over the Willamette River. Sixteen-year-old Matt joined me for this moment and observed me sipping wine. "Can I have some?" he asked. After a quick question and answer session in my head, I said, "Sure."

I figured we were in for the night and I'm here to watch him, so I saw no harm. Father and son sat and imbibed in what I believed to be his first alcoholic beverage. I began to pour more in my glass as Matt reached his glass over as well, so I poured.

As we sat, Matt talked a lot, which made me chuckle. After a bit, he placed his glass on the table saying, "I'm going to call Nick," his best friend.

After a while, I thought it best to check on him. I found him in his bed fully clothed, lights on, the phone to his head, mouth wide open, and passed out cold. The phone beeping into his ear had no effect, so I flipped off the lights saying, "Good night, champ."

Whenever I traveled with the show, I normally stayed under an assumed name. Listeners would call at all hours, which is what dictated this. There were times when they would knock on my door.

Most times, I was listed as either John Burrows or Dr. John Carpenter. These were the two names Elvis used when traveling. Dr. John Carpenter was Elvis's character in *Change of Habit*, his last film. The only other name I would sometimes use was Bob Jones, a radio jock who actually existed.

The legend of Bob Jones was known to most air personalities, though not in an endearing way. There was an air-check that went around that most jocks either had a copy of the tape or had heard it. The air-check featured Bob in the early morning hours at KQUE in Houston.

Bob was having a particularly rough night. Things started out fine, but as the hours ticked, Bob began to slur his words, and it went downhill from there. Bob would accidentally leave his mic on while the record was playing, and you could hear him wandering the studio, mumbling to himself. Then, we got the first real indication that Bob was not in control.

As Bob was talking and not making much sense, suddenly his private thoughts were blurted out on the air, seemingly without his knowledge.

"And if you see Trudy's mother, have her call me. Wait, on second thought, never mind, I don't need those kinds of problems."

There were long stretches of dead air with no sound of any kind, except for Bob, who had again, unknowingly left on the mic. He was wandering the studio mumbling, seemingly unaware that nothing was playing. And just when it couldn't get any worse, Bob puked into the trash can, which was clearly audible.

While this was unthinkable for any radio talent, there was also great sadness that Bob was unable to control his actions. As I heard it, Bob got his life together and back on track, and it would seem without the help of Trudy's mother.

As we approached the Christmas Show that December, we had a wonderful problem we were more than happy to deal with. From the moment we announced the news, it became the single focus of our program. This is what happens when you're going to have a living legend standing on your stage, a far more famous "Bob." It was impossible to answer the phones, because all anybody wanted was to win tickets. It was the first and only time in our history where we had to do a daily allotment; only twenty tickets a day would be given out, because everybody wanted to see Bob Hope read, *Twas the Night Before Christmas.*

On the morning of the show, there was an unmistakable energy to the house. All our Christmas Shows had a buzz, but this was different. All were there to see the legend, and out he came. The standing ovation lasted three minutes, and it floated in the air like waves. It seemed for a time like it might not stop.

His wife Dolores joined him since Bob was 91 years old. Bob

would open and close the poem, and his wife would do the rest. And, to celebrate the season, Bob wore a green jacket, his wife wore red. Nice Christmas touch, guys!

There is a term known as "Bob Hope jokes." That's a joke only Bob Hope can deliver and make funny, because it would fall flat for anybody else. Case in point, the opening of the Christmas poem included a Bob Hope joke, which he killed with, simply because he's Bob Hope.

After the ovation had waned, people settled as Bob began, "Twas the night before Christmas, when all through the house, not a creature was stirring, *not even my agent.*" The place fell out, and the ovation started up again. As his wife beautifully read the rest, we all just stared at Bob, as he stood there doing nothing. Bob then closed it, "And to all, a good night," then another standing ovation. Only a legend can leave the stage in the middle of a standing ovation, and not have it seem rude. Thanks for the memories, Bob!

In late 1995, we signed a new five-year deal with KLOS, and I wondered if we would survive the full five. Something wasn't right, and I don't mean with the deal, I mean with me; something was off, I wasn't myself. It just started out of nothing and suddenly, I felt shaky. It was like I was nervous about something, but I was unaware of anything I had to be nervous about. This may be the time I was the most worried because I didn't know what it was, and it seemed to get worse by the day.

The Orange County Fair was the best run fair I'd ever seen; well organized, top to bottom. Every year we would make an appearance there. The crowds that came to see us now were quite a bit smaller than years prior, but that was not only understandable, it was also a good thing, honestly. In our crazy white-hot years, the crowds were so big we couldn't get to everybody, and I seriously hated that. People stood in line for hours, and we didn't get to meet them due to time constraints. You simply can't win in that situation.

The OC Fair was a summer event, so our crowd would stand in the hot sun to say hello. When I hugged some of them, I could feel the heat on their backs. We would see everything from super fans who always showed up, to people who had no idea who we were. I asked one guy why he waited so long if he didn't know who we were and he said, "I saw a line, so I got in it." Fair enough (see what I did there?).

As a bystander myself, my favorite parts of these events were the super-hot women who came to see Brian. You could tell they spent hours getting ready for their moment. They would reach us and make their play for the tall, good looking, blond guy. I always enjoyed listening to Brian whisper his comments to me after they had left. I could always tell the ones who had an actual shot because Brian wouldn't say much to them, he would just stare. I wound up doing most of the talking since I had nothing to lose or gain.

A very nice family stepped up to our table, mom, dad, and three beautiful kids. They stuck out to me because they were so well put together, which is always mom; she makes sure everybody is ship-shape. You could also tell she dressed dad, and we dads love that because it's one less thing we have to think about.

Mom and the kids did all the talking. Dad just stared at us with his big, goober grin. Mom leaned over and whispered, "My husband is a huge fan, he's just shy." As dad stared, we signed everything and off they went.

After the event, I was walking to my car when the goober-grinning dad stepped up to me; his grin had disappeared. His family stayed back, which struck me as odd. When I looked at dad, I saw he was fighting his emotions. I lost my smile and said nothing, knowing he had something he needed to say.

He fought to keep control as he said, "I've been a fan from the beginning, you guys make my day. Last year my mother got cancer, and I spent every day going to the hospital to be with her, to hold her hand on chemo day, to comb her head where hair used to be. It was a really tough year until she left me, and through all of that, the only smile I got was you guys. I wanted you to know that." Tears streamed down his face as he gently shook. I welled up, too and hugged him.

I got into morning radio to entertain people as they went to work, have some fun, achieve my goal, and that was it. I never realized that what we did could possibly help someone when they were in need. It never crossed my mind, until that moment.

I don't remember hearing the radio on my drive home, my thoughts drowned out all the sound. I thought I was done growing up, but I was wrong.

The single biggest drawback to doing morning radio was the hours. For the better part of thirty-five years, I got up every day at 3:30 a.m. You get better at doing it, but you never get used to it, if that makes any sense. You walk through each day in a kind of fog. It goes against every fiber of our being to get up that early. While technically it's morning, it's also the middle of the night. Every early morning person does it differently, but the one thing we all have in common is, we are exhausted by noon.

For me, I learned to remove all decisions from my morning process. I would lay my clothes out and load my briefcase the night before, so all I had to do was grab and go.

My morning began with the alarm clock. I had two alarms, one main, one backup, both battery, and both on a table across the room. I had to get out of bed to turn it off, on purpose. I've never been a snooze pusher, too much can go wrong. Being late for a morning air shift is unacceptable. It will lead to your demise!

I would shut off the alarm and head straight into the shower. Some morning people don't shower before a show, but it was an absolute must for me. Then dress, coffee up, and hit the road.

I first noticed it in the shower. The only way I can describe it is that an uneasy feeling had washed over me and remained there. There was a slight tremble in my hand as I poured coffee, and the trembling got worse as the morning progressed. The closer I got to work, the more intense the uneasiness became. Before, the feeling seemed to come and go, but now it was my constant companion. There was clearly something wrong, and that terrified me because I had never felt anything like this, and the most worrisome part was my inability to control it.

There was also something wrong with Amy because apparently

the poor child couldn't spell for shit. She was about to start the first grade, so on the morning of her first day, Lynda dressed her to the nines and took 6,000 pictures to get one. Our monthly film developing usually cost the same as our mortgage. With two grandchildren now, whoever invented digital photography, muchas gracias! Anyway, Amy was grinning ear to ear, but her grin disappeared after she took her first test. It was obviously spelling, and she flunked it, as in F.

She was crying when I arrived home, and Lynda had warned me what to expect. So, I put my arm around her and said, "Listen, this is nothing to worry about. Next time, just try not to be so stupid."

See, I was using reverse psychology. I was trying to catch her off guard with a joke, to get her laughing. And, it was a colossal failure, she burst into tears. I'm a tad vague on Lynda's reaction, but I seem to remember she felt I should've gone a different route.

Amy might've been flunking but our syndication company was flourishing. We had added KRQR, in San Francisco, which I was jacked about. My goal was to be in major market, now I'm in two.

We agreed to fly up and do our first show live, and man did we. We toured the city while broadcasting, including going to the home of the mayor of San Francisco, Frank Jordan, who was running for re-election.

The interview was typical political junk, but when Mayor Jordan said he needed to wrap-up the interview to shower, we suggested we shower with him. During the commercial break, Jordan's advisor tells him he thinks the shower idea is great, just what voters would find funny. Brian and I sat and watched this unfold. But when Frank's wife said she thought he should do it, that was all it took.

The photographer started frantically getting ready, and I made him promise I wouldn't see my penis in the newspaper the next day. So, there we were, Mark, Brian, and mayor, taking a shower as the camera clicked away.

The story hit and the voter's reaction was pure hatred. The mayor was getting skewered, so he released a statement, "At least you know I run a clean campaign." I thought that was a great line, one that should've calmed the storm, but it only made things worse.

Then, the inevitable happened: Mayor Jordan denounced the

Image courtesy of Billy Douglas of www.billydouglas.com

shower stunt. He said it was a bad judgement call, and that he was sorry. In my mind, he simply became another politician apologizing for whatever.

He lost the election and Mark and Brian were blamed. And it doesn't matter, Frank Jordan is a nice guy who fucked up when he apologized for a fun, ridiculous thing like taking a shower with two strange men he had just met.

That is what you call a hot first show for KRQR's new morning show, and we lasted less than a year in San Francisco before they dumped us. Same thing in Las Vegas, and San Diego. As I said, if the station isn't healthy, we can't help them, nothing can.

Lynda noticed I was quieter than usual. I guess when something is stirring within, you tend to remove yourself from things without realizing it. After repeatedly saying, "I'm fine," I finally explained in the best way I could what was happening, while being careful with my words. I didn't want to alarm her, because then she would dote on me, and I didn't want that. As I spoke, I was embarrassed saying the words from fear that it was all in my head. We both agreed I would see a doctor. She did poorly at hiding her concern, but it did feel good to tell someone.

The doctor ran a battery of basic tests and confirmed I was physically fine, other than higher than normal blood pressure. After I shared my experiences, he said it sounded like anxiety to him, and wanted me to see a therapist. Given a choice, I would listen to nails on a chalkboard or even Roseanne Barr serenading me, before going to therapy. He gave me the contact for a therapist he liked, and a prescription for something called Xanax. Lynda filled the prescription and I stuffed the therapist number in a drawer.

I took one of the Xanax pills and moments later, I knew I would never take it again. Not only did it remove the uneasy feeling, but I felt great, almost euphoric. I knew this must be what many get addicted to. One pill today means two tomorrow, and then you're hooked. I threw them in the drawer with the therapist's number and decided to just get over it.

The year 1997 wasn't destined to be a good one. The fun for me had gone out of doing it. It had become a job I didn't like, and for the first time ever, I dreaded going to work. I can honestly say it was here where I started earning my money. Prior to this, it was the work that made me happy; not anymore.

To open the year, Bill Sommers retired. Bill was the one who hired me, and to that point, the only GM we ever had at KLOS. I liked Bill, and I knew how he worked. Bill could be harsh when he was upset, but he would let you have it right to your face, so I always knew where I stood with him. He never talked behind my back or was launching some devious plan with me in mind. Bill was tough and fair, and I liked the playing field. I always knew what was out of bounds. Now I would have to adjust to a new GM.

Bill was replaced with Maureen Lasourd. I don't think I was ever officially introduced to her. I saw her a handful of times, and not once did she look my way. It was as if I wasn't in the room, and I felt she was purposely avoiding me.

The first moves she made were on KABC. I was hallway friends with Michael Jackson, one of the most respected talk show hosts in LA. I would run into Michael in the men's room, him in his three-piece suit and tie, and me in shorts, IHOP T-shirt, and flip flops. Michael was always entertained by me, saying, "What kind of trouble are you and your partner into today?"

Michael was the "Talk Show Host of the Year," and Ms. Lasourd removed Michael from his full-time shift and demoted him to one shift on the weekend. Maureen quickly became, as *Variety* magazine put it, "The most disliked woman in LA radio."

After she was done with KABC, Ms. Lasourd took the old KMPC and changed the call letters to KTZN, The Zone. She staffed it with mostly females, and it catered to a female audience. It simply didn't work. The Zone was abandoned after six months.

On a visit to my aunt's farm, I once tried to name one of her chickens, and my aunt told me I shouldn't. She said, "We don't want to get to know them too well. Eventually, they'll be our dinner." I was positive Mark and Brian were next on Maureen's dinner menu, and maybe that's why she ignored me; she didn't want to know me too well.

Under her tenure, 1997 brought the end of what had been a great segment for us called, "What Would You Do for Super Bowl Tickets?" People would tell us how far they would challenge themselves to win two tickets to the game, and we would select the best five. Those five would compete on the Friday before the Super Bowl. All five competitors would show up with their bags packed, and the winner would leave from there for the game.

There were many great entries over the years, but I had two all-time favorites. One extremely hairy guy shaved off all his body hair with a disposable razor, which took thirty blades. He was covered in blood from the shaving nicks and then dove into a kiddie pool filled with pure rubbing alcohol. I had never seen a person bolt straight up and sprint like he did, as if he suddenly caught on fire. He went to the Super Bowl, bloody nicks and all.

And this last one makes me nauseous to type it. A guy ate a huge plate of raw pig guts and raw goat liver. He then forced himself to puke into a plastic bag, and then took a fork and ate all his own puke from the bag, but he wasn't done. He then took a straw and slurped up every, last bit of the *puke juice*. I couldn't watch it, so Brian had to do the play by play. Yes, he went to the Super Bowl.

Under the new management, we were told all entries had to be run through the company's legal division. I don't have to tell you

where *that* went. They threw out all the great ones and left us with lame *no risk* entries, so instead of lame, we cancelled the segment.

The oddness of '97 continued, with Mark and Brian receiving our star on the Hollywood Walk of Fame. It should have been joyous, but it felt empty for me. It turned out to be an odd moment, during a strange time, and that shouldn't have been the case.

I don't know the reason, but we had been alienated from KLOS. The station itself made no mention of the ceremony. During a moment that should've been a proud career achievement, it felt more like a birthday party our parents didn't attend.

Being fair to the station, our ratings were not good. We had fallen out of the top 10. And my relationship with Brian was dismal, at best. The special communication we once had was now almost non-existent. We were no longer on the same wavelength, with the show, or each other. So many things had gone unspoken, important things.

We were five years removed from our dominance in ratings and that reality had built a wall that neither of us attempted to scale. It was like one of us had cheated, and the idea of even saying the words would bring shudders. I regret now not sitting down with him and saying, "We need to talk about Howard."

We not only lost our dominance in morning ratings, but we lost ourselves in the process. Brian basically went from waiting tables to becoming a radio rock star, and he very much liked his newfound persona. So, it must have been devastating for him—as it was for me—and we clearly needed to discuss it. Instead, we both fell into a kind of crippling silence. I was worried that having the conversation would make matters worse, and it probably would have for a time, but at least it would have cleared some of the air between us.

That period of my life felt like I was living in a Winslow Homer painting; a man alone in a small rowboat, trying to navigate turbulent waters in an open sea. Our reigning world as kings had collapsed around us, and the kings' court no longer bent the knee. It also felt like Brian blamed me for what had happened and that he no longer trusted my comedic instincts. I deeply regret not at least sitting down with him and having the conversation. It might have made things uncomfortable but at this point, things between us couldn't have escalated much worse. When we were off the air, we barely spoke.

With station management remaining a challenge, the handcuffs we wore from ownership and a lack of support from the station, I was wondering what my personal future would be. So yes, everything pretty much sucked balls!

Regardless, on October 4, 1997, Mark and Brian stood before a small crowd in the rain on Hollywood Boulevard and accepted our star. I chose the spot our star would be placed for two reasons. First, it was two spots down from Elvis, and it was in front of the Hollywood Wax Museum, the worst wax museum I'd ever seen, which I found funny.

We had invited John Travolta, Billy Bob Thornton, and Kevin Pollak, and all three attended. We were standing in the waiting area with various dignitaries, when John's limo pulled up, and we got word that John wanted to see us. We both loaded into his limo, and John congratulated us on the honor. I told him, "I don't think you know how much it means to us that you would come down for this," and John replied, "Yes I do." I loved the honesty of that answer.

My biggest regret of this honor is that I didn't invite Bill Sommers, and that truly hurt Bill's feelings, something I would never knowingly do. We were being honored with this moment because Bill had the vision to take a chance on us. He should have not only been invited but featured. I have apologized to Bill repeatedly because this was my error. He has forgiven me, but I haven't forgotten that one thoughtless lapse on my part could bring hurt to someone I love, respect, and care about.

My favorite moment of the morning was Amy. Lynda brought the kids down in a limo. They pulled up to the red carpet and eight-year-old Amy was about to get out, when Lynda told her, "Amy, stay by the car. I have to get Katie out of her car seat, and we'll walk down the carpet together."

As soon as Amy stepped from the car, the crowd began cheering and her little brain said, "Fuck it, I'm going." Amy started walking the red carpet alone and waving like a star. I included the photo here, one of my favorite pictures.

The only head scratching moment of the day was Gary Coleman showing up. He wasn't invited, but he was clearly welcomed.

We always tried to be as charitable as possible. Over our time, we released three CDs full of comedy bits and music from the show, with all proceeds going to charity. On November 19, 1997, we released *You Had to Be There*. It debuted at #1 in Los Angeles and #48 nationwide.

As we approached the end of the year, we were informed there would be no Christmas Show. Ratings were not where they needed to be for the budget of a big show. The idea of selling tickets came up but I refused to charge listeners. I would rather not have it.

So instead, we did something that made me quite proud. We put on a live production of *A Christmas Carol*. We harkened back to the days of live radio productions, the way it was done in the 1940s, when the family would gather around the refrigerator-sized radio in the living room.

We hooked up with Sound Deluxe, a studio with full capabilities for live orchestra, live sound effects, and live actors. Kevin Pollak was Scrooge, Jenna Elfman also joined us, but the star performance belonged to Mark Hamill, who played several characters to perfection. Because it was live, there were obvious screw-ups but for the most part, it was a straight-forward, professional production of the timeless classic.

Sadly, this fantastic live production came and went. Not much was said about it in the media. If we had done this in our early years, we would've been highly praised. It wound up being an unnoticed, unheralded, yet remarkable achievement.

It kind of signified the way things felt in those days. We were there, doing good stuff, but people didn't seem to notice. But 1997 did end on a high note. Maureen Lasourd resigned as president of KLOS/KABC after one year on the job.

The financial issues that prevented us from doing a Christmas Show that year would show itself many times in our future. We would have to find ways to do things on a small budget. The following year would bring us a moment captured in time, a photograph that you weren't supposed to see. And it would be as good as it gets, boys and girls.

EASY NOW

1998–1999

> 66 Every man must do two things alone; he must do his own believing and his own dying. 99
>
> —MARTIN LUTHER

I remember driving to work those days, my car knew the road and drove itself as I was lost in thought. Each morning's drive felt like it might be my last. We were still making *big boy* money, which should've been compensation for big boy ratings, but that wasn't the case anymore. We were no longer in the top 10 and slipping more in each ratings period. As far as LA proper, we were almost non-existent, far removed from our days on the throne. I wasn't thinking of LA while doing the show anymore, I was thinking of our syndicated cities, where we were still riding high. We no longer made outside appearances in LA—it was too risky—we only did Mark and Brian events. Once you've been booed by 60,000 people and rushed by a guy who wants to do bodily harm, it tends to alter your thinking.

Every day I drove in, I just knew this was the day we'd get fired, but we never did. It was no secret, our show had not aged well, and neither had I. I was looking a tad like Abe Vigoda.

The building Mark and Brian built was also showing its age. A coat of paint was in order, the carpet was peeling up from the corners, and rust was climbing up one of the stalls in the men's room. I know this sounds odd, but I have fond memories of that bathroom.

You've got this huge building in LA, home of the stars, that houses three radio stations and there's only one bathroom for men. It stands to reason that the level of celebrities shuffling through there would be rather high, because even celebrities have to pee. That was clearly the case as I bumped into many, but I will give you three that I had the unique opportunity to stand next to and take a leak.

To begin, I stepped up to the urinal and noticed another guy next to me, the back of him seemed familiar. I glanced over to see that it's Terry Bradshaw. If that name is unfamiliar to some of you, he's the Super Bowl winning quarterback from the Pittsburgh Steelers who played in the 1970s. He now works for Fox as part of a primetime football broadcast team and also has made several guest appearances in film and TV.

I opted not to pee so I could do some business with him. As soon as Terry zipped up, so did I. We both headed for the sink and while there, I told him who I was and asked if he would pop in for a quick hello. In case you also don't know, Terry is a party walking. He came in for one break and wound up doing an hour. Once the phones got going, you couldn't have forced him from the room with all the compliments he was getting, and I had snatched him out of the bathroom.

Next, I was already at the urinal when I heard the door open and a guy stepped up next to me and started talking. I look over and it's Andy Dick, who talked the entire time about weird shit. I had to leave to make it stop.

And last, I walked in to wash my hands. I was aware someone was at the urinal as I heard him flush, zip, and approach the sink area. I then heard, "How are you?" in this deep, resonate, familiar voice. I glanced in the mirror to see Charlton Heston washing his hands beside me. I responded, "I'm good, Mr. Heston, how are you?" As he dried his hands he said, "Blessed my friend, blessed," then exited. And all I could think was, "Moses just spoke to me."

I'll share something here I find oddly interesting about myself. I don't care for my laugh. I realize I'm known for it since I did so much of it, but I simply don't enjoy listening to it. To be brutally honest, my own laugh grates on my nerves. It doesn't bother me when I'm doing it because I'm not thinking about it, but I just don't like hearing it played back to me. Seriously, it's like nails on a chalkboard for me.

And another thing, I've never enjoyed hearing the Mark and Brian program. Each morning as I drove in, KLOS played "best of" moments from the day before, and I never listened to it, not once. Maybe because I helped plan it, I clearly was there doing it, and I knew what was coming, so I found no joy in listening to it. I think it's like a musical artist who doesn't like listening to his or her own records. Or maybe, it's because I'm laughing all the way through it.

However, laughing obviously was our business because we both thought it would be funny to launch a Butterball turkey on top of a rocket to celebrate the joy and togetherness of Thanksgiving. I find that a dead bird sent thousands of feet into the air speaks volumes for the holiday.

It doesn't matter how we got on the topic of launching a turkey, we knew it needed to happen. So, for stupid shit like this, you start at the beginning. We needed a rocket that could achieve the given task, so we went to our resourceful listeners.

We got a call from a guy who was a level three model rocket builder, which requires certification from the Federal Aviation Administration. This guy was a model rocket pro. He told us that sending a frozen turkey up would be no problem for him, but we would have to do it at the salt flats, meaning the desert. He said it would require a specially built rocket, and he would start building right away.

We drove up to the chosen launch area the Tuesday before and checked into the only hotel within 5,000 miles. It was an old school motor hotel, where you park your car in front of your room. It was a mom-and-pop place, where mom had knitted the doilies that were on the chairs in my room. I love that kind of shit.

The morning of the launch, I had on the TV and a couple of lights, but I made the critical mistake of turning on the blow dryer at the same time, and I blew out the electrical system for the entire hotel. That's not a joke, it really happened.

In radio speak, there is a group of listeners categorized as "the active listener." These are people who call the show, appear at events, buy station products; in other words, they actively participate. The active listener represents only three percent of the listening audience, meaning 97 percent do nothing but listen.

Having said that, when we arrived at the launch site, there were 5,000 active listeners waiting to see a Butterball turkey fly, in the middle of the desert. God bless all of you.

The guy who built the rocket had assembled a wooden dowel on top of the rocket. It looked like a paper towel holder sticking straight up. He had inserted a female receptacle inside the cavity of the turkey, so it simply slid down on the dowel. It was designer's perfection; this guy was exceptional at his rocket turkey craft.

It was so utterly ridiculous to see an eight-foot beautifully built rocket with a frozen turkey perched on top. The Mark and Brian logo was all over the rocket, and the turkey.

We did the countdown with the crowd, and this turkey took off at lightning speed. I thought the weight of the bird would slow it down, but it was as if the twenty-pound beast wasn't even there. It came down majestically with a parachute, which brought a tear as I watched it. Those in attendance wildly cheered the stupidity.

The turkey launch was a complete success, so we officially proclaimed that Thanksgiving would be allowed to take place. We had thereby ordained it with *flying frozen fowl;* that's some sweet alliteration right there, my friends.

On-location broadcasts are physically exhausting. You are dealing with the technical side of the broadcast and the crowd at the same time. It didn't help that I got zero sleep the night before in the mom-and-pop motel; the doilies kept me up.

Truth is, I hadn't slept in a while because this anxiety thing made nights the worst time for me. I would get in bed and couldn't keep still, so I would writhe back and forth. From fear of keeping Lynda awake, I would eventually get out of bed. I tried sitting but couldn't. It seemed to help if I kept moving, so I would walk our hallway back and forth, careful not to wake the kids. If I was experiencing anxiety then it was getting worse, which was frightening because I had no way of managing it.

Some nights, if I walked long enough, I could fall into bed and maybe get a half hour before the alarm went off, and then it started all over again. There was no rest from it, being 24/7 now, so I made the decision to look into the therapy thing. At times I was afraid that I might not be able to continue working, and that was terrifying to me.

It's not that 1998 was bad, it just wasn't good, either; it was indifferent. When I think about the uncertainty of the entertainment business, I think of Steve Harvey, and for good reason. Steve has been around for a long time, and during those many years he's been both up and down. His approach, he once told me, was to hang around and make sure you're relevant when things open back up, because they will.

There are many great comedians, but few I respect more than Steve. He was around when *Family Feud* was looking to make a change. Steve single-handedly took that tired, old franchise and rejuvenated the show. *Family Feud* is great again because of Steve.

We had him on the show many times, and during a commercial break once, I asked him where he got his style of comedy. He said, "There are two kinds of comedians . . . there are the ones that say funny things, and there are the ones that say things in a funny way. I do both."

Steve is correct, that's his style, and it's the same in radio entertainment. If you don't have your own particular style, you won't be around long.

My first time in Birmingham, I was doing some of the best radio of my solo career. I was doing things people had never heard, because I was being myself, and no one can do that better than me. It made me unique in a world of bland air talent, or copycats who tried to sound like someone else.

Each morning I went into the station, there was a huge pile of stories that developed overnight. I would pour through them, selecting the ones I wanted to use. Out of sixty stories, I would get maybe fifteen, and I was aware my competition had the very same stack. I would think in terms of, "What can I do with these that my competition won't?" That's what set me apart. I would make unique, off center choices, and start compiling music and sound effects to get them ready for air.

As an example, if Brian and I had been on the air during the Trump years, we would've known that most of our competition would be doing a straight-up Trump impression with the same tired jokes. Maybe, instead of us talking to Trump himself, we would take a call from *Trump's hair.* It's already unique, even before you add jokes, because nobody else is going to do that. The idea itself is original, which made us stand out in a pack of the same old thing. But you can't fake it, it must be genuine, or the audience will sniff you out. They always know when it's bullshit! Without your own unique style, you're just another person on the radio, and in life.

As mentioned, thanks to Florence Henderson for starting the trend, Brian and I enjoyed a myriad of guest appearances on television and film. We appeared in the background of various shows with our only requirement being, you must be able to clearly see that it's us, not buried in a group shot. By this point, we had stopped doing them, or they had stopped asking, so I thought I would give you a quick roundup of my favorites.

Married With Children — I hear a lot about this one. Apparently, the show is big in syndication, and friends of mine see this even now, and ask if it's me. We play waiters at a wedding, and I've never been around so many super-hot twenty-something girls wearing next to nothing. We're clearly seen at the wedding reception, and the artwork that was my mullet shines brightly for all to see.

Cheers — We stepped in a mess on that day. Apparently, there is a pecking order with extras on shows; the longer you've been there, the more seniority you possess. On *Cheers*, the coveted moment is for an extra to sit at the bar, and when the producers marched us up and placed us at the bar, the stink-eye we got from the extras was palpable. We were stealing their moment, and I would say I'm sorry but I'm not. Every single one of them can kiss every inch of my ass.

Star Trek — This one was both stupid and well received by their fans. Like idiots, we agreed to play lizards, which meant we were in full lizard suits, meaning you couldn't see our faces, not even a little. So, you have no idea which lizards we are, but the Trek-kies know. It's one of the collectable cards I still sign to this day. These Star Trek fans are ravenous for anything to do with their show, even Mark and Brian as lizards.

Rocky 5 — We were reporters in the opening scene when Rocky arrives home after his fight in Russia. The fun here is we hung out with Sylvester Stallone all day. It's interesting to see how people handle Sylvester. He's a big star, and he's treated like one.

Escape From LA — Same thing here. We play guards with full gear, including helmets, so you can't tell which ones we are. We got to hang out with Kurt Russell all day, so that made it worth the trouble. Kurt kept waiting for the sun to set for what the business calls, "magic hour." That's when the sun has set but it hasn't become completely dark yet, and the lighting you get is amazing. At Kurt's insistence, we walked to the top of a small hill behind the studio, with Kurt in his full Snake Pliskin costume, and we took a picture; a picture I've never seen. It's out there somewhere and I hope to run across it one day.

Friday The 13th, Part 9 — Hands down, my absolute favorite of the bunch. We were on the show chatting about a movie we would like to be in, and I said, "I would love to be killed by Jason Voorhees." Within minutes, the director of Part 9, Adam Marcus, was on the phone telling us he could make it happen. We were on screen for two minutes, we had lines, and Jason kills us by smashing our heads together. We appear in the comic book of the movie, and we are a collector's card. We are officially victims' #263 and #264, killed by Jason. It is considered an honor among actors to have been one of Jason's victims. If you don't believe me, ask Kevin Bacon.

We also did *Darma and Greg* because Jenna Elfman was on the show, but that's not why I bring it up. No, this is about Jenna's birthday party I was invited to. By the standards of other Hollywood parties, this was on a much smaller scale, but the power in the room was the biggest I had witnessed.

The party was at Dar Maghreb on Sunset, where you sit on the floor and eat with your hands. I do that at home, so no instructions needed here.

I assumed it would be the cast from her show, but Jenna's friendship circle travels far beyond that. It was a small, but powerful grouping that included Tom Cruise, Cameron Crowe, Richard Dreyfuss, and Lisa Marie Presley.

Tom had been on the show, so I briefly spoke with him, but I made sure Cameron Crowe felt my love for his film, *Jerry Maguire*. And no, I didn't. You're thinking I cornered Lisa Marie and bothered her about her father. I had already done that when she was on the radio show. Richard Dreyfus, however, didn't seem approachable. I hear he can be snarky. For the record, Jenna is one of the nicest, kindest people I've ever met.

As I talk about my brush with the celebrity world, it should be understood I mostly felt on the outside of it. I never felt like one of them. It was more like I was visiting that extraordinary world. In my mind, they were stars, I was radio. I enjoyed meeting some of them because you realize they're just people, like us, and while it was exciting, I was mostly uncomfortable, because I knew I didn't fit in. I experienced some incredible things in that world, and some I wish I hadn't.

Brian and I were making an appearance at some charity function, which was semi-heavy with B celebrities. There was a stage show of some sort, so we were all lined up to be introduced. Behind me in line were the Olson twins, maybe five years old, all dressed up in their cowgirl outfits. What struck me about them was what they *weren't doing*; they weren't acting like little girls. They looked miserable, staring straight ahead, not moving, not talking, just standing there. I kept glancing back in hopes of some glimmer of kid-like activity, but there was none. They looked as though they would rather be anywhere than there. And this wasn't the only time I saw this sort of thing.

We had Haley Joel Osment on the show, maybe ten at the time. When he was brought into the room with, I assume his father, Haley was beside himself with excitement to be in a radio station. He would pick up something and say, "This is so cool, what is this?" Unlike the Olson twins, he was very animated.

We were just about to come back on the air so we started putting on our headphones, while Haley continued to marvel at stuff. His father then sternly said, "Haley!" This little boy bolted up straight, at attention. It was as though he had received his command, and he had now been programmed to work. No more play, no more inquisitiveness, he was at the *ready!*

I've never forgotten either of these moments. To say that I was saddened by both would be understating it. I would love to say I'm not judging, but I clearly am. I felt terrible for all three of them, and I'll leave it at that.

What those kids needed was a clown and boy have I got one for them. I've been waiting to tell you this story because out of twenty-seven years with Brian, I think this is one of my three favorite moments, for a slew of reasons. The main one being, throughout this story, I was laughing *at* Brian, not *with* him. We had so many fantastic moments on the show, it's hard to pick one, but this one *really stands out*.

As mentioned, we were on a strict budget now and it was Brian's birthday. Back when we had great ratings, money flew out the window on birthday shows; helicopters, renting stadiums, flying in major bands, the works. Since this was no longer the case, this would be Brian's birthday on a shoestring budget, and this boy holds his birthday up there with Christmas, so I had to come up with something I thought he'd like but spend very little in doing it.

Brian told me a story from his days in Chicago. He waited tables, did improv, anything he could to earn a buck. He then auditioned for the part of Bozo the Clown, for WGN's Bozo TV show, and it was down to Brian and one other guy. Clearly, the other guy got it, Brian was the no-go Bozo. So, my idea was to turn Brian into Bozo the Clown for one day, which I thought was brilliant . . . and it was.

I contacted Larry Harmon, the original Bozo, and the owner of the rights to Bozo. I told him Brian's story and arranged for him to fly to LA, bring the original Bozo costume, huge shoes, hair, makeup, the works, and transform Brian into Bozo. Boom, *Bozo Brian*.

The day before Brian's birthday, it hits me. Brian always comes to his birthday shows dressed nicely because he and his friends like to go out and celebrate afterward, so there is no way Brian is going to agree to this Bozo makeup job, Larry Harmon or not.

My only option was clear. I drove to the liquor store and bought two large bottles of Patrón tequila. Larry would arrive at 7 a.m., giving me an hour to get Brian's drunk on. It's a challenge, but I know Brian, and I'm thinking I got this.

The next morning, the control room was decked in birthday crap, and Brian is dressed very nicely as expected. So, I told him that we had a special birthday planned for him and that it would be best if he took the edge off with a shot or two. My goal was to get five shots in him before seven.

I poured his first and he threw it back, then I decided to hit it while the liquor's flowing, so I poured a second, and he threw that one back. I realized this wasn't going to be a problem, this man came in to have him some birthday, so let's have some Bozo birthday.

It was imperative that I sell this Larry Harmon thing to Brian. We had KTLA Channel 5 coming in to broadcast all of this live, but Brian isn't drunk enough to know that yet, because if Brian refuses to put that Bozo shit on, I'm going to fucking kill him.

Now, it's 7 a.m. and Brian is well-oiled with six shots down. I hit the air with the story of Brian's failed Bozo audition, and then

I said, "So, since you didn't get to be Bozo then, you are going to be Bozo today. Please welcome the original Bozo the Clown, Larry Harmon." Larry walks into the room and Brian's face lit up as if the good Lord himself had just entered. Brian was genuinely stoked to meet him.

It took an hour for the transformation from Brian to Bozo, and Brian continued his tequila shots during the process. When Larry was finished, I knew Brian was

Image courtesy of Teri Garza

in there somewhere, but with the costume and the perfect makeup, the finished product was truly amazing. That was clearly Bozo staring back at me, and Bozo was drunk as fuck.

Thinking we might take Bozo out somewhere, I had the engineering department get the Mark and Brian mobile ready. The idea of having Bozo do a short show for some kids was appealing, so it was decided we would head to Carl's Jr. since we might find a few kids there, and it was close.

Driving up La Cienega with Bozo sitting next to me in a convertible was perfection. Bozo's hair was flapping in the wind, and listeners were following us blowing their horns.

Bozo hit Carl's Jr. *show ready,* and the kids never knew what hit them. Bozo made some balloon animals in his show and then took a few whacks at a Bozo piñata since it was Cinco de Mayo.

But then came my favorite moment, and no one knew it happened but me. While Bozo was doing his show, he went silent for about five seconds, then I heard, "Easy now," but not in Bozo's voice, it was Brian's. Later, Brian told me that with him forcing out the Bozo voice and laugh, combined with being drunk, that he almost passed out. When he said easy now, he was talking to himself.

How funny would it have been if Bozo had passed out cold in front of the kids? Well folks, we were almost there.

Then came the infamous photo. I loaded Bozo into the Mark and Brian mobile for our short ride back to the station. On the way, someone snapped a picture of drunk Bozo sitting in the convertible, enjoying a post-show smoke. His eyes were tiny slits and his Bozo wig had started to slide back on his head, allowing a little bit of blond hair to show. The photo says it all, and it's *so* good, I put it on the back cover. It is, without question, my very favorite photo of all time. Hey kids, that's Bozo Brian's last show!

This was clearly a fun moment, one where we could put aside all the crap and simply enjoy being ourselves again, which felt rare in these times. Everything seemed so heavy. I understood our ratings weren't what they once were, and that reality brings change. I completely get that, but it doesn't make it any easier to go through.

Losing our number one position was devastating. When you're on top and the world is at your fingertips, it never dawns on you what it would be like if and when you lose that privilege. I guess it's a little like going through a divorce, which people say is their worst moment in life. Everything that was there before goes away, and you're left with less, less of it, less of you. You were the king and now you're crap, and everything changes. You're not special anymore, and that's really hard to deal with, especially when you once were.

I didn't call the therapist my doctor recommended. Through a friend, I called a doctor of psychiatry, who specialized in anxiety and panic attacks. In the early stages of these sessions, we talked about stuff that didn't seem to matter, so I called him on it.

"I've already learned a great deal about you," he told me. "I've learned you're very driven, which is why you're so impatient. This won't be a quick fix, so I would appreciate it if you would stop pushing and allow me my process." I told him he wasn't much of a psychiatrist since he didn't have a couch. "Would you like me to get one?" he said, smiling. I refused to answer since I was positive that was a trick question.

All I learned from that exchange was that he was way smarter than me, and this was going to take fucking forever.

henever Lynda and I would get away for a quick weekend, we very much liked Santa Barbara. It wasn't far there or back, and the pleasantness of the area felt right to us. Plus, Lynda loves the beach and I like looking at it, from afar, because sand gets everywhere. I don't like sand as a rule, it's small and gritty and it gets in everything, and frankly, I don't trust it. I'm fairly certain sand has some sort of hidden agenda, and I'm not well liked in that world.

On our first night there, we would normally eat at the hotel restaurant. We had just arrived, we were tired, so it made sense. On this trip, the restaurant was closed for renovation and a makeshift restaurant had been set up across the street at their beach club, so we walked over. They had basically put tables and chairs in a small conference room, but the lights were low, we could see the ocean, and the food was—as always—pretty good. Plus, we had the entire place to ourselves.

We chatted as we sipped wine, when our solitude came to an abrupt end. The maítre'd was seating another couple. I glanced over as they passed us, and I had to stare to make sure, but as life would have it, the maítre'd was seating Rick Dees and his wife, Julie.

How odd this was, that two well-known LA morning radio personalities would be the only two tables taken in the entire restaurant. Besides the obvious history between us, we now had a new distinction in common: We both know what it's like to lose the #1 position.

It must be understood how much I respect this man. He was, and still is, an icon of my chosen profession. It had been ten years since we first met, and he made the first move then, so now it's my turn, and I walked over.

I first introduced myself to Julie, who is quite the radio personality herself. She seemed excited to meet with me, warm and very cordial. I'm sure being the wife of Rick Dees teaches you many things. I wondered what those were.

She offered me a chair, but I declined, then turned my attention to Rick. The moment we shook hands and he smiled, I knew this time I was meeting the man, not the personality. There were no characters, no shenanigans, just the guy. We quickly chatted about shit that doesn't matter, and I returned to Lynda.

Within ten minutes, the maître d' appeared at our table with a bottle of wine that we hadn't ordered. He opened it with all the fanfare one does when the bottle is of a certain respect. As he placed the cork on the table, he said, "Compliments of Mr. and Mrs. Dees." The wine was Shafer Select, so I knew before I looked.

Rick and Julie stopped by the table on their way out, and I thanked them for the wine. However, I said I couldn't allow them to absorb the expense of such a nice gift, and then I paid for it. Rick responded, "Well, I can't leave here without giving you something," as he reached into his wallet, withdrew a Rick Dees pocket-sized calendar and laid it in front of me. I cracked up and thanked them both.

As a young radio jock trying to climb up the ladder, the name Rick Dees was constantly around me. Rick had set an unreachable bar in his career. There would always be Rick Dees, and then the rest of us. The fact that I would have any kind of history with Rick, where I was considered an equal for just a moment, let me know just how far I had come. And for the record, I still have the calendar.

However, Rick wasn't my only LA radio contact outside of KLOS. There was also Ryan Seacrest, and on a much more personal level.

When Ryan first appeared on LA radio, I was impressed by his natural, on-air presence. His form was impeccable, and it was clear that he loved radio like I did. He was close to the best I had ever heard, so I reached out and told him so. We talked for twenty minutes and found a natural bond with both of us being from the south.

So, we began our bromance with dinners whenever we both could work it out. Ryan always said the same thing before every one of our dinners, "Bring ideas for TV shows." I always did and he never liked any of them. I once asked what his goals were, and he told me, "To create and own television game shows." Ryan had tremendous admiration for Merv Griffin.

Early on, our dinners were just the two of us, but then we branched out to me bringing Lynda, and Ryan bringing his co-host, Lisa Foxx. We went to places Lynda and I would've probably never gone, one being The Ivy in Beverly Hills.

For that one, Lynda and I reserved a hotel room at the nearby L'Ermitage. As her dinner guest, Lisa brought Leif Garrett. If memory serves, Leif was a bit of a mess. I remember simply wanting to get through dinner without setting anything on fire.

Leif kept wanting all of us to go back to our hotel room and eat and drink everything in our mini fridge. This is a five-star hotel, which overcharges for everything. If you consumed everything in that fridge, you would be talking about possibly five grand. Leif clearly didn't do the math.

Ryan and I finished the evening with cigars and cognac by the pool of the L' Ermitage, overlooking Beverly Hills. It was a wonderful friendship, one that I treasured.

Ryan's TV shooting schedule began to overtake his spare time; he was constantly shooting something. Then, he got *American Idol*, and he quickly became "Ryan Seacrest, the TV star."

I didn't see him for a year or so, until one night after a movie screening, I ran into him on the theater steps. Excited to see him, I gave him a hug, and I noticed he didn't return my embrace. As I pulled back and looked at him, he stared at me as though he didn't know who I was. Our conversation was short and awkward. I was embarrassed as I walked away, and I didn't know why at the time.

If I'm guessing, I was no longer in Ryan's league. What was once a strong friendship had become a forgotten memory. I felt like one of the little people who was around when he was one of *us*. Looking at it now, it was probably silly of me to think that things would've been the same, and I don't blame him. If I did or said anything to offend him, then I'm unaware of it, and I refuse to judge him. But I will never forget the blank way he looked at me. It broke my heart, and that was the last time I saw or spoke to him.

So, I was pretty sure Ryan wouldn't be trick-or-treating at our house and that was his loss, because Halloween was a big deal in our neighborhood; every house gave out full-size candy bars. We lived in a gated community and every Halloween, our neighborhood would open the gates for walk-in trick or treaters (cars were strictly forbidden). We would have as many as a thousand trick or treaters, and I'm not kidding. Every year, Lynda would buy a large amount of candy, and every year I would tell her, "Go back to the store and triple that." And every year she ignored me, and every year we wound up giving out pop tarts at the end of the evening.

Several families would visit our house for cocktails and pizza before the kids went begging for candy. As always, I would go to the liquor store and load up with everything since I normally didn't even keep a bottle of wine in the house. Other than an occasional glass of wine at dinner, I had never been much of a drinker, especially at home.

The doorbell would start around 5:30 p.m. Groups would come, as many as fifteen at a time, and we were the first house in the neighborhood, so we stayed busy. Once the crazy period started, the rule was "closest answers the door."

The guys would hang in the kitchen to drink and talk about their work. I've never understood why guys feel compelled to constantly talk about work, until it finally hit me: They were trying to one-up one another with how important their job was. Once I realized that, it was comical. This was just short of them measuring dicks.

From boredom, I poured myself some scotch and took a sip, doing the typical rookie grimace, but it made listening to them slightly more enjoyable. Within minutes, I finished my drink and poured another. I noticed this anxiety of mine had waned with my drink. For the first time in a long while, I felt normal.

You know where this is headed. I got myself pleasantly drunk, had a great time at the party, and slept for the first time in as far back as I could remember. I hate to spoil it for you, but this newfound remedy I had discovered would not end well.

We've all had them, moments in our lives we would rather not recall. You were there, but you have little to no memory of how you got there, or what went on. But this is something each one of us must face at some point, we certainly have that in common.

I honestly don't remember the first time, or any of them for that matter. I assume I shaved and showered, then had to think hard on how to tie a necktie because I seldom wear them. I must have climbed into my black suit, hoping it would fit since it's the only suit I own. I did this same ritual three times in the span of eighteen months, and I don't remember a single moment of the three. You don't care how you look when you're about to bury the people who raised you.

My sister Tracey was in remission from breast cancer. She was always reminding people that there was an E in her name. She would tell them, "It's not c y, it's c E y," and I would tell her, "Nobody gives a shit."

Tracey called to tell me the cancer had returned. It was in her brain, and several organs. I didn't have to look that up to know what it meant. We talked a lot in those next months. Being five years apart and very different people, we were never very close. It probably didn't

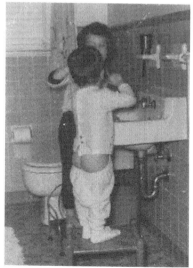

help that when she was fifteen and I was ten, every morning I woke up that summer and tried to come up with annoying things that would ruin her life. I was entertained by it, but she was not. Tracey was the solid, grounded one between the two of us. She took care of our mother since I flew the coup for my career. Mother had advanced Parkinson's disease, and Tracey was there at every horrible turn.

My conversations with Tracey those months would be our last, and we both knew it. I tried to keep it light, conversation that would bring a smile, and she would tolerate it clearly knowing I was avoiding the obvious.

I once asked her how she was doing. She said, "I'm actually fine. It's having to take care of everyone else that's the hardest part." That was her telling me she was going to die, and she was okay with it. I never asked that again.

Her husband Dane called a couple of months later and told me I needed to come. She had no energy when we arrived, she just sat. I wasn't sure if she knew I was there, but Dane told me she did.

These things are so weird, and hard. I was seeing my sister for the last time. I didn't know how to do that, and I don't want to say the wrong thing, but I'm afraid not to say my truth to her. I finally settled into simply letting it be weird, because it is the strangest thing you'll ever do.

She and I were finally alone. I'll keep my last words to her private,

but I did tell her that I loved her, and I said goodbye. When I hugged her, she could barely hug me back. Eight days later she died while her husband was holding her.

At Tracey's funeral, my mother wanted to see her, so I helped her up from her wheelchair and held her so she could see her daughter for the last time. No parent should witness their child die. A month later, almost to the day, my mother died. She spent her last moments in a hospital bed, gasping for breath. The nurse told me she could hear me, and though I didn't believe her, I still talked to her.

On the evening of her funeral, I wrote these words in my journal: *I always felt like a big man in my mother's world, and now that world is gone.*

With my father now alone, and my sister no longer available to care for him, I realized he needed help. I called him to check in, and during our conversation he asked me what I did for a living. It turned out my father thought he was talking to his brother John who had died forty years earlier, so I brought in a qualified caregiver to tend to his needs.

My father served in the Navy and was stationed at Pearl Harbor on the U.S.S. Maryland when the bombing began. The movie *Pearl Harbor* was about to come out and I thought it would be nice for Matthew and me to take him to see it so father, son, and grandson could sit together and relive a proud moment from his past. His health was deteriorating quickly, and I felt this might be my last opportunity to see him, and possibly address our lack of closeness. Matthew and I made the cross-country flight only to discover my father had already seen it, against my wishes.

As I angrily packed to fly back home, it was my fourteen-year-old son who reminded me that I had come here to address my issues with him, and that I would regret it if I didn't.

My father and I sat on the patio, the very same patio that massive flames shot through whenever he would light the gasoline charcoal. I interrupted our mundane conversation by saying something cliché like, "I wish we could have had a better relationship." My comment was met with silence, then my father—who didn't look at me—told me a story.

"When you were growing up, I always wanted you to know the meaning of hard work, but every time I had a job for you, your mother would whisk you away. Finally, I put my foot down. There was a pile of leaves in the backyard, and I insisted you were not to leave until you raked every leaf. I watched from the window, and you couldn't make a dent in the pile. So, I grabbed a rake and tried to help, but the pile barely moved. Then I set them on fire, and as the smoke curled into the air, our relationship seemed to go up with it. We were never the same after that."

My father had just told me a story that was thirty-five years old, and I distinctly remembered the moment, but differently from his account. My weekly chores consisted of washing his car, cutting the grass, polishing his shoes, taking out the trash, and raking leaves in the fall. Our yard was close to an acre, and he's pissed that I can't move a yard full of wet leaves at the age of ten?

I've thought about this moment often since my father's patio confession. In my ten-year-old mind, I thought little of the moment when it happened. I had failed him yet again, which was a frequent occurrence. Now, I see the moment quite differently. When my father found that he, too was incapable of moving the pile, he realized he had expected too much of me. He demanded something of his son that even *he* couldn't do, and that must have been traumatic for him. Talking honestly about it decades later, some fathers might have thrown out an apology, maybe something to help repair the relationship. But just as the words "I love you" had never passed his lips to me, neither had "I'm sorry." This man was simply not capable of saying either, so instead he just fell silent and gave up, on both of us. His confession to me rang true then, that we were never the same after that day.

This would be the last time we would speak. He died several months later in his sleep, and I don't say this to be cruel or dramatic, I say it because it's true. Mostly I just felt guilty because I was indifferent about his death, and I knew I should feel something, but I didn't. I remember something my sister once told me about how badly she felt when we were kids. She said that our father would be hugging her and then turn to yell at me, which he often did. I guess

I blocked it out because I didn't know what she was talking about. But I knew this, that I didn't feel anything about his passing because my father was right, our relationship burned up in that leaf pile a long time ago.

Having served his country, he received a military funeral. Eight Naval officers in dress whites stood beside my family. As my father's hearse passed us, all eight stood at attention and saluted him. The bugler belted out taps, and as the twenty-one-gun salute began, I stood and placed my hand over my heart. I felt my tears land on my sleeve, and for what felt like the first time in my life, I became my father's son, and yet I knew I would never understand him. And I suppose that's fair because he never understood me.

As we walked to the car after the funeral, I remembered something. Years prior, my father had said to me, "I want to be cremated and have my ashes spread on some good farmland." I located the funeral director and he assured me after everyone had left, they would take my father back and fulfill his wishes.

With his ashes in my possession, I drove down to Opelika, Alabama, my father's birthplace. The farm where he was raised was still there, and my cousin Cary lived on it. When I arrived, a preacher was sipping iced tea in the porch swing with Cary. All three of us loaded into Cary's barely running truck and drove to the top of the back pasture. This was the same land my father worked as a child, so I knew this would please him.

The sun was fading behind the trees while the preacher said his words. I opened the canister as the wind took my father's ashes with no effort from me. As his ashes circled above, a flock of wild turkey scampered across the pasture below, the setting sun reflected brightly off their backs as they cackled softly. I stood there and quietly wept.

In the span of eighteen months, I had lost my entire immediate family. My tears were for them, but I also wept for myself. The 1990s had started so brilliantly and ended so harshly. I felt sorry for myself, but only for that moment.

It was hard not to feel down. It seemed as though life had it out for me. But you can't allow these natural, negative emotions to control your reactions to things. Life unfolds according to its order, but these things didn't happen to me, they simply happened. You are the only person who determines how you react to adversity. Actor James McAvoy said, "You should take all of it seriously, and none of it personally."

I dealt with every ounce of it, heavy as it was, and then flew back to LA and went to work. My only focus was to keep it moving, *keep the show going.*

EVERYBODY REMAIN CALM

2000–2003

66 Well, I've been afraid of changing, 'cause I've built my life around you.99

—STEVIE NICKS

If you experienced the New Year's Eve of 1999, then you experienced the turn of a new millennium. Did you ever consider what small fraction of human beings get to see that? I considered myself privileged. I wondered if it might bring new hope and new breath to Mark and Brian. It didn't! Same shit, different century.

But I was entertained by people who thought our computers were going to stop working. The fear was computers weren't programmed for 2000 and beyond, so the ticking clock was counting down to the end of the world. This may have been my first glimpse at widespread mania, though harmless, and stupid.

The clock on Mark and Brian was still figuratively ticking, and I felt it had ticked past its expiration date. Maybe we shouldn't have worked beyond our glory days of the early '90s. There was no part of us that was standing on solid ground, with the station, or each other. I couldn't believe we were still there, or to better state it, *that I was still there.*

We were allowed to continue because the company was still making money from our brand. If they felt they could make more money with another show, we would've been gone faster than Popeye can suck spinach through his corn cob pipe. The only loyalty in the corporate world is to money. They don't care about people; they care about profit.

Our show, regardless of our ratings slide, was still the best option for the company because we still made a profit for them. But what about *my* best option? We were no longer relevant, and I had known that for a while. I began to seriously consider removing myself from whatever it was we had become.

Many years prior, we had David Lee Roth on the show, and he said something about being with the same people for long periods that stuck with me. He said, "We would be in some hotel room eating room service, and I would look at Eddie and say, 'you know what man? I hate the way you chew.'"

Brian and I were in a marriage of sorts. The beginning was joyous, effortless, and we had seven wonderful years, but when ratings fell, so did we. There was doubt and second guessing between us every day. The show itself was still viable, but it was off the air where we had issues. We hated the way each other chewed.

We decided to bring in a comedy writer to help with show ideas and possibly bridge this disconnect between us. We paid the writer's salary since the station wasn't going to. We went through several writers before we found a good one, Eric Lola. He was even-tempered and very funny, but most important he was dependable. He always had the script ready for air.

I sat with Brian and Eric each day after the show in a *think tank* situation where we would discuss possible ideas, and when someone landed on a good one, we would throw ideas at that to formulate what could be a funny script.

Over time, it became clear to me that my ideas weren't being used. It seemed Brian mostly sided with his own comedic thoughts. I felt I had been omitted, so since I wasn't contributing to the process, I stopped attending.

Eric was with us until the end and his addition proved extremely valuable. Eric wrote a comedy piece that is one of my all-time favorite moments from the show. If someone walked past my tombstone and wondered who I was in life, I would like there to be a big red button on top of my grave marker, and when pushed it would play Eric's bit. That's how much I loved it.

With me being out of the loop on writing scripts, I never knew what they were, and I never read them ahead of time, by design. I would highlight my parts without reading them. When I did the bit on the air, I was hearing the jokes for the first time, so my laughter was genuine. This would show itself to be valuable on this particular bit.

Eric came in one day with the "Krugers Meat Department" sketch, something he wrote completely on his own. This sketch had to do with the way the butchers of Krugers would prepare their meat to make it so juicy and tender.

We did the set up as the music bed started. Brian was doing a character voice, kind of a nerdish sounding guy, which got me tickled from the beginning.

The sketch opened with what a nice store Krugers was, and then it started to praise the award-winning meat department. I then began to hear myself say things that were so incredibly wrong that I started giggling at the wrongness of it, then Brian would come in with something even more wrong.

As the sketch progressed into things that were simply vile, I was having trouble saying my lines through my laughter. Two thirds of the way through, I was having to wipe tears so I could see the lines I had never read and appalled that I was laughing at what I was saying.

By the end of it, everybody within earshot was on the floor. It must have been a proud moment for Eric to listen to something he created that knocked it out of the park. And though I had nothing to do with its creation, I am incredibly proud of that moment. As they used to say in '50s live television, "Funny is funny, and funny is in."

If you want to hear it, go to YouTube and type in, *Mark and Brian promote Krugers Supermarket*, or you can simply tap the red button on my tombstone and enjoy it there.

The company brought in a new GM, John Davison, my third at KLOS. He seemed pleasant, had a nice smile with a bunch of pretty teeth, but my initial impression was he didn't listen, he just waited for you to stop talking, so he could.

Shortly after John's arrival, I noticed the music of KLOS—once piped through the building—had been turned off, along with most of the lights in the hallway. I realize it's a minor thing, but it made a difference. The hallways used to be cheery, now they were like a dungeon, dark and silent, much like my therapy sessions.

The good doctor and I always sat across from each other with maybe two feet between us, and he watched my every move. If I lifted my hand to scratch my nose, he observed it.

"How long have your hands been shaking?" he asked.

"Ever since I started coming to this shit," I joked, not even drawing a slight grin from him. We had been muddling through these sessions for a while, and I had been completely honest about everything. I kept waiting for some big reveal, like I hate my mother or something. There was that one dress she wore I didn't care for, but I didn't hate her; I hated that dress, though. I tried to be patient, as requested, but it seemed a waste of time.

"Are we getting anywhere?" I blurted.

"We are," he said, as he put down his pen and faced me. I was thinking, *here it comes*. He paused, searching for the right words. "You have success in career and a home, money, fame, all the things people associate with happiness, yet I see no joy in you. Why do you think that is?" He stared, but I had no response. I didn't realize I was joyless. He continued, "There is something that gives you pleasure, and that something is missing. Any idea what that could be?" I pay crazy amounts of money for him to ask *me* the questions?

My anxiety was raging now, naps were no longer possible, so I created things to stay busy during the day. I'd never known this kind of exhaustion, and liquor was the only thing that brought sleep, but I refused to day drink, which would mean I have a problem. The idea of walking the halls at two in the morning locked up with anxiety was terrifying to me. The intensity would ramp up as evening approached from fear of that. I would binge drink every night. If I could just get some sleep, then I could deal with this, I kept telling myself. The single thought that drove me, as it often did in those days, was to keep everything moving, and keep the show going.

Like most of my friends from high school, I spent two years at my local college, taking classes in the morning before work. I attended the University of North Alabama, since Harvard rejected me for being ignorant. I had a speech professor who told me he thought I was a natural actor, and I immediately dismissed him as drunk.

At one point in the latter '90s, I decided to listen to that professor and take acting classes, and where better to study acting than Los Angeles? I couldn't have known how deep down the rabbit's hole I would go, because I loved it. The school I chose was Playhouse West in North Hollywood, an intensive study of the Meisner technique. Not only did I enjoy it, I was also good at it.

Once you reach intermediate level at the Playhouse, you were encouraged to write your own scenes. A scene I wrote would eventually turn into a well-received motion picture, one of my earliest efforts to write anything.

I reached out to several actors who had become friends and asked if they would be in my film. Joining me were Dana Delany, Kevin Pollak, Jere Burns, Garry Marshall, David Keith, Joe Mantegna, Charles Durning, and a friend from my acting class, James Franco.

We filmed a ton at KLOS. It felt very much like a neighborhood film project: small budget, small crew, but it was professional from top to bottom. We won best picture at most film festivals we attended; I won best screenplay, and Kevin Pollak won a couple of best acting awards. Leonard Maltin said this about *Mother Ghost*: "Refreshing. An American film that's willing to deal with a real-life adult situation. I admire this film." Leonard also gave it three out of four stars in his book, and with all those accolades, every distributor passed on the film. *Mother Ghost* collected dust in my attic for several years before the movie was finally released.

Shortly after, my manager sent me on an audition for Reba McEntire's sitcom, *Reba*. When I arrived, the waiting area was packed with well-known comedians, and I actually thought about leaving. I stood no chance with these guys, so why was I there?

I walked into the audition with a defeated attitude. My thinking was *just do it and leave*, but an odd thing happened: The casting director laughed at something I did. By the time I arrived at my car, my manager called to tell me I had been invited for a call back.

When I walked in the lobby for the call back, there was only one other guy and me. The longest ten minutes of my life was waiting for them to call me in.

As I entered, I was greeted by fifteen or so people, all staring at me. I was so busy noticing them that I missed Reba standing next to me. I would be doing the scene with her, which clearly surprised me. We quickly got to the audition. I put my arms around Reba and started the scene. My stare never left her eyes, and the scene went about as well as one could hope. I knew I had gotten the job, the phone call from my manager simply confirmed that. As I drove home it hit me: *I'm Reba's new boyfriend.*

My character was scheduled for two episodes, but the first episode went so well that the network decided to do a one-hour special.

I made a rookie mistake at the end of the first night's filming, though. I saw the cast lining up for introductions, so I got in the back of the line. I noticed a few glances until the stage manager came over and quietly pulled me aside saying, "Mark, only the main cast gets introduced. Sorry." I slinked away realizing I've spent my entire life making an ass of myself, why should I stop now?

For the record, Reba is one of the nicest big stars I've ever been around. She was great to me for the month I was there, and I will always hold her in the highest regard. Plus, she's one hell of a kisser!

And I can't seem to get away from her. Several years after I did *Reba*, I was in Gadsden, Alabama, on a boating trip with friends. I was standing in the lobby of a Ramada Inn at seven in the morning trying to check out, and in a hurry to catch my boat. There was a guy standing next to me at the counter who held his stare much longer than normal. I was half awake, dreaming of my moment at the coffee station when he said, "Were you on Reba?" I confirmed I was, and he then bolted from the counter shouting, "Wait there. I have to get my wife!"

I completed my checkout as this guy and three women poured out of the elevator. I'm about to get on a boat so I haven't showered, I've had zero coffee, and I'm taking pictures with these three women. I can only imagine what I looked like. But the ladies got a kick out of it and I made my boat. Thank you, Reba!

In my quarter century of doing the Mark and Brian program, I was privy to some unbelievable live musical performances, done not more than four feet from where I sat. From as far back as I can remember, music had been a huge part of my life, and I don't think anyone could've enjoyed what I was fortunate to witness more than me.

Like the time we had this new band come in and perform when their debut album, *Woodshed Diaries*, hadn't even been released yet. We took a chance having this new band on that no one had heard of named Matchbox Twenty. They performed live for an hour and brought the building down. Just prior to release, they changed the album's name to *Yourself or Someone Like You*, and the rest is musical history.

The musical moments on our show speak for themselves, but there was one in particular that stays fondly in my memory, and the music had little to do with it.

Lionel Richie was coming in and scheduled to perform. He sang every hit, we laughed and took calls, and it was a truly memorable

two hours. I had a story I very much wanted to tell him and thought he could relate to, since he's from Tuskegee, Alabama.

When I was a kid, my father would load us all into the car for the six-hour ride down to Tuskegee to see my Aunt Mutt, who lived there on a 300-acre working farm with her own lake. My early memories of time on this farm included many firsts. I had never experienced chickens pecking at my feet as I walked; the smell of diesel fuel when my cousin cranked the tractor; or to lie in the stacked bales of hay in the barn and have a corn snake wrap itself around my arm. But my favorite was watching cows chew their cud. It's hypnotizing and I could watch it for an hour without looking away.

My greatest joy on those trips was walking the mile or so up the road to the Torch Cafe. The Torch pumped gas and worked on cars, but they had a small restaurant where truckers could get a bite to eat. I would sit in the only corner booth they had, watch the trucks roll by, and eat an excellent cheeseburger, fries, and a Coke.

I told Lionel that story and he stared oddly at me saying, "Are you fucking with me?"

Surprised, I said, "No, being from there, I thought you might know the Torch."

He sat back, realizing my story was genuine, and said, "When I was in college at Tuskegee Institute, I had to work hard as a student since it didn't come easily to me. I was in the Commodores and we were struggling to make it, so every Sunday morning I would go to the Torch Cafe to grab a bite, sip coffee, just relax. It was my only moment of the week I had to myself.

"One of those was a beautiful sunny morning and I didn't feel the weight I carried, just for those few moments, and I thought to myself how easy this is. *It's easy, just like this morning.* So, I pulled out my notebook and I wrote, 'It's easy, like Sunday morning,' which turned into my song 'Easy,' and I wrote that song sitting in that same corner booth you sat in, eating your cheeseburger."

You can imagine my face. I had no idea any of that was his reality, but it happened. The only part I hated is that it wasn't on the air because that was maybe the single greatest story I have ever been told. Lionel and I hugged just before he left.

If you talk with anyone who listened to us on a regular basis, and you asked them their most memorable moments, you will get a varied array of responses, but many would say our broadcast from the morning of September 11, 2001. I hear that one the most often. The memory of how we handled that morning has stayed with people, and I completely understand why.

As I arrived for work that morning, I saw on the news that an airplane had crashed into one of the World Trade Center towers. I took it as a freak accident and though shaken, went about my business. Then, breaking news of another plane having flown into the second tower made it clear, this was no accident.

As we went live at six, we immediately began reporting it. There was a television in between us, and we went back and forth from live network audio to us discussing what we were seeing. We goof around for a living; trying to cover this tragedy is not what we do, and we were clearly out of our element.

We were holding our own until the towers began to crumble. No matter how prepared you may feel as a seasoned broadcaster, nothing can prepare you for this. Two of the most famous buildings in New York were on fire and crumbling to the ground, causing countless deaths, and this isn't halfway around the world, this is right here where we live.

I was like everybody, watching this happen in real time. The difference is, I was live on the air, with frightened people listening to my words. I kept repeating, "Everybody remain calm." I was in the middle of this anxiety thing and this event took it sky high. When I kept repeating *everybody remain calm*, I was also talking to myself.

I had experienced two enormous doses of breaking news, situations prior to this in my broadcasting career. My first and biggest was only a few years after my entry into radio. In those days, the 1970s, every radio station had an Associated Press (AP) machine, a giant monolith of a typewriter that never stopped churning out news on a fat roll of paper. This is where we got our latest news and weather, and it was so loud it had to be isolated in its own small room so the constant clicking wouldn't drive people crazy.

One day during my air shift it stopped typing and remained silent for what seemed like an eternity. These contraptions typed around the clock, so the long period of stillness was highly unusual. I remember the station engineers started to gather around it, puzzled, checking the machine for a malfunction. Suddenly, it seemed to power up again, ready to go and typing only one word over and over in capital letters: URGENT, several times, and then it stopped again.

Word of this spread through the station and every employee in the building came to hover around the silent AP machine to see what came next. It's not like we could turn on the TV for the latest; we *were* the latest. Every broadcast station across the country depended on these AP machines for the latest news. Finally, the machine started to run again, typing only one sentence:

Elvis Aaron Presley was pronounced dead today at his home in Memphis, Tennessee at 2:42 p.m.

Then the machine fell silent again.

I interrupted the record I was playing and read the lone sentence, then went into an Elvis record. Pandemonium immediately set in; the phones exploded, station employees were crying, cars lined the road in front of our radio station to see if we were playing a joke. I was 22, it was August 16, 1977, and this was my first experience with mass hysteria. It was both terrifying and exhilarating.

I was also on the air when John Lennon died, so I had some experience at these intense, real-life moments. But nothing compares to the events of September 11, because this wasn't one, singular shocking moment, this was ongoing terror where each passing second surpassed the one before, taking all of us into unknown levels of fear and anxiety. Our country was being attacked.

Each morning following was odd, to say the least. When do we try to get back to normal? There's no guideline for something like this. It was a couple of weeks before we talked about anything other than the events of 9-11, and when we would venture into calmer topics, we were never far from the tragedy.

Everybody processes things like this differently. I was a bit removed from the sheer reality of this because I dealt with the side of "serving the community," which to some degree, removes you from the reality of it.

My moment came three months later when U2 performed at the Super Bowl. When Bono opened his jacket and showed the Stars and Stripes as the inner lining, I hit the floor. It all resurfaced at that moment for me. I wept uncontrollably.

I believe listeners remember this moment because it was clear we were shaken, just like they were. The two idiots who make you giggle each morning were showing themselves to be real people, in a real situation, just like you. But I also think we were always perceived as real people to our listeners, not just radio personalities. Along with trying to entertain you, we showed real emotion at times, tears of joy and tears of sadness. We revealed ourselves to you, as much as we possibly could, anyway. People tend to bond in moments of tragedy when fear runs rampant. We look to each other for strength and connect in a way that becomes a bond that never goes away. People hold each other up in trying times, and I believe that's what happened here; we connected as we all sought a place of solace, and we found that in each other. We became as one in a moment of fear and anguish, and that became our unity.

talked earlier about special musical moments from the show, and though it truly is difficult to choose only one, this particular moment in time is probably the single greatest I ever witnessed. It took two hours of drama for it to play out, but I guess that's allowed because *it's Stevie Nicks.*

Stevie and Lindsey Buckingham were going to be on the show, and were scheduled to perform, so we heavily promoted it. Lindsey had been on the show many times, making him a friend of the show.

The morning of their appearance, Stevie was the first to arrive. They were scheduled for a 9 a.m. appearance, and Stevie got there at seven. She was taken to the green room which has one door with a small window. She requested the window be covered up, so Preva (switchboarder) did as requested. This may have been a precursor to that "don't look at me" thing, and a warning of what was to come that morning.

Lindsey arrived around eight and began warming up on his guitar, which was amazing to watch. We then received word that Stevie had decided she wasn't going to sing. Drama had now raised its unwelcome head. Upon hearing that, Lindsey promptly placed his guitar back on its stand. You could tell he had been through this routine with her before.

We were now approaching airtime and Stevie was being escorted from the green room to our control room. A guy named Tito, who ran our syndication system and was a bit of a hippie, was quietly waiting in the wings as Stevie walked by him. Tito gently offered her a small bag of hippie shit tied together with a leather strap. It was as though the skies had opened and the tears of baby angels had come flowing down from the hippie heavens. Stevie and Tito stood there and embraced for the longest time as they whispered flowerchild shit to each other.

Stevie was now late for her appearance, but the sheer glow of her embrace with Tito kept us all warm. As she entered the control room, tightly embracing her beatnik bag, she announced that she was going to sing, and without skipping a beat, Lindsey had his guitar back in his hands and started warming up . . . again.

Stevie stood at the microphone clutching the leather pouch Tito had given her and poured forth the most breathtaking rendition of

"Landslide" one could ever hope to hear. Stevie wrote that song prior to Fleetwood Mac, when she and Lindsey were a couple of musicians who were romantically involved. She was torn between leaving him and returning to school or staying. She said her personal life—at the time—felt like a landslide. And now she is singing this piece of her heart, accompanied on guitar by the same guy she wrote the song about. No matter how you slice it, moments like this simply don't come around, ever.

I've always enjoyed hearing the stories of how certain songs got started. More often than not, the origin of some songs are such simple things that turn into massive hits; a moment in time becomes an idea, and that idea turns into gold.

Case in point: Hoyt Axton's mother Mae was sitting on the floor one day reading the newspaper when she read a story of a man who had committed suicide. The man left a note with one line saying, "I walk a lonely street." Mae then put pen to paper and wrote "Heartbreak Hotel," in mere minutes.

I once asked Gino Vannelli what his motivation was for his biggest hit, "I Just Wanna Stop." He told me, "My brother Ross was my motivation because he wrote it, not me."

After being a fan of Gino's for years, I met him when we had him on the show. We established a friendship that included dinners when possible. I found him to be fascinating, an artist who refused the ballad singer assembly line orchestrated by Clive Davis. He bought his way out of his Arista contract and moved to Portland, where he built his own studio. I traveled to Portland several times a year for KGON, so we dined on some of those trips. I even used Gino's music in *Mother Ghost*.

Gino called one day, telling me he was going to be in LA to film a documentary for the show, *Soul Train*. Gino was the first white artist to perform on that show and he invited me down to watch filming and then grab dinner.

As I walked in, I saw Gino talking with Smoky Robinson, so Gino introduced me to him. After he filmed his part, we hopped in my car and headed to the Polo Lounge at the Beverly Hills Hotel to meet his brother, Ross, for dinner.

It was a beautiful evening, so we sat outside on the patio, which was packed. Since it had been a while, Gino and I caught up and I got to know Ross a bit. As the evening progressed, we chatted over wine and salads when I suddenly felt a bit of gas come up. The bathroom was all the way downstairs so I began to calculate ways I could expunge myself there from my seat.

Since it felt sizable, I wanted to diffuse any audible noises during its escape. I felt my best chance was to part my cheeks to allow free flow. My maneuver was simple: As I leaned over for the saltshaker, I slid my other hand down and separated the cheeks to allow uninhibited passage. I then unclenched and let it ease out.

I immediately realized it wasn't gas I felt. I had inadvertently released the chocolate man into my drawers, and the immediate concern was how much. As I slowly sat back up it was clear, I had unloaded a sizable pile of my own feces into my pants.

Here I am at the Polo Lounge with Gino and Ross Vannelli, who were oblivious to my situation. These are the two men who wrote and sang, I Just Wanna Stop, and now, I too wanna give anything to just stop. It was early in our evening, and our entrées hadn't even arrived yet. So, I had to *sit in it* for the next hour and try to act as though everything was fucking great.

As we neared the end of dinner, I began to calculate how I would make my daring escape. I was wearing shorts, and the possibility that some of my droppings might fall out onto the floor was horrifying to me. I glanced down at my seat cushion and saw that it was now damp from where the eagle had landed. Luckily, I had my briefcase, so my plan was to hold my brief behind me to conceal the obvious moist spot. I was aware that would look odd, but I had no other alternatives.

We waited forever at valet since there were maybe fifteen people waiting with us, and some had noticed I was holding my briefcase behind me. My car finally arrived, so I hugged Gino with one arm and bid him adieu. I had to crack the windows on my drive home.

I arrived home late, so everyone was in bed, thank God. I went into the laundry room and removed my underwear and for the first time, gazed upon my ploppage. It was astoundingly substantial, and wholly unpleasant. I tiptoed across the hall into the guest room and cleansed myself, which no one should ever have to do. I then walked up the stairs naked except for my shirt and slinked into bed.

The next morning, I scrubbed quite well in the shower, dressed and went to work. Lynda texted me mid-morning and asked, "WHAT HAPPENED LAST NIGHT?" To my horror, I was so distraught the night before that I left my shorts on the laundry room floor, complete with my diddly, to be discovered by Lynda the next morning.

Obviously, I told this story on the air. I also shared the story with Gino, and he didn't seem overly entertained by it.

Many years later, my broadcasting days now behind me, I got a call from Gino who presented me with an idea. He said he had always wanted to do a segment in his live shows where he and a friend sit down and talk about music, and then organically sing one or two of his songs acoustically. He asked if I would join him at the Saban Theater in LA to do exactly that.

The Saban was sold out because Gino has many loyal followers. I didn't quite know how I would fit into this sit-down thing, so I just decided to be myself.

I hung out backstage with Gino and his wife before he went out and did about an hour with his band. Then, as two chairs were placed, Gino introduced me. We sat and did as Gino had hoped, and we talked about his beginnings which led him into an acoustic version of "Powerful People." I then talked about getting to know Gino when he came on the Mark and Brian program. Gino then said, "Mark, why don't you tell them about our dinner at the Polo Lounge." I stared blankly at Gino, not believing those words just exited his mouth. I then looked at the audience and realized I'm about to tell this packed house of strangers that I shit a football in my pants at dinner with Gino.

I had promised I would be myself, so I lunged into my story. I had forgotten how great it is to hear 2,000 people laughing so hard that I had to pause in places before continuing, and Gino sitting there stone-faced throughout the entire thing made it even funnier. *Kiss my stinkin' ass, Gino!* See if I ever come to your show again.

When I would hear people talk about anxiety, I just thought they were a little nervous about something. I could never have imagined it was this.

It's hard to put into words but it felt like my chest and head were constantly in a vice. I would grind my teeth without realizing it, causing bad headaches. There was continual fear and a sense of dread, but I didn't know of what, exactly. My body tingled most of the time. My heart was beating so hard I was certain people could see it, and it was nonstop. If I was lucky enough to get sleep, the moment I awoke I had only seconds before the beast was back on me, and by the time I walked from bed to shower, my hands were shaking. I learned that if it became difficult to get a breath, then a panic attack was near, and they came without provocation. Those were like someone hit me in the chest with a sledgehammer. It would roll over and through me on a wave, and it would take what little breath I had, which brought on vertigo. The one thing that helped was heavy walking. I would power walk, sometimes for an hour until exhaustion overtook the anxiety, and I could at least sit down then.

I had two physical side effects: My hair started falling out and I lost a ton of weight. The very thought of food made me nauseous, and whatever food I could get in I had to choke down.

I went everywhere with Lynda because anxiety makes you afraid to be alone. We got back in the car one day after loading groceries and she started cracking up. She told me that since I had lost so much weight, and that I constantly took walks, I was thin and tan, and women were checking me out in the store, and I was completely oblivious to it.

Your thoughts become irrational. You begin to fear things you once enjoyed. I had generalized anxiety, meaning your fear can go to anything it chooses. One year, I became terrified that I would puke during the Christmas Show in front of everyone. I assume this was born out of my fear that people would discover my struggles. Of course, in many cases, you get to the moment you have been dread-ing and it's nothing. I remember feeling silly that I was ever afraid of the Christmas Show, but that's what this stuff does.

This is also a big lesson: You cannot let fear win. You must face it, no matter how terrifying it may seem. You must show yourself to be stronger than the fear, which I believe is a big part of beating it. But even that doesn't make it go away completely.

One of the worst things I experienced was the self-imposed loneliness. I felt I was the only one going through this. I hope you never experience the trauma of facing each second of every day with overwhelming terror.

Until you fix what's causing the anxiety, it's your constant, unwanted companion. The only respite I had was drinking. Liquor made me feel normal and would allow me a few hours of sleep. The doctor had me try every kind of pill, but nothing worked like liquor.

There is great power in being who you are. There's no replacing genuine individualism. One of the things I've always done when it came to ideas for the show is go with my gut. If I found it funny, I always went with it.

I ran into such a moment one year when the Atlanta Falcons won a playoff game and they interviewed the head coach, Dan Reeves, after the game. As many athletes and coaches often do, Coach Reeves thanked God, but he went on thanking God for close to thirty seconds, on national television. It's fine to give praise, but Dan was all in. It went on so long it became odd, and I found that funny. Since a lot of our listeners probably saw it, too, it was a perfect moment for parody.

The next morning, I mentioned it to Brian as a possible character bit, a guy who no matter what he talks about, goes over the top in thanking God for it. Though I was no longer part of writing scripts, I would still throw out an idea when I had it; use it or lose it. Brian was hesitant at first, thinking it might come off as poking fun at religion. My feeling was that if he went way over the top, it would become obvious parody. In my mind, you aren't making fun of religion, you're pointing a finger at fanaticism. I've always found anyone who is way over the top about anything to be oddly entertaining.

Brian chose the name Reverend Joe Don Faircloth, funny right off the bat. There was a script, but Brian used it sparingly, which was one of his superpowers. His ability to rant off the top of his head—this Jesus jargon with the passion and fervor of a religious fanatic—was mesmerizing to watch.

Of all the Reverend Faircloth bits we did, my personal favorite was when the Reverend took on Paris Hilton and her sex tape. It was inspired. Brian was never able to fit Reverend Faircloth inside the standard two-minute radio bit. I would have complained if he had.

One of the reasons I wanted to write this memoir was that I knew I was privileged. Being half of a high profile, LA morning radio program showed me so many things most people never dream of. One of these moments was without question the strangest thing that has ever happened to me, and the moment it occurred, I knew I would one day write about it. Every time I share this story with someone, I'm greeted with mouth open, wide-eyed stares, and it came at the hands of one of our show's dearest and most beloved celebrities. Plus, while I'm dolling out strange moments, I'll also throw in some of the oddest guests we had through the years. If you liked Tina "Parasol" Louise, you'll love these.

COULD YOU STOP TALKING, PLEASE?

2004–2007

> **❝** I don't mind gearing my life toward privacy. It's my nature.**❞**

—JOHN TRAVOLTA

This period was strange. On the surface things were fine, but behind the scenes the beast was swimming just beneath the surface, and about to come up for air, so beware of the blow hole!

I know I've made it sound like everything was falling apart, and the main reason I do that is because it was and would continue. But even in the middle of all that were some good experiences, which I learned a great deal from. However, what made things even worse for me was *me*. I've been completely forthcoming that I am an idiot by default, but what helped me through that is the fact that I'm also married to one. It wasn't always me that innocently fucked up.

Case in point: In my house, I was the cook. Lynda somewhat cooks but she doesn't really enjoy it and I do. We didn't eat at home all that often, for example when Lynda yelled "dinner!" the kids ran and hopped into the car. But on the nights that dinner was at home, I cooked it.

Every morning around 7:30, I would text to ask Lynda about our dinner plans. If I'm going to cook, I wanted to know it. Lynda got a text one morning asking about dinner for that night, and Lynda texted back, "Why don't we eat each other?" The moment she sent it, she realized it was our son, Matthew, who was asking and not me! My wife had just told her son, *why don't we eat each other?*

She screamed, which frightened Amy and Katie. Lynda then had to tell her daughters what she had just done. At that moment, her phone dinged, and it was Matt who texted, "Mother?" It's wrong and sad and disturbing and illegal and hysterical.

So, let me stay with Lynda for one more second. We were on a dinner date while the kids were at home with a babysitter. The plan was dinner and sex, but the problem was dinner didn't take very long. It was 8:30 p.m. as we were driving home, and the kids weren't in bed yet. We thought maybe we could sneak up the stairs and slip into our bedroom but decided that was too risky. If we get caught, we're stuck with no sex and stupid kids everywhere.

Lynda then said, "Exit here." The exit took us to our local Costco. Lynda directed me to park as far back as I could. We had sex in our car in the warm glow of the Santa Clarita Costco sign. I still hear about this one, as listeners have sent me pictures of where they think we did it. Apparently, sex in a parking lot is one thing, but sex in a Costco parking lot is a completely different deal.

Now, why would something someone else did negatively impact Mark and Brian? In fact, it affected the entire broadcasting world, and it only took one second to do the lasting damage.

Two words: *Janet Jackson*. Miss Jackson decided to do the Super Bowl halftime show, February 1, 2004. Somehow, Janet's left boob was shown on worldwide television, and viewed by all who were watching it, including children. One second of airtime sent the broadcasting industry into a wholesale panic. You know the story, so I'll cut to the chase.

Since her naked lady part was viewed by the world, the Mark and Brian program went from a hard PG-13 to a soft G. The FCC was awakened from their nap and was asked how this could be allowed to happen, and all of us in broadcasting paid the price.

The FCC was now listening, so from fear of hefty fines, every broadcast company was bearing down on their air talent.

It was bad enough that we were owned by Disney, but now one left boob made everything on our show so bland and milk toast that it honestly wasn't much fun to be there, especially for two guys who made their living by pushing the envelope. We were forced to wear "content cuffs" for years. Thank you, Janet, hope your career is going great. And don't anyone forget Justin Timberlake's role in this fiasco. Justin reminded me of Joe Keenum, a kid from my childhood who threw a baseball through Mrs. Irons' kitchen window and promptly ran home and hid, leaving the rest of us to take the blame. *I see you, Justin.*

We never had Janet on our show, but out of twenty-five years of being on the air, we had a ton of celebrity guests. I'll take a wild guess and say 10,000 people joined us to promote whatever they were selling, and 90 percent of them were completely and utterly forgettable, while some were actually boring. So, that leaves roughly a thousand guests that were memorable, by being funny, or outrageous, etc. But some were memorable because of how odd they were.

For example, the Monkees. All four members were on the show, but I only remember them because of what they *wouldn't* do. They each refused to be in the same room with the other three, so we interviewed them separately. When Davy Jones entered the room, Peter Tork went the other way; they refused to even pass each other. That's kind of hard to forget, but I have four others that I remember quite well, simply because of the unique strangeness of their visit, or in some cases, pure rudeness.

I'll start with one that's no surprise he was odd, but I was hoping for a much different outcome. We begin with the talented Christopher Walken. Like many of you, I love Christopher's work, so it's disappointing that I share this but it's precisely what happened.

Christopher was scheduled to promote his role as Max Shreck in *Batman 2*. Reportedly, Tim Burton was initially hesitant to cast Christopher because the actor frightened him.

Traditionally, I was the one to greet all guests. Producer Ted brought Christopher in, and as he took his seat I asked if he needed anything. I would normally use those few minutes to try and make a guest feel at ease. If I can make them feel comfortable, you simply get a better interview. That wouldn't be the case on this day.

As I spoke, Christopher looked at me and said rather coldly,

"Could you stop talking, please?" I clearly heard what he said but I stared for a moment, thinking he was kidding. He wasn't, so I stopped mid-sentence.

Above our heads were the studio speakers. These are normally quite large, which is why we hang them from the ceiling to get them out of the way. Christopher pointed to the speakers and asked, "Could you turn these off, please?" Frank Sontag, who was running the board, did as requested.

So, we sat in complete silence for a full five minutes. This is not the atmosphere I would ever hope for to start an interview. There is simply no way this can go well.

Once we got on the air, it was two and three-word answers to every question. No matter how praising the question was, he simply wasn't having it. He clearly didn't want to be there. So, I thanked him and got him out.

There is a clause in every actor's contract that states the actor must promote the movie. My guess is that he was forced by the studio to do this interview, so he took it out on us, and you. I've seen Christopher interviewed many times by other media without incident. Maybe, he simply didn't like me.

Second, there's Jamie Kennedy. Ted brought Jamie into the room, and he sat down in his chair as he pulled the mic close to his mouth and lowered his head. He was wearing a hoodie, so his face was completely covered. He mumbled short answers with zero energy, you could barely hear him, and not once did he look up from the floor. He was there for maybe sixty seconds before I got rid of him. I don't know what was going on with the dude, and I don't care. Why even bother coming in?

The third is Rosie Perez, though she wasn't the problem. It was who she brought with her, actor Danny Glover. As it was put to me, Rosie was a bit media shy and wanted Danny with her for comfort.

We spoke mostly to Rosie during the interview. However, Danny decided this would be a good time to clip his fingernails. Yes, you read that right. He pulled out his clippers and while we were on the air, he clipped all ten fingernails. You could clearly hear the snip, and the nail clippings landing on the console around us. He even talked while continuing to clip. Thankfully, he didn't reach for his shoes.

And fourth is Robert Blake. We had Robert on once before and had a blast with him. Robert would often do the *Tonight Show* with Carson because of that very reason, he was simply a wonderful guest, always very up and full of funny energy.

One day during the show, Ted came to me and said Robert Blake was in the green room and wanted to go on the air. What made this odd is that he wasn't invited or scheduled, plus he was waist deep in legal troubles concerning his wife. I considered the situation and agreed to his visit. I told Ted we would have him in as soon as we could clear a spot.

Thirty minutes later I told Ted to fetch Robert, that we were ready. Ted left to grab him but quickly returned saying, "He's gone." I assumed Robert thought better of the interview and decided against it. From where I sat you can only imagine what that interview might have been like, considering his situation. And dats da name of dat tune!

Periodically, I would befriend a guest of the show, and would try to take the relationship beyond the confines of the radio station. One such person was Thomas Haden Church. I love that guy. He's funny, engaging, high personality, my kind of dude, so I mentioned grabbing dinner sometime, and his response was favorable. Every time I would see him, I would bring it up with the same response from him, "Yeah, let's do it," only to never happen.

Finally, we were on the set of *Wings* as one of our concerned onlooker roles, and I'm standing with Thomas chatting and I brought it up again.

"Let's have dinner sometime," I said. I think he must have realized I wasn't going to let this go, which I guess forced him to be honest with me.

"Listen, I don't hang out with married people," Thomas replied. I was positive I heard what he said but I wanted to make sure.

"What?" I asked.

"I don't hang out with married people," he repeated.

I bring this up because I just didn't expect to ever hear anyone say that to me. For the record, I love that any human being has personal rules they follow, all respect to that. I've just never heard *that* particular rule. I didn't ask why, though I wish I had. I would love to hear his reasoning. But it doesn't matter, I still love him.

After that, Brian and I were doing one of our drunk shows and we thought it would be funny to have a guest to interview while we were drunk. Thomas was the obvious choice.

We were several shots down when he arrived and to our surprise, he joined us. He wanted to know how many shots we had so he could catch up, and he did.

We wound up heading to the Carl's Jr., the same one where Bozo did his show, and we were plowed by that time. Brian and I leaped over the counter at Carl's and began eating fries right out of the tray, and Thomas was right there with us. That's why I love the dude, and always will, married or not. By the way, that was apparently a workday for Thomas, so he went to the set of *Wings* in bad shape and promptly passed out. I heard that the show's producers did not take kindly to his napping on *their* time.

For the entire run of our show, we were always big on annual events. They call them "tent poles" in the marketing world. Ours were simply big events we held each year that folks could look forward to. Some were always with us, like the Christmas Show and Halloween Drive-in. Others would run for a while and then disappear, such as our Super Bowl ticket giveaways, or our Thanksgiving parades. One event that stayed with us for several years was our annual football bets.

The game was simple. All family members of the show would pick an NFL team they felt would have the best record. At the end of the season, the person whose team had the best record was the winner, and the winner got nothing and did nothing, which makes no sense. We should have thought that through. But all others had to pay their debt by performing a punishment from a list we all agreed upon. Clearly, the point of this whole thing wasn't winning, but punishing people for the entertainment of those listening.

My team finished up somewhere in the middle, so the punishment I chose was to perform the duet "Sisters" from the film *White*

Image courtesy of Rudy Daniels

Christmas, and I had to perform it with a drag queen. I couldn't have known what an eye opening, wondrous experience this would be.

Producer Ted had found a drag club called The Queen Mary, which agreed to host the event. On the first day of rehearsals, I met Maximilliana, the queen who had agreed to perform the duet with me. I told Max that the only way for this to work would be for us to give it 100 percent, costumes, wigs, the works. If we half-assed this, we would be booed off the stage. When he saw my enthusiasm, it was on.

There were about ten queens who came to pitch in. We rehearsed every day, working to match the choreography from the movie; costumes had to be made from scratch. One day I had to show up for my wig fitting, something I'd never done before. These drag queens worked this like their job.

Even though we were different people from different worlds, we came together for a common cause, the show. These men chose to be there, donating their time doing what they loved. The bitch-fights were scary and hysterical, but we worked hard to put on a good show.

Although the subject never came up, I was aware of some of the hurtful things these men had faced in their lives, such as ridicule, judgment, verbal abuse, sometimes violence, and why? Because they were simply different. Being around them, you wouldn't know the hardships they endured. They were happy being part of something they loved.

On the night of the show, the place was standing room only. There were two queens assigned to me, hair, makeup, dress, the whole deal. When I turned to view the female version of me in the mirror, I gasped, because I looked exactly like my sister.

The show itself was flawless, if you're into watching a middle-aged straight guy trying to dance in high heels. Max was the show, he smoked it! When we finished, the room exploded. We did our very best and the room knew it.

But my thoughts were on the group of men off to the side volunteering their time to help pull this off. Our success brought them joy, they couldn't have been prouder, and I was genuinely happy for them.

So, what have we learned? If you have a show to pull off and you need help, call a drag queen, and your worries will be over.

One of the perks of doing what I did was the iconic celebrities I got to meet, and sometimes sharing in a real-life moment with them. Enter Tina Turner, the *Queen of Rock 'n Roll.*

There is something about Tina that exudes sexy, even when she is just sitting there. Mostly, I remember how comfortable and confident she was with herself. That's hard to believe after all she had been through in her life, or maybe it was because of it.

Producer Ted was running around grabbing stuff and asking me questions about the next day's broadcast. Tina asked me, "Are you not going to be here tomorrow?" I explained that I was getting a vasectomy the next day on the air, and we were getting ready for that. She got this huge grin and then offered two words of advice, "Don't move," and giggled.

We started the next day's show from my home. Since I would be wide awake for the procedure and thought it would be funnier, I decided to drink, meaning Lynda had to drive a drunk Mark and Brian to the doctor as we broadcasted.

The vasectomy came off without a hitch, so to speak. When I got home, there was a gift waiting on the kitchen counter. It was a very phallic looking cactus and the note read, "The first cut is the deepest. Regards, Tina."

The year 2005 was coming to a close and I was shocked we were still there. Our demise should have come in the late '90s, but one thing prevented that. After all these years, we were still the company's best option. There were still very few shows out there that were our equal. The company kept throwing up large amounts of money, and I kept taking it. I was fully aware I would never again have another opportunity to sock away this kind of security for my family's future, but I just couldn't do it again.

I've said it privately and I've said it publicly, I had to get out of there.

I felt like shit. Anxiety takes all joy out of life, and I just wanted to stop all this. I was no longer receiving any pleasure from it, and I was in a dangerous place, in that I no longer needed the paycheck. And on top of all that, the chilly weather inside the hallways of KLOS had been *jacket required* for some time now, and I was fresh out of parkas.

I went into 2006 with a firm decision made. I would leave the show at the end of this current contract. A sad part of this new phase was the absence of life in the building because it used to pulse with excitement, with optimism. Back in the day when things were healthy, there were three radio stations cranking 24/7 with 400 to 500 employees. Now, I could hear my own echo in the hallways. Being in that building now was like dating Bette Davis, dark and scary. I know it seems as if I didn't like John Davison, but I liked him fine. I just didn't care for the way he managed KLOS.

Bill Sommers would walk around the station most every morning, coffee in hand, and visit with people. I guess he liked a few quiet moments before he chewed your ass out. I saw Bill, without fail, every day; I never saw John. Morale in the building was not only low, but there was also a weird vibe, which happens when people don't trust the front office. I've seen it before, just not at this level.

I felt alone in all of it, mostly on the air. It felt like I was doing one show and Brian was doing another, we just happened to be doing them at the same time. It was no longer a united front. We had lost any and all connection.

The only thing John did, as far as our show was concerned, was *Two Strangers and a Wedding*. This was, as John put it, "reality radio." Basically, a slew of complete strangers competes for the chance to marry each other.

We started by introducing the bride, a beautiful woman who had agreed to marry a stranger. Then, through a series of interviews with potential grooms who also wished to marry a stranger, the bride would choose a man she's never met to take as her husband. The whole thing culminates at the wedding, attended by listeners, who witness the bride and groom meet for the first time at the altar and say, "I do."

In truth, this was a packaged radio promotion purchased by the radio station. The guidelines dictate exactly what to do and how to do it each day, from beginning to end. It was kind of like following the assembly instructions to a dining room table from IKEA. The promotion is geared to incorporate on-air segments, intertwined with social media, and all of it aimed at getting people to talk and listen, which is supposed to raise your ratings, therefore raising revenue.

In my mind, this was programming for female demographics, maybe a station like KOST, not KLOS. This made me question if John knew what music KLOS played. As I was told, it did nothing for our ratings. I disagreed with it from the start, and I said nothing because I was finding it difficult to care.

When I think of Two Strangers, the word "gimmick" comes to mind, because that's exactly what it was. Gimmicks have long been used, in all forms of business, including entertainment and politics.

Take, for example, Tiny Tim on the *Tonight Show*. Tiny Tim was a tall, rather awkward looking guy, who played his ukulele and sang "Tiptoe Through the Tulips" on the show, and people loved the oddness of it. Johnny Carson went to the bank with the Tiny Tim side show, having him on many times, then capping off the gimmick by staging the wedding of Tiny Tim to his fiancé, Miss Vicki. The ratings were huge, and that gimmick brought major financial gains for Johnny and NBC.

And then politically, George Wallace promoted his stance against integration by standing on the steps of the University of Alabama, determined to physically stop African-American students from entering.

This gimmick brought Wallace national attention, but President Kennedy signed an executive order demanding that Wallace step aside, which he did, allowing the students to pass through the very doors that Wallace was supposed to block. This particular gimmick brought national attention to George Wallace's failure. Clearly, you can live or die by the gimmick, so tread carefully.

I learned the power of the gimmick through my own ignorant stupidity when I was in Montgomery. I've made clear my devotion to David Letterman. I tried many times to secure an interview with David on my show, only to be rejected each time. My problem was that each call I made to NBC was live on the air, so everyone listened to my failed attempts. So, I did what most would in this situation, I decided to *mail myself* to David.

I took a large cardboard box and cut holes in the top and sides, and I headed to the airport. Most local TV stations carried the story with me stepping up to the airline counter with my head and arms sticking out of a box and a mailing label on the front, David Letterman, NBC Rockefeller Plaza, New York.

When I stepped out of the cab in New York and stared up at 30 Rock, I thought—as I would several times throughout my career—what have I done? I have very publicly come to New York to interview David Letterman, and I don't have an interview scheduled. No one at David's show even knows I've done this. The reality of the situation hit me in that moment. If I go back to Montgomery with no interview, it's over, and no one to blame but myself. This was sink or swim for me and my career.

I found a pay phone and called the NBC publicity guy who told me no every time I called. I filled him in on what I had done, and that I was downstairs in the NBC lobby. I'll never forget his response, "Oh my God! Stay right there! I'm coming down!"

He took me upstairs to the studio where David does his show, and placed me behind the cameras saying, "You can watch the show from here. I'll come back to get you when it's over, and for God's sake, don't do anything!"

I don't remember anything David said during the show. All I knew was that my hero was ten feet from me, so I laughed where I thought I should.

When the show was over the publicity guy took me to a small hallway, placing me by the wall, and whispered, "David is going to come through these double doors to get to his office. You cannot approach him. But if he approaches you, then do your thing."

Hanging from my shoulder was the very same cassette recorder and microphone that Brian and I used at the post office, and I was noticeably shaking.

An NBC page opened the double doors, so I hurriedly pushed record and brought the mic close to my bone-dry mouth. David then walked through and was coming down the skinny hallway, right at me. He glanced over and smiled, then started walking toward me. He might have said something like, "Hi there," but I don't remember. All I know is that David Letterman was standing one foot from my face, and I said, "Hi Paul!" It's true, my very first words to David Letterman were, *Hi Paul.* David could tell I was nervous and said, "It's okay, I answer to many things."

We had a five-minute conversation, and I don't remember a single word of it. I only remember that he was very kind to stop, and he could tell this was special to me.

If I ever speak with David again, I will tell him of this moment, and he will respond with something like, "Oh I remember that, you were wearing a pink chiffon thing."

As soon as I could get to a phone, I called the radio station. They were awaiting my call, so I was immediately put on the air, where I announced that I got the interview, and I would air it the next afternoon at five.

When I left Montgomery for this gimmick, I was an up-and-coming radio personality, but I returned a local celebrity. My successful quest was all over the news, and if I had accepted no for an answer, then this would have never happened.

This moment in time showed me the power of sticking your neck out, but at the same time, I was honest with myself because I got lucky. This could have so easily failed.

I do, however, have one major regret. I can't recall the publicity guy's name at NBC who made this happen. Whoever you are, sir, your kindness wound up being a game changer in my first gimmick, so thank you, from this first-class package!

Let's go from gimmicks to ridiculous boasts from a morning radio show. The idea that Mark and Brian could determine which season it was always made me smile. As you're aware, summer didn't commence until we deemed it so. You were not allowed to swim, frolic in the sun, or even think about sand until we said you could. And we couldn't possibly deem it summer until Mark and Brian had gone swimming in a celebrity's pool. *Let it be said, let it be done.* And so, it was!

Out of all our celebrity summer leaps, the best was our buddy, John Travolta. He agreed for us to broadcast from his home and jump in his pool so summer could take place. It needs to be clearly understood, I love and adore John. He did so many things for us, and I'm not dissing him, but if he were standing in front of me right now, I would tell him to his face that this moment was weird.

John was nice enough to send us a limo, though I found it odd there was an assistant in the car with us. As we approached the area of John's home, the limo pulled over and the assistant handed us two blindfolds saying, "You'll need to wear these for the next few minutes," and he wasn't kidding. To be honest, I didn't blame John. I wouldn't trust the likes of me, either. I've got that beady-eyed look, and I'm clearly on the prowl.

There we were, riding along wearing blindfolds. I assumed the reason was to prevent us from knowing where we were going, or where we had been. It was clear that John didn't want people to know precisely where he lived. I remember thinking, if I ever write a book, I have to put this experience in it.

We were allowed to take off our blindfolds in his driveway and escorted to the backyard, where John stood to greet us wearing swim trunks and a Hawaiian shirt. We were welcomed with a full breakfast spread, and his wife Kelly was outside with us the entire time.

When the moment came, we all jumped in the pool and officially declared that summer could begin. Several of John's employees jumped in as well, fully clothed.

Later, I had a quiet moment with John that stayed with me, because what he told me actually works. We were standing in the shallow end of his pool, off the air. I had noticed how happy he and Kelly seemed, which inspired me to ask, "You guys seem content. Is there a formula?" He told me, "You should always have something you're looking forward to, something today, tomorrow, next week, next month. And if you don't have something, you should create it."

To this day, I will often ask my family, "What's your John Travolta?" And they always have an answer. John was nothing but kind to me, and I have nothing but goodwill toward him. He has had some incomprehensibly difficult periods in his life, and he's often in my thoughts.

One day, I walked into Amy's room as she was cleaning out stuff. We had sold our house, and I told the kids to decide what you're each taking and throw out the rest. She had a small pile in the middle of the floor, which was her keep pile, and in it was an old VHS of the movie *Grease*. "Why are you keeping a VHS tape?" I asked. She said because John Travolta had signed it for her.

I stood there wondering if I should tell her the truth. John was coming in on the show and Amy had given me the VHS for John to sign. I put it in my briefcase and completely forgot to have him do it, so when I got home, I took a sharpie and signed, "Love you Amy, John Travolta."

I decided I couldn't let her go through life with a VHS of *Grease* signed by *me*, so I confessed. I now know what the face of true disappointment looks like. It's amazing what a shit father I am capable of being, but it's so funny the things a parent will do while trying to avoid looking like an asshole.

Throughout our twenty-seven years of morning radio, we had a smorgasbord of crazy shit happen on the show, but some of them aren't big enough to warrant a full story; maybe just an honorable mention. And as wacky as it sounds, there was something Elvis once said that enabled me to stop drinking, and it was only three words. And no it isn't, *thank you very much*, because that's four words.

THIS IS WHY YOU'RE STILL IN FRESNO

2008–2011

66 We all think of ourselves as Bugs Bunny, when in truth, most of us are Daffy Duck.**99**

—CHUCK JONES

Things were looking up, at least for me, because I had finally set a date for my departure. However, this period would also bring an incredibly wonderful change for the better, unfortunately it would be too little, too late. But no matter how good or bad things were, I always had my wonderful therapy sessions to rely on.

Have you ever heard the term, "Moving slow, like molasses in wintertime?" Why doesn't the therapist just tell me what's wrong and give me a pill, or slap me? But I did learn one thing about the therapeutic process that I found really smart: Therapists will share one small bit of information about you at the exact right moment so you'll think about it, and later process it.

He told me I was joyless and after processing it, I didn't disagree. I've had happy days before and these ain't them. I'd been going to these therapy sessions for some time, and I felt no improvement. I had learned that therapists don't like direct questions—I guess it messes with their timing—but I needed answers.

"Why do I still have anxiety?" I asked.

"Because you want to," he said, exhaling deeply.

In my mind that was a bullshit response, so I asked the obvious.

"Why would I want this?"

"Because something isn't right," he said, "and your problem will continue until you find what's off and change it." On that, he leaned in, "You're the one who's causing your anxiety." He started writing on his notepad, and then looked at me over his glasses, "And normally, it's something very simple."

That didn't sit well with me, and he noticed that, then smiled.

"You won't understand this, but you already know what it is," he said.

"But I don't," I blurted out a bit too forcefully. It felt like a standoff because he became firm.

"You do! And whatever it is, it's what made you who you are, and that part is missing!" On that, we both fell silent.

I'd seen a lot better days and Lynda certainly had. She felt a lump in her breast while putting on lotion, and immediately went to the cancer center and had it biopsied, so we waited for the results. Shortly afterward, *Mother Ghost* was finally being released and we were having its premiere. Many of the cast including Garry Marshall, Charles Durning, and Kevin Pollak would be attending. Lynda found out on that afternoon that she had cancer. She insisted we go to the premiere despite her diagnosis saying, "There's nothing we can do about it right now."

No matter who you are, cancer is a scary thing, but she met this hurdle head on. The moment she could have the operation, chemo, and radiation, she did it. The problem wasn't going away on its own, so she did what had to be done as soon as possible. Lynda was pronounced cancer free and as of this writing, the cancer has not returned, though it crosses her mind every day.

Lynda also learned a harsh life lesson as she worked her way through this difficult period. During her chemo days, she was at the grocery store when she saw a friend in the aisle. Lynda had on a scarf covering her hair loss, and witnessed her friend see her, and then turn to go the other way. People, for some reason, think cancer is something they can catch, or maybe they just don't want to be confronted with it. This was around the time I found it difficult to like most people. Clearly, I was in *a place*.

On the topic of things that come out of nowhere, John Davison told the programming department to tell us, "Mark and Brian have lost their biggest fan." To this day, I have no idea what we did or said to provoke the president of our company to say he didn't like us anymore. *I was unaware he ever did.*

Brian and I were preparing for our 20th anniversary on KLOS by having listeners vote for their favorite moments from the show's past. We had compiled a list of the top 20 and were going to play them back over anniversary week.

I hadn't heard any on-air promotion on KLOS about our celebration, so I went to the programming department and confronted them. I was told, "We don't feel the Mark and Brian program is in any condition to promote."

These last two stories I've shared are verbatim. This was the environment we were existing in and had for a very long time. I was amazed at how we could close the control room door and put on a good show when it was obvious to me, no one in the building gave a shit. It's hard to come to work and do a comedy show when you know you aren't liked, or respected, by the people you work with. It didn't feel like the building that Mark and Brian built anymore!

Mother Ghost had been out for a year by this time and had been well received by those who saw it. The problem was, very few did. I was hoping for recognition of my acting and writing that might lead to work since I felt I might need a new job, but that hadn't happened. So, I concocted a simple plan to write a script so good that the film business would notice and move it into production.

It took me a year to write *2:13*, a psychological thriller. I met with numerous investors, and all were impossible. One guy offered me $5 million, but only if he could rewrite the script and the female lead be played by his girlfriend, not his wife, apparently unafraid to reveal he had both.

At Lynda's urging, I funded the film myself. We shot in the summer of 2007 with a strong cast of Kevin Pollak, Jere Burns, Dwight Yoakum, and Teri Polo of *Meet the Fockers*, as the female lead.

We found distribution almost immediately, and just like *Mother Ghost*, no one saw it. The distributor later closed shop and moved to Canada, then went bankrupt along with my money.

Regardless of the outcome, I'll never look back with regret. I gave everything on both films, and I'm proud my name is on them, and their names are on me. I had my right arm tattooed with both film titles.

However, the strength of writing on my films did help. I was hired by Morgan Freeman's company, Revelations Entertainment, to adapt James Patterson's book, *Mary Mary*, into a screenplay. Morgan had played the lead character, Alex Cross, in two previous Patterson films, so Morgan's company was preparing *Mary Mary* as the third film in the series. The main part of the book had a character named Mary (of course), with a brilliant story arc that I kept. Not only did I keep her, but I expanded her.

I then sat down with Lori McCreary, the head of Revelations and her staff. They gave me a massive list of notes, and that became our process; write, get notes, rewrite.

It took a year of writing, until Lori said she was going to give the script to James Patterson for his review. Word came back quickly from James. He had no notes, except to say that *Mary Mary* was the best Alex Cross script he had ever read. In the film world, that usually means the script is going into production. We already had the star, the script, and a proven franchise with a guaranteed audience.

I began to realize I would be sitting in a theater and watching my name fade in, *Mark Thompson, Screenwriter*. I also had found the character I wanted to play in the film. They couldn't say no to me, I wrote it.

Then, the phone call came; it was Lori and Morgan. I could tell by Lori's tone this wasn't good. Morgan then spoke with that incredible voice of his, "Mark, I guess you'd better sit down." I knew then, this would be the worst possible news. "James Patterson is pulling the film."

I won't bore you with the rest of the conversation, the film was completely dead. A year of work and it amounted to nothing after a five-minute phone call.

I heard later that James Patterson wanted to establish a younger Alex Cross, and Jamie Fox was being approached. *Mary Mary* was never made, and years later, a completely different Alex Cross movie came out with Tyler Perry as Alex. I didn't see the film, but I didn't hear good things, either.

As for *Mary Mary*, it's sitting in a file on my computer. I pulled it up a year ago and read it again, which reminded me of what a shame it all was.

Our Mark and Brian syndication company had started picking up several stations along the west coast, and our San Luis Obispo station asked us to come to their state fair and introduce Jay Leno, but it was scheduled on a Wednesday night. We didn't have time to drive up, do the gig, and get back for the next day's show, so we passed, but then received word from Jay Leno's people that we could hop on Jay's Learjet with him.

As we flew, Jay's head writer handed him a stack of 3x5 cards with potential jokes for the next night's monologue. Jay went through the stack, and those he didn't like were thrown on the floor, the ones he held made the cut. This elimination process would take place numerous times throughout the next day until Jay literally stepped in front of the cameras for the next night's monologue.

After our arrival, we all huddled up backstage with the stage manager from the fair. He told us some television guy from Fresno would speak, and then introduce Mark and Brian, then we would introduce Jay.

So, the Fresno guy walked on stage and did his thing, and then introduced us. We go out, about to speak, when the Fresno guy grabs the mic back and says, "Ladies and gentlemen, would you please welcome . . . Jay Leno!" To his surprise, Jay didn't come out. I was fuming at this Fresno pig, and as I grabbed for the mic the Fresno guy did it again, "Ladies and gentlemen, would you please welcome, Jay Leno!" Once again, hysterically, Jay refused to come out. I grabbed the mic from his hand and introduced Jay, and out he came.

Afterward, the stage manager let the Fresno piece of shit have it, and I mean really lit him up good. I then leaned over to the shitbag and said, "This is why you're still in Fresno." He reminded me of the kid at the playground who would suddenly push you out of the way when it was your turn on the slide.

The next morning on the show, we told that story. A San Louis Obispo listener called and told us the Fresno dude showed footage of himself introducing Jay and had edited the tape to look like Jay walked right out. Enjoy, Fresno dude! That is small town shit, and you will always be small town, you *fucking slide hog.*

When we landed back in Burbank, Jay invited Brian and me to see his hanger of cars, where he has hundreds of them. Jay opened the hood of a Rolls he had just acquired and showed us the engine. Based on our reaction, Jay said, "You guys aren't into cars, are you?" We admitted that we weren't. As we left, Jay threw on his overalls and jumped under the Rolls hood and couldn't have been happier. Jay was always great to me. He's also one of the good ones.

I have been fairly open concerning my displeasure with the way John Davison managed KLOS, and his self-admitted lack of support for Mark and Brian, so this should come as no surprise. Mr. Davison optioned out of our contract window. Mark and Brian's final day would be August 17, 2009. However, as Phaedrus once said, "Things are not always what they seem." Andy Griffith said it even better, "We're picking our peaches before they're fuzzed up good."

I stated earlier that I was leaving, and now I've just been handed an earlier release date. Lynda and I had been talking about looking for a home on the lake in North Carolina, so we began actively looking. The plan was to purchase our home and after my final day, move there.

We flew into Charlotte and looked at seventeen homes in one weekend, found one we liked, and bought it. We spent all our vacations and holidays there. I was also sprucing up our Santa Clarita home in preparation for putting it on the market. The plan was solid, and then . . . John Davison was either fired, or he quit, not sure which, nor do I care. However, his optioning out of our contract still held, our last day was still set as August 17.

So now, we have another new GM coming in, and since Bill retired, I haven't liked anything that came through that door. Lord, please let it be porn star Ginger Lynn. She'll run the place into the ground, but she'll do so naked and it'll be a blast watching it all happen.

But life can be so entertaining sometimes. Enter Bob Moore as our new GM. Bob was the former GM of KLSX, the guy who brought Howard Stern to LA, and by doing so dethroned Mark and Brian. I held no animosity toward Bob. His bringing in Howard helped to make him #1, and I respected that.

On Bob's first day he came straight to us. He told us the number one thing on his "to do" list was to re-sign Mark and Brian, and that things were going to change. "You will no longer be disrespected under my watch," Bob said. "We are going to do things the way they used to be."

I had waited so long to hear someone say something like that. I felt like I had been in prison, and someone just unlocked my cell. Bob was obviously a sales guy, you must be for that job, but most importantly he was a radio guy. He understood air talent and where they're coming from. If Bob promised you something, it was in the bank, and a man of his word is rare in any business! During Bob's first week, the hallway lights were back on and KLOS was blaring from the hallway speakers again. It was like finding out Santa Claus is real.

I told Bob privately that I was done and moving to North Carolina, but Bob then threw a wrench in my plan, telling me he would build a studio in my North Carolina home and I could do the show from there. Lynda and I were on our boat on Lake Norman watching the sun set when I officially agreed to the job opportunity. I agreed to a three-year deal, and construction began on my new studio immediately.

Facing the reality that Brian and I would be 3,000 miles apart while doing the show, we had a big problem. Doing a live show in the same studio, one of us might get an idea and we could turn off our microphones and discuss it quickly, and then launch into the new, wild scheme. No longer being in the same room made that impossible, so I requested a small button be installed on my studio console. Whenever I pushed this button labeled *Brian*, he and I could communicate during the show without you hearing it. Adding this one small button allowed us to continue exchanging ideas, from opposite sides of the country, and you were completely unaware it was happening.

Speaking of unaware, it would appear Richard Lewis could use a crash course in what "friendship" means.

KLOS wanted to do a live comedy/rock show and call it "Livestock," and we were asked to invite some of our stand-up buddies. Whenever Carlos Mencia or Richard Lewis was on the show, they always brought the funny, so we invited both. Some of the musical acts were my buddy John Waite, Midnight Oil, and Cheap Trick. It felt ripe for a fun event.

At the well-attended shindig, Brian and I went on stage to introduce Richard Lewis. As we were about to bring him out, Ted whispered, "Richard isn't ready," so we continued vamping for what seemed like forever. Finally, Ted gave us the okay, so we brought him out.

Backstage, Ted told us that Richard arrived in the limo we provided and refused to get out until he was paid. This was our buddy; he knew he would get paid, but he allegedly stayed put until his check was brought to him.

I don't know what Richard said when he went on stage, but the crowd started booing him loudly, and it continued for the rest of his set. Richard made sure he was on stage for twenty minutes, which is what his contract called for. As soon as Richard came off, we quickly got Midnight Oil on stage.

As they say in the business, we had *lost the crowd*, which is not usually what you want. As soon as Carlos arrived, we explained what happened and that he needed to get them back. You could tell Carlos loved the challenge. Within five minutes of going on, Carlos had the crowd on their feet.

Several months later, Ted told us Richard wanted to come on the show to apologize and explain. My response was *absolutely not*. Whatever his reasoning, we had invited him out of friendship, and what he did isn't something you do to a buddy. We never saw or heard from Richard again.

The first broadcast from my North Carolina studio was September 17, 2009. Brian and I could see each other from a high-quality video hook up. You couldn't tell we weren't in the same room together, which was the point, but I let things slip on many occasions. I didn't care if people knew or not.

The benefits of an in-home studio were numerous. No longer did I rise at 3:30 a.m. and make that thirty-mile drive to KLOS. I would get up at eight and walk leisurely downstairs. It's amazing the difference this made, in so many ways.

I did wonder, however, how doing the show remotely from my home studio would change the experience for the listener. Over the years at the KLOS studio, there were many moments that occurred on the show that were unique and memorable, in many cases because we were all in the same room. Most don't warrant a full-blown story, but they all deserve an Honorable Mention. So, while we're on the subject, let's take a brief ride down memory lane and hand out some awards.

In the category of "That Never Happened Before or Since," we had some big-name guests who brought large groups of handlers, but none could match the size of Mel Gibson's group of sixteen people. We used every chair in all the studios, then went to the sales department for more. It was entertaining to watch that many people trying to protect their percentage.

From the "Best Dressed" category, enter Chuck Jones. Chuck was the creator and animator of most *Looney Tunes* characters and the Grinch. Chuck was on many times and each visit he wore a suit with his signature bowtie—not a clip-on mind you—and he tied that junk himself.

On one visit, Chuck asked for a picture of my son. During the interview, Chuck was sketching and at the end, handed me his rendering of the Grinch holding up three-year-old Matthew smiling at each other. That sketch is framed and hanging on Matt's wall.

From the category of "Coolest Move," this award goes to Brett Favre. As Brett walked into the room, he grabbed his Green Bay Packers Super Bowl ring from his finger, placed it on the counter and slid it across to me. I still remember the sound the ring made; it had some real meat on that bone. He knew it was the number one thing his fans wanted to see, so he didn't wait to be asked.

And now I give you "The Only Guest Who Frightened Us." Mike Tyson was about to do our show. On the day of his visit, it also happened to be Arbor Day. Obviously, Brian and I were going to take a jack hammer, dig a hole in the asphalt of the parking lot, and plant a tree to celebrate.

As we were blasting away, Don King's limo pulled up. Don took the jack hammer and started hammering, as his tall, wild hair hysterically shook back and forth with each divot. Then, Mike Tyson's limo pulls up and Tyson was so upset by what he saw that he refused to get out. He sat in his limo the entire time we planted our tree and sang the Arbor Day song.

We then moved to the studio with Don, and Mike again refused to join us. So, we have the heavyweight champion ten feet away, and he's pissed off at us. Eventually, Don talked him down and walked Mike in. Things were calm for the interview, but I never took my eyes off Mike because it almost went very badly for about a half-hour there. And you really don't want to get that *look* from Iron Mike.

So now, we go from Don's hair and Mike's glare to Dolly's boobs with "The Best Joke from a Guest." Dolly Parton was late. As we were explaining her tardiness, she walked in saying, "I'm sorry I'm late boys, but it takes a long time to look this cheap." Now, that may be one of her standard jokes but I had never heard it, and I fell out. It's hard not to love a gal with that hair, those boobs, that kind of attitude, and great one-liners!

And on the heels of that, I give you "The Best Answer to a Question." We had the founder and leader of Parliament and Funkadelic, George Clinton on the show. I asked George what the difference was between the two groups. George said, "Funkadelic gets more pussy."

We've all heard it's important to make a great entrance, but what about "The Best Entrance?" Jim Carey was coming in to promote *Ace Ventura*, but he also was late. As we were talking, the control room door burst open and Jim leapt into the room, landing on his knees. He leaned back, spreading his arms and yelled, "I am the way and the light!" Brian and I "borrowed" that phrase and started calling ourselves the way and the light. Thanks, Jim!

Giving the right gift that fits that moment, and is hysterical to boot, means you've done your job well. I therefore award, Kurt Russell with "The Best Gift Ever." Brian and I were talking of our admiration for Kurt, and I stated that if Kurt ever wanted to be with a man, I would gladly give it up for him. The next day, two dozen roses were delivered, and on the card, "If I ever lean that way, I'll let you know. I love you, Kurt."

And now, up for grabs is the "Best Surprise" award. One morning, we were doing a Neil Diamond Tribute Day, for absolutely no reason whatsoever. The whole thing was tongue in cheek, and we did this for the entire show. As we were coming to a close, I looked at the phone screen and line fifteen read, "This guy says he's Neil Diamond," so naturally we took the call. It only took a few seconds to realize it was, in fact, Neil Diamond himself. He had been listening for two hours and was cracking up. And the bastard never called again.

And then there was the "Best Disagreement." We periodically did a thing called Celebrity Sellout if we had a prize worth the trouble. On this occasion, we had two courtside seats to a Lakers playoff game, clearly worth the trouble. Listeners would give us the phone number of a celebrity, and if we got that celebrity on the air the listener would be in contention. Then, at the end of the week we would vote on the biggest celebrity name of the week, and that listener would win the tickets.

A listener called and said he had Jack Nicholson's phone number. It rang five times before someone groggily answered. We spoke ten minutes to a barely awake Jack Nicholson, and then sent him back to bed.

The disagreement came when Brian didn't think it was Nicholson, only a good impersonation, but I knew it was Nicholson. How many people can do a drop-dead impression of Jack Nicholson just waking up? I will go to my grave knowing that was Nicholson. By the way, that listener got the Lakers tickets.

I now give you the category of "How Cool Is That?" Early in

Image courtesy of KLOS Radio, LLC

1995, Rita Wilde handed me a VHS tape saying Miramax Studios strongly believed in this film and wanted me to watch it, with the hope I might be interested in the writer, director, and star.

I viewed the film and loved it, so we welcomed the film's creator, Billy Bob Thornton on the show. We fell in love with Billy's laid-back style and humor, and we heavily promoted the release of *Sling Blade*. I told Billy that I strongly believed he and his film would be nominated for an Academy award and he responded, "I tell y'all what, if I get nominated and win, I'll come in the next morning with my Oscar in my hands."

Billy Bob was nominated in several categories and won best screenplay. The next morning when I arrived at the station, Billy Bob and his entourage were waiting in the green room. He was still wearing his tux from the night before, including his ZZ Top hat still on his head. He kept his promise and stayed for two hours. Honoring his word is truly what Billy is all about and he was so thankful for our early support of him and his film. *How cool is that?*

In the category of "One Is Odd, Two Is Creepy," I sadly bring in Jonathan Winters and Chris Farley. The visit from these men was separated by a decade, but their visits triggered the same uneasy feeling, even ten years apart.

Jonathan was great on the air. The problem was getting him to leave. Well after we had ended the show, Jonathan remained doing shtick for anyone who was around. Bob Coburn, a long-time KLOS jock, had to do his show around us because Jonathan wouldn't leave. He was doing characters, bits, jokes, anything for a laugh. It wasn't until he got a super big laugh that he finally exited.

Then, there was Chris Farley. It didn't matter if the microphones were on or not, the gags never stopped. Anytime anyone would enter, he would do his thing for them. It was hard to find anything funny with Chris sweating profusely, and it wasn't hot.

I share these stories alongside each other because I think both suffered from the same thing: their desperate need for laughter, or maybe, acceptance. In both cases it became sad to watch and anyone near it was uncomfortable. Both men suffered greatly in their private lives. Chris was a hopeless addict, having tried many times to get clean only to die from an overdose. Jonathan was in a psychiatric hospital on two occasions, suffering from a host of issues, bipolar disorder being one of them.

The very thing that made these men famous also made them sick. It would seem when these men were alone with themselves, those became the moments when they were most troubled. Without someone's laughter to bring comfort, to bring a kind of approval or appreciation, they had nothing, which I'm assuming put them in an anxious state. Many times, genius comes with nasty demons, and I witnessed both, and both times it made me sad.

I have to make room for the head scratching category of "Are You Fucking Kidding Me?" One day in the mail I received a sizable package which contained a carefully wrapped, very old and tattered poster promoting an Elvis Presley concert from 1956, and it was signed by Elvis. The letter that accompanied the poster was from a male listener who shared this story.

His mother went to see Elvis when she was a teenager. After the show, word spread that Elvis was behind the venue signing autographs. The guy's then sixteen-year-old mother took off running and snatched this poster from a pole and reached Elvis to sign it. He told me that being the Elvis fan I am, that I deserved to have this very collectable item.

I took impeccable care of the poster through the years, until one day I was on the phone with the curator of the Rock and Roll Hall of Fame and I told him that story. He got excited and asked if I would allow him to put the poster on display at the hall for fans to see. I told him I would be honored. He requested a picture of the poster for verification.

A week later I get a call from him saying, "Both the poster and the autograph are fake." Incensed, I tore through my files where I had kept the guy's letter and called the number provided. The guy who sent the poster had since passed away, and in retrospect, I'm relieved he had. What if I had told him of this forgery, and it wasn't his lie, but his mother's? I would've become the pig who told him his own mother made the whole thing up and lied to him. No matter how you look at it, either this guy or his mother was full of shit. Are you fucking kidding me? Who does that?

Oh shit, wait a minute, I did that to Amy with the John Travolta tape, but that was way funnier, right? Well, at least I told her the truth, so there's that.

And finally, "The Two Dumbest Shows," and both were my fault. We were talking about Bigfoot one day (ya know, like you do), and we get a call from a guy in Seattle who says he's a Bigfoot specialist and has proof the mysterious creature is real. Okay, we'll bite as we often do, so we flew up and did a show from the forests of Washington and featured this specialist.

During the show, this "specialist" told us Bigfoot walked into his camp and said, "Arrrr Garrrrr Larrrrrr Garrrrrr." I sat there staring at an insane man who is claiming Bigfoot told him, "Arrrr Garrrrr Larrrrrr Garrrrrr." And that was his proof?

Any responsible broadcaster would've picked up the phone and checked this person out, and I didn't do any of that. So now, we have camped in the middle of the fucking Washington forest and are on the air with a man who probably lives in his mother's basement, and claims his best buddy is Bigfoot. And his Arrrr Garrrrr Larrrrrr

Garrrrrr thing was his only story, he had nothing else. We had three hours and forty-five minutes of show remaining and nothing whatsoever to say, and it was all my fault. It was completely on me, and you can *Arrr Garr Larr Garr my ass, Mr. Specialist*!

And right alongside Bigfoot are the Smothers Brothers. We were asked to broadcast from Dick Smother's house where they would announce their next big thing, and we jumped at it. During the broadcast, they announce their next big thing is "The Yo-Yo Man." Tommy Smothers then proceeded to do Yo-Yo tricks, the problem being—as I'm sure you've figured out—is that we're on the radio. The Yo-Yo doesn't make any noise and we're on the fucking radio. Yes, super silent Yo-Yo tricks for an hour, ladies and gentlemen! Jesus, I wanted to kill everybody who was there but mostly myself.

This has been *Honorable Mentions*. Actually, it's little more than a collection of quick stories I couldn't find any other way to use but in this segment. I hope you enjoyed!

I once heard Elvis say something that stuck with me. It was the movie version of Priscilla's book, *Elvis and Me*. Elvis would visit Priscilla at all hours after their divorce and beg her to come back. Elvis was lost in prescription drugs, and Priscilla pleaded with him to stop. Elvis responded, "I need them," and I thought how sad that sounded. This man, who had everything—talent, fame, looks—had flushed it all for a bottle of pills. He clearly didn't need them, but he was addicted. I could never have known that the three words "I need them" would eventually save me.

The calm the liquor brought from anxiety had become a nasty habit. I was dependent on it to bring sleep, the only thing I found that did. I was correct about Xanax being habit forming, but I was wrong about liquor being a safe alternative. I never enjoyed the taste, which I thought would keep me safe, but you already know how wrong I was.

I was married to the belief that I needed liquor for sleep. Never having been a drinker, I didn't realize you can build a tolerance to it. What started as a couple of drinks, became a bottle of wine and half bottle of scotch every night. I would drink, stumble to bed, and pass out every night.

The enormity of the problem showed itself when I had no recall of the night before. I couldn't remember dinner, not just what we ate, I couldn't remember eating. Lynda confronted me on several occasions, but I would always say, "I'll do better, I promise."

The bottom started at Christmas while my kids were visiting. I drank my usual amount, which brought concern from the kids. I am so embarrassed that my family saw me in that way. I apologized the next day and still didn't stop. Months later, I fell trying to get into bed and couldn't get up. Lynda had to lift me into bed.

The next morning, I had no memory of it and Lynda left for errands in tears. When she arrived home, she confronted me again, and it was then that I heard myself say, "I need it." I was shocked when those words came from my mouth. I realized I was no better than any addict. I had a problem, and only I could do something about it. Every person's bottom is a little different; my bottom was saying those three words.

My first night of abstaining from alcohol was a challenge. I didn't know what to do with myself. The hardest part was waiting for bedtime, convinced I wasn't going to be able to sleep. I spent most of that night plotting which hallway I would walk. I settled on the bottom floor since it makes no noise when pacing.

I tossed for two hours and was considering heading downstairs. The next thing I knew, Lynda was waking me saying, "Are you going to get up?" It was 7:30 and for the first time in years, I slept without liquor, feeling stupid for allowing myself to become addicted to anything. I had heard all the horror stories and never dreamed I could become one of them. It happens that easily, I'm proof.

Other than boredom, not drinking hasn't been a problem. Once I debunked the warped belief that I needed alcohol to tame my anxiety, I haven't had any urge to drink, and haven't in years. I fully realize it's not so simple for others who suffer from substance abuse, whether it's alcohol or another drug. Every person's experience is different with a unique set of circumstances. By no means am I suggesting that *my* journey can be the same for everyone else. However, in sharing my story and struggles, my hope is that others who are suffering from something similar can see a way out, or at least a way through. I was able to find help, and I had support, and I implore you to seek the same.

I expected to look and feel better once the drinking ceased. But I wake up most every day feeling fairly crappy, and I look like massive amounts of ass. I do take pride, however, in fixing a major problem when no one except me could do so.

The rumors had been swirling for a while, and they came true. Cumulus Broadcasting had purchased ABC/Disney Broadcasting, which was comprised of several hundred radio stations. This purchase made Cumulus one of the biggest owners in the country and solidified the new wave of broadcasting.

All their stations would be run from the central office of John and Lew Dickey. The Dickey brothers made all decisions for all their stations, then the local GMs and PDs would do as they were instructed; there was no decision-making at the local level.

The blood bath began on day one. The moment the acquisition was made final, John Dickey walked into Bob Moore's office and fired him. A great many people lost their jobs in the coming weeks, not only at KLOS/KABC, but nationwide. It was a slaughter. Though I was in North Carolina, my phone blew up all week, getting calls from people who lost their jobs. In some cases, entire divisions were completely dissolved.

It's sobering to look at workmates who are frightened that they're next. I know this happens at most companies these days, but that doesn't make it any easier. And sadly, it now seems commonplace, and will probably get worse.

As I've shared, I spent a fuck-ton of time in therapy trying to find the cause of my anxiety, which I finally did, so I'll explain this in the simplest way I can.

When we lost our #1 position, I too was lost. I'd never been in that situation before. Everything changed around me, the listeners, the staff, but mostly Brian, who seemed to veer off on his own after that. It didn't seem the right time to argue about how we were going to fix this. Instead, I went into the mode—as I had done before—of just trying to keep the show moving.

In my attempt to keep the peace, I became a completely different person. I've always derived great pleasure in knowing how to put on an entertaining show and doing it well. I pushed aside that important part of me and became someone I didn't recognize. I became a "yes" man, to anything and everything concerning the show, even though that's not who I am at my core.

I ceased being a leader and became a cheerleader. This was the nucleus of my anxiety. I had lost the essence of who I was, replaced by some stranger I didn't recognize. My inner self spoke up saying, "I don't know who you are anymore, but there's no way we're doing *this*." Call it what you want, my conscience, my internal voice, but something inside started pushing back, triggering my anxiety.

Think of it this way: Your house has an electrical circuit breaker. When a surge of too much power comes through, your circuit breaker shuts down so the surge can't do any damage. Then what happens? You discover there's a problem. That's what happened to me, my circuit breaker clicked itself off.

My therapist told me I was joyless because something that gives me great pleasure was missing. Therapy doesn't hand you answers in a tidy box saying, "Here's what's wrong and here's how you fix it." Instead, it gives you a dimly lit path through the maze of confusion and fear. Once I was there, *I saw it was me* that was missing. The pleasure I derived from orchestrating a great show was gone because I wasn't truly present to conduct that show. I allowed things to happen that I should've ended before they started. I agreed to the hiring of people who weren't qualified to be there. I agreed to ignorant moves that management wanted. And I should've responded to Brian in a much different manner by being firm on things I knew greatly mattered.

I should've stood up and said no. I had the power to do that, and unknowingly I relinquished that power by doing nothing. Power is like a muscle: If you don't use it, you lose it. I had lost my true self in the mess we'd become. To be brutally honest, though, even if I had done things my way, sadly it may not have made a difference anyway. We had our day, and that day was long gone. It might not have changed the outcome, but at least it would've been on *my terms*. Yet I did nothing, and I paid the price.

At night when you lie down, sleep comes because you are at peace with yourself. Well, sleep wouldn't come for me; *I was at war with myself.* I had created a monster which I had no control over. Understanding the source of my anxiety helped me find the only possible path back to the guy I knew as me.

WHO HAVE YOU TOLD?

2012

❝ This is the end, beautiful friend.**❞**

—JIM MORRISON

My very first radio job outside of my hometown was in 1977 at WKMX in Enterprise, Alabama, a tiny little town in the deepest part of the state. The gig itself was whatever; I didn't really lose or gain anything, but I became a man on the six-hour drive down to it. As I drove away from my hometown, I left behind my innocence. I learned how to live on my own in Enterprise, to rely on myself because I was all I had. I slept, cooked, and paid my bills, all by myself. In short, I matured there.

A year was about all I could take of that place, so I looked for employment anywhere but there. I landed what was considered a dream job in Knoxville, not realizing this is where I would have my "lightbulb" moment that would change everything for me.

I finished my last WKMX air shift at midnight and bolted to my apartment to load up and go. The idea of using moving boxes never occurred to me, so I backed my U-Haul up to my front door and threw all my belongings into it and hit the road.

The only road out of Enterprise is Main Street. If you turn left or south, you're in Florida, and if you turn right, you're headed into your next adventure. As I was leaving town, I did something spontaneously I've never forgotten. It was 2 a.m. and I was the only car on the road. I stopped in the middle of Main Street and got out. As the lone streetlight flashed yellow, I stood there and looked back at Enterprise, because I knew I would never see this place again. I wanted to remember what this was, but mostly what it wasn't. If I was going to make major market, then my job choices simply had to improve. But now, looking back, I see it in a much different light. My car sat on a road that led to somewhere, *out there*. The turns I took were up to me, but I apparently made wise choices because that empty road in Enterprise would lead me to Los Angeles.

I joined KLOS in 1987, a mere decade since I stood on Main Street and quietly said goodbye. Now, twenty-five years later, I was about to drive away from KLOS as well. During my tenure with KLOS, I worked for four different owners, six general managers, and nine program directors, all at the same job, and only one of them had taught me anything. And now Cumulus had just purchased KLOS.

My departure would be a delicate situation. I knew I would get pushback from people who stood to lose money from my absence. This would need to be handled with intelligent timing, like a hand of poker; I'm not going to show my cards until I must. Everyone involved was going to make a play, and I realized I had no more skin in the game, but there was still great benefit in executing this wisely.

My only reality was that my current contract ended in eight months, but I believed Cumulus would try to keep us, which would be their smartest move. I would let the cards be dealt, then see where I stood. I've won games of poker by holding and letting everyone else fold, then I win the pot with lousy cards.

I was in LA on my twice-yearly visit from North Carolina when I got word the new GM, Marko Radlovic, wanted to meet with us. Marko wasn't calling the shots—the Dickey brothers were—so this meeting could only mean one thing: The Dickey brothers wanted to keep Mark and Brian. If that weren't the case, they wouldn't have asked for the meeting. I entered Marko's office to also observe one, key moment, how Brian would react to the news.

As expected, Marko informed us Cumulus wished to retain our services. As he talked, Brian was listening and asking questions. I sat quietly, but engaged, nodding my head at the proper times. I could always tell if Brian was listening, since he wasn't good at faking it, and he was clearly tuned in. I realized then, I have to tell Brian right away that I'm leaving.

As we walked from Marko's office, I asked Brian if I could have a few minutes with him. If Brian was going to consider staying, he needed to know that I wouldn't be sitting across from him. We sat out back of the station on those two cheap patio chairs as we had many times before. I got right to the point.

"I won't be continuing with the show," I said. "I'm leaving after this current contract is up."

Brian nodded and looked down, seemingly unphased, then asked only one question, "Who have you told?"

"You're the first," I assured him.

He asked me to keep the news quiet for a while so he could put some things together. I agreed and drove home.

Having said those words to someone other than Lynda made it real, and I found that calming. I knew I would never regret this move and I haven't, ten years later. After twenty-seven years, I was done! It was important for me to exit the way I entered, on my terms. I decided to do the show, and now I've decided to leave it. *My decision, my terms.*

The Christmas Show was coming up and I wondered if I would be a nostalgic mess, looking back, reminiscing, regretting. I was standing in the wings waiting to be introduced, and I already knew how removed from this I had become. Brian whispered, "This is your last one." I nodded and smiled, saying nothing. I couldn't wait for it to be over.

This wasn't my Christmas Show anymore, it hadn't been for years. I had no emotion invested here. It was supposed to be a free ticket, our thank you for listening. In another moment of weakness, I yielded to the plan of selling tickets instead of giving them away. It stopped being my Christmas Show then. I should've stood up and flexed, but instead, I stood there completely empty.

Although billed as the Mark and Brian Christmas Show, it was now the KLOS Christmas Show, basically just a rock show. We hosted without having anything to do. It's amazing the things you don't see when you're not capable of looking. I don't remember anything about the show except the end. I was told to wait backstage to introduce Billy Idol, only to be told by the stagehand, "Billy doesn't need an introduction, you're done." *Yes, my friend, I am.*

It was now early spring of 2012, and I let Brian know I could wait no longer. I was planning to tell station management of my departure. My attorney broke the news, and my phone immediately blew up. I just didn't want to deal, so I let it ring and then listened to the voice messages later. As I'd hoped, they wanted to know if there was anything they could do to keep me. This kind of positive attitude was important because I very much wanted my exit to be respectful. I wanted to have my last day and walk from the building with pride for a job well done. It may seem trivial to some, but this was important to me. Mixed messages in something of this nature can cause bad feelings, which can result in messy endings. Clearly, not what I wanted. I felt I had played my cards admirably.

The station did request that I keep the news to myself for a while, from fear advertisers would drop the show if news leaked out. I agreed to hold my announcement to the staff, but made the station aware, it would be brief. I wanted the staff to have ample time to find jobs, if needed. And why does everybody I tell want me to stop talking about it?

It's now June (three months have gone by) and the staff still doesn't know. In two and a half months I will exit this building for the last time as an employee, and the station realized they could no longer dodge the unavoidable. We agreed I would tell the staff on the Thursday after the show, three days away.

On Wednesday night, Marko called me and requested that I pop by his office before telling the staff. I agreed, but all the while thinking, "Here we go with another round of poker."

The next morning, I asked the staff to please wait for me in the back studio. I went to Marko's office, as agreed, and found that another player had pulled up to the table. Standing to greet me was John Dickey, the owner of Cumulus Broadcasting. This was my first time meeting him, and the fact that John flew in for this meeting means he plans to make a major play. Anything less and he would've had Marko do it. His presence was a surprise, and I was anxious to hear what was about to exit his mouth.

"Mark, are you mad at money?" John said.

I stared at John, then at Marko, who was at his desk pretending to write, then back at John. "Um no, I don't think so," I replied.

"I'm going to make this very clear and very quick," he said. "I want you. And I don't care where you do the show from. Do it from North Carolina if you want. Do it one day a week, three days a week, do one hour, two hours, I don't care. You can keep whoever you want, hire anybody you want, fire anybody you want, it's completely up to you, completely your call. All you have to do is say yes, then write the check so I can sign it, but I want you."

I tried not to appear as shocked as I was. I take pride in forecasting these types of situations, and I thought something big might be coming, but I never imagined something like this. People dream of this kind of offer, and I was now on the receiving end of it.

I told John it was an extremely kind offer, that I needed to think it through, and I would let him know. He stood and shook my hand. "You have my number," he said. And with that, I left the room. This is one of those times where you kind of float, not walk. It's always good to know you're wanted. I decided I would process this later. I had to focus on telling the staff I was leaving.

Everybody was huddled in the back studio. I thanked them for waiting and got right to the point. As I spoke the words, there were no gasps, no surprise, no shock, from anyone. Clearly, someone had already told them. I held my anger as I informed them my last day would be Friday, August 17, and immediately left. Sometimes, it does no good to try and do the right thing.

I already knew my decision the moment I left John Dickey. I declined John's offer for one reason. This wasn't about money for me and never was. I truly believed the show was over, and there was nothing left to salvage. It wouldn't have mattered if the very best version of me put on the best radio anyone had ever heard, nothing could save it. There was no juice left in the fruit. The show was dead, and I felt strongly enough about that to turn down the kind of offer very few people on this planet ever get to hear. I never once looked back and thought, "What was I thinking?" Some decisions take a long time, some don't. I think it depends on how clear you are with who you are, in that moment, and I was crystal clear.

It was mid-June when I told the audience. Brian chimed in that he was talking with the station about staying. Through the next few weeks, Brian told the audience several times that he was still negotiating with the station and thanked everybody for their well wishes.

It was billed as my last appearance. It would be the Wednesday of my final week and staged at the House of Blues on Sunset. It was a workday, and the place was packed out. A lot of folks took the day off for the show, and that meant a great deal to me.

There was live music and celebrity appearances; it was a typical farewell show and I thought Brian might announce he was continuing with the station. This was the perfect place for that, but he announced he was still negotiating, and thanked all the well-wishers. That announcement landed oddly for me since our current contract would expire in two days. His deal should've been done and signed, and I wondered why it hadn't been.

My last show with Brian was August 17, and I believe it was the only time I didn't do any prep for a show. No bits, no gags, because shows like that have an energy of their own. I was excited for the wrong reason. I just wanted to get it over with. Lynda and the kids were coming to witness me crying through my goodbyes.

When I arrived at the station front gate, security guard George was sitting in the station van, so I rolled down my window and asked what he was doing. He had been told no media would be allowed in and he was to block their entrance. I was very aware at the oddness of that policy. Why would the station not want media coverage on my last day? But I honestly didn't care and drove on through.

When I got inside, Brian and several of his friends were already there. Brian had never been early for a show in his life, so why were his friends there? He wasn't leaving, I was. To be honest, there was a strange vibe in the place. I noticed it but didn't think too hard on it.

My most vivid memory of that final show was the 7:30 break. Brian started addressing his status, and before he got to the details he broke down in tears, which is never good in this situation. He proceeded to say that he had called off negotiations the night before, and that he would not be remaining with the station.

I had no prior knowledge of this news. I learned of it when the audience did, and this left me with a question I still haven't answered, because now things don't match up. This was now the end of an era; this was suddenly the last show for Mark and Brian. So, why did KLOS put George at the front gate to block all the media? Mark and Brian's last show was fairly big news on the west coast, so what concerned KLOS so much that they didn't want any media present? I will always find that perplexing.

By the final hour, the control room and hallway were packed with employees. My goodbyes were a gush-fest, as expected. After I kissed and thanked everybody in the hallway, I walked outside to hop in my car and drive through those gates for the final time as an employee. Brian was sitting in those same crappy patio chairs with his friends. I shook his hand and wished him well.

After I left the building, the morning show staff was called into Marko's office, and fired. With the decision that Brian would not remain, a new show would be coming in and they would bring in their own staff.

Several years after the Mark and Brian program had ended, my family and I were packed into a party van headed to the Bruno Mars show at the Forum. The driver took us down La Cienega Boulevard, so I was excited to see the station for old times' sake.

When we approached 3321 La Cienega, it was gone. The building that Mark and Brian built was no longer there, torn down for the next new thing. Without warning, all the moments and memories flooded me. Twenty-seven years of guests, gags, and bits, in both the old and new buildings, came rushing through me, and that's when I saw it. The building was gone, but there it was, *still standing.*

When we first started at KLOS, we worked out of the "old building," as it's referred to. As soon as you turned off La Cienega into the radio station, you had to drive through a small common area. The only thing there was a flagpole with a small cinder block circle at its base for flowers.

Each morning, I had to drive around it to get to the gated parking lot. This common area was special since it featured the infamous fun zone, and the flagpole was the dead center of it. It was here we dipped ourselves in chocolate, and Barney Fife handed me a bullet. It was here where listeners came in droves to witness us being us, and it was here where they stood. We held many events in the fun zone in our early years, and the flagpole always attended to bear witness to the stupidity.

When they tore down the old building to make room for the new one, the flagpole and cinder block planter remained. This area of the fun zone was in the corner of the parking lot, so when they put up the security fence for the new building, this area was fenced off, leaving the flagpole in unused dead space.

As the years rolled on, the grass grew long and covered up what was once the asphalt floor of the fun zone. You could no longer see the cinder block planter, but the flagpole remained, standing tall above the weeds for anyone who cared to look, and I did.

During my troubled times, I would drive beyond the parking lot into this forgotten area, and stare at the flagpole that stood so strong and sturdy behind the fence. I never questioned why, but I did this on several occasions. I suppose I was remembering when things were great, and almost effortless. Seeing it was comforting, and I suppose I needed that reassurance.

As we drove past 3321 La Cienega that night, I saw the empty hole where the new building once stood, and the beginnings of construction for whatever they were putting up, and that's when I saw it. The flagpole was still there, relegated to its fenced-in corner, having survived the demolition and creation of three different buildings. By its unlikely existence, it seemed determined to remind anyone who cared to look that this was the fun zone, where the seeds of something great were once planted. Thousands had stood beside it and watched a new kind of crazy and stupid unfold before them, and now the flagpole stood alone, *forgotten but not invisible*. And on this night, the flagpole conveyed a comforting message. It reminded this old radio jock of the great and memorable events that once thrived here, in a moment he needed a reminder the most, because emotions are strange and wonderful things.

When we started, Brian and I were as one. If you look at the period when it was purest, it's clear to see. Our beginning had no producers, no assistants, and no writers. Those years were just the two of us, and we were never better. We were comrades in arms, rising to new heights together, and we had no equal. Though unaware, we were destined to create a new kind of morning entertainment. We were connected, and it was the most magical time of my life.

Through most of our later years, we somehow lost that and it never returned. It seemed like we existed on separate islands, with no real bridge to connect us again.

The flagpole became a lighthouse on that night, reminding me of the brilliance that once shone brightly there. During our many years, there was joy, heartbreak, accomplishment, defeat, dreams fulfilled, and daily struggles, but considering it all, it was still the single, greatest era of my life, and nothing will ever change that fact.

THE ROAD I TRAVELED

2012–Ongoing

❝ We keep moving forward, opening new doors, and doing new things because curiosity keeps leading us down new paths. ❞

—WALT DISNEY

As I drove through the gates of KLOS after my final Mark and Brian show, my phone was exploding on the passenger seat beside me. I let it ring and ding as I drove to our hotel where the kids were meeting us for a well-deserved afternoon by the rooftop pool. Since the media wasn't allowed through the KLOS gates, they came directly after me. As the family drunkenly played some card game called "bullshit," I did one interview after another while laying poolside wearing sunglasses and trying to look as "LA" as I possibly could. It didn't work, I looked like the displaced redneck that I am.

The next morning, Lynda and I drove to Santa Barbara for a three-day reprieve, and for the first time in twenty-seven years, I didn't have to race back to LA for the next show. Monday morning, I rolled over and glanced at the bedside clock and saw 8:00 a.m. staring back at me, so I drifted back to sleep, relishing the idea that this was my new life now, which felt better than you could ever know.

I've watched many of radio's biggest personalities either leave radio or get pushed out, and many had gone over to podcasting.

They were doing what they wanted, and I very much liked the sound of that, but what would my podcast be?

Lynda and I have always had a sense of play between us, and I wanted to take that playful banter and display it on a podcast. I was convinced that listening to a long-term married couple with attitude would be decent entertainment. So, October 22, 2012, the "Mark and Lynda Podcast" made its debut into the podcast world. We were always in the top 100 comedy podcasts and many former Mark and Brian fans joined us.

Shortly after we began, I experienced something that proves a point I made earlier. I said that, as a society, we need celebrities to admire, cheer for, and then rejoice in their downfall. I tried hard to never allow myself to buy into the celebrity trap. I was simply filling a role and refreshing myself of this notion seemed to keep me grounded.

After Mark and Brian left the air, "Heidi and Frank" were set to replace us. KLOS asked if I would join them on their first day to pass the baton, as it were. I gladly obliged since I had always liked them, and they seemed to like me.

A few months later, I asked Heidi and Frank if I could drop in and promote the podcast. As I sat in the KLOS green room, the fact that this was my first time in that room as a guest—not a host—wasn't lost on me.

As I sat there listening to the show, I heard Jason Bonham promoting his next gig, and it reminded me of all the times he was on Mark and Brian. His manager was always nice to me, since I had dealt with her on many occasions. I can always tell when someone is comfortable with me, and she was; maybe *too* comfortable, as I would soon discover. I hopped up and went to find her to say hello. She always watched through the studio doorway, and there she was again. When she saw me approaching, she flashed her big smile and said, "Hi sweetie, could you get us some waters, please?"

I had interacted with this woman every time Jason was on the show, and she had no clue who I was, and guess what? I left and got the waters. The experience was eye-opening, surreal, and yes, hysterical. Even though I knew my place in the world of celebrity, I was a bit surprised when I proved my own point, and I wasn't necessarily prepared to be right.

Now that I was no longer tied down to a paying job, I wanted to find my way into a bit of acting. I played the white supremacist, Randy, in the TV show, *Black Lightning*. My scene was with Black Lightning, played by Cress Williams, and Cress and I were put in the same dressing room. Cress was in his Black Lightning outfit, which lights up and takes hours to put on him.

As we chatted, he asked if I'd always acted, and I told him I had just returned to it since retiring from radio. He inquired where I did radio and I replied, "Have you ever heard of the Mark and Brian program?" Cress bolted out of his chair and stared at me, yelling, "Are you *that* Mark?" There was cause for concern now because I have a seven-foot-tall, totally energized superhero peering down at me shouting, "I loved you guys! That was you?" A bear hug might have crushed my ribcage.

I also played a doctor on *Star* with Queen Latifa. We had her on the Mark and Brian show many times and I had a scene with her, but I wasn't allowed to approach her. There is an unspoken rule: Day players aren't allowed to approach the star, so I said nothing.

Whenever Lynda and I were in LA we would use one of the studios at KLOS/KABC for the podcast. While there during one trip, the PD of KABC offered me a job. He seemed to think my presence there would bring new life to the station, but KABC was a dead radio station, and it wouldn't have mattered who was working there, nothing could help them.

The first offer I received after Mark and Brian was KGON in Portland. While flattered, moving to Portland didn't fit my lifestyle, in fact none of the offers I received did, until this one. It was mid-2014 when 100.3 The Sound first contacted my attorney about me doing their morning show. It had been two years since I left Mark and Brian, and there was a part of me that wanted to show what I could do on my own.

When I looked at the whole picture, trying this made sense. It's a return to a classic rock audience, I can hire anyone I want, and I will do it mostly from North Carolina. Most importantly, Bonneville Broadcasting, which owned the Sound, is not like the corporate radio world I talked about earlier. This would be as close to a mom-and-pop operation as I would ever get; I liked my chances.

My first "Mark in the Morning" show premiered February 1, 2015. The assembled staff of Gina Grad, Andy Chanley, and my daughter Katie were firing on every cylinder, and we got better as the days unfolded. Katie's natural ability to entertain in her "Chick on the Street" segments impressed even me. She killed it every time!

Within six months, we were the #4 morning show in LA. That summer we had a meet and greet at the Orange County Fair, and the line was so long we had to call the station to announce there was no more room. We were riding a radio hot wave because this show was great, and the ratings reflected that, for about eight months.

The news then broke that Bonneville had sold the Sound to Entercom Broadcasting, which owns 235 radio stations. I knew then, this was over. If Entercom had been the company that reached out to me about this job, I would've declined right up front. I couldn't win in that setting.

Entercom started firing people and shutting down entire departments. But I knew my future when they started making changes to my show.

I recently heard a former NFL head coach say, "They fire you for what they hired you for." The same person who begged me to come out of retirement for this job is the one who fired me the next week.

Even with that, I'm glad I did it. I chose to be judged by how good the show was *before* Entercom bought the station. It was some of the best morning radio I've ever been a part of, and I'm still proud of it.

Once back in North Carolina, I was down for all the obvious reasons, but the biggest hurt was my love affair with radio had ended. The radio I fell in love with was gone. As I processed it, I made the clear decision that I would never take another radio job, and the finality of that realization was painful. My career, and my first love, were both over.

Lynda and I returned to the podcast, but only once a week. I'd lost the desire for the daily grind; the fight had left me. Everything around me had changed and therefore I had, too.

At that moment, I got a phone call from my friend David A. Armstrong. David was the director of photography on my film *2:13*, and he was about to direct a movie of his own called *The Assassin's Code*, and he wanted me to be in it. I'm being honest when I say it was as if God had intervened. This was exactly what I needed, to get my ass up, fly off to some distant destination, and throw myself into a completely different world. But God also has a wicked sense of humor, right? I had to fly to Cleveland for the film.

I wound up doing well in the film, and I found it oddly calming that my character was not a nice person, so climbing into his dark existence made me feel pretty good about my own. Without being overly dramatic, this opportunity was a life changer, allowing me to see my own dark period as a mere bump in the road. My character took a bullet that ended his life, but he deserved it; I didn't! It gave me a fresh perspective.

But there was another life changer in my future, and it would take me back to familiar territory, whether I wanted to go there or not.

A lot has been said and written about the fact that Brian and I didn't speak for seven years after our last show, and that's true. And why didn't we? Because we were sick of each other! But at least judge us knowing all the facts.

On our shortest workdays, we were together for seven or eight hours straight, facing each other four feet apart, and talking constantly. Our longest days were eighteen to nineteen hours, and that's no exaggeration. Then on weekends, we would make appearances together for four hours minimum, and we did that for twenty-seven years. We were good friends, better than some, not as good as others, but we were never best friends. We were best workmates, who were better than most at what we did.

Also, factor in our differences. There was a four-year gap in age. I'm married, with three kids living in Santa Clarita. Brian is younger, single, no kids, living in Beverly Hills. Yet we worked together at an impressively high level for a very long time, and we needed a break from each other, so we took one for seven years. As normally happens in a situation like ours, the day we met up by chance our conversation seemed to flow easily with lots of laughter, as it did so often during those early days.

When Lynda and I were visiting LA, we normally stayed at a hotel in Beverly Hills. The kids would visit us for cocktail hour and then walk to Il Pastaio for dinner.

As we waited outside for our table, I heard Katie say, "Oh my God, there's Brian." He was crossing the street right into us. It was completely by chance that we were both in the same place at the same time.

We hugged and chatted as we allowed the moment to roll over us. Then we took pictures, and I asked his permission for the girls to post them. I let him know this would be a *thing* if the photos went up.

Our table was ready, so Brian joined us for a glass of wine, and some of Amy's food. We laughed and caught up, and it was exactly as I had always said, we fell into our familiar rhythm.

Quite a bit has been made about this chance meeting. Listeners were convinced it was planned and we were cooking something up.

It wasn't, and we weren't, but something *did* change. There was a certain heat about us after that day. The photo of us on a Beverly Hills street corner was everywhere, and listeners were eating it up.

I boldly told Brian on our last show that I would see him again at our Hall of Fame induction ceremony. I always firmly believed that we deserved to be there saying, "If you don't put us in, who *do you* put in?" And I meant that!

There was a growing rumble of like-minded thinking along those lines, mostly from Switchboarder Laura. Beyond liking our stuff, she always felt it was "important work," as she once put it. Had it not been for Laura, I don't believe we would have made the Hall of Fame. Laura was a one-woman wrecking crew, mounting a massive campaign for something she truly believed in.

As part of it, Laura and Rita teamed up to produce a Mark and Brian segment on the 50th Anniversary show for KLOS. We were half of that, so it made sense. We did a one-time, four-hour reunion show. In planning that show, I felt people who would be listening wanted to remember, and not just be reminded. So, we did exactly that, and folks sucked it down like sun brewed tea. It was a reunion at Mark and Brian High.

The Radio Hall of Fame is just like any other, the voting process is long and multi-layered. It seemed I would get a call from Laura every other day with her telling me, "Well, you made it to the next round." We were chosen for induction on October 29, 2020.

When Brian and I did the Heidi and Frank Show for our induction, the first question they asked was, "Do you miss it?" I answered "nope" and that's true, but I do miss the process. The show itself was the "sandbox," and I spent multiple hours each day loading that sandbox with toys, and that part was the process. Building the pieces that make up a show and having them work was my drug. No pill or drink can give me the high I enjoyed from airing something I concocted, and hearing people talk about it.

The chairman of the Radio Hall of Fame, Kraig Kitchin, told me, "Mark and Brian were chosen for induction not because of the twenty-seven years, but because of the first five." I've always referred to that period as our *sweet spot* because it truly was. We were doing

MARK AND BRIAN

RADIO
HALL OF FAME

a new kind of morning radio, and the radio world took notice. Maybe that's what Laura meant by *important work*. We were inducted because of those groundbreaking few years.

I found it unique that my induction was the official end of my radio career, yet in my acceptance speech, I mostly talked about the beginning. This Hall of Fame honor made me think about my mother. If she had been at the ceremony, she would've taken a picture with every person there on her Kodak Brownie and made all of them sign her program. That lady loved her boy, and she would happily tell you so while pulling press clippings from her purse as I'm standing right beside her.

My bank president father would've been proud, but he wouldn't have been able to say it. He wanted me to follow in his footsteps. For him to admit being proud of my success would've meant he was wrong and controlling people don't apologize; that signifies defeat to them. Instead of saying "congratulations," or "I'm proud of you," he would've simply said, "So, what are you going to do now?"

For the record, I never blamed him. Bluntly, neither one of us was what the other wanted and sadly, I think that happens quite often in familial relationships.

If I could go back and live my adventure again, I would do it this instant, and I wouldn't change a thing, even when the power company was banging on my door for payment. All I needed to say was, "Listen, I'm sorry I haven't paid the bill, I'm in radio." He would have understood, told me to forget the bill, and then walked away while whistling "Smoke on the Water."

I see this honor for what it is, that I am now a proud member of an elite group of men and women who are considered the best to play the radio game. To say I'm honored is cliché. This honor simply means that my family is proud of me, and that fulfills me completely.

One day, my grandchildren will learn of this honor, and they will ask, "Grandpa, what is the Radio Hall of Fame?" I will tell them, "That's a big building with some very smart people who know good shit when they hear it."

The road I traveled during my career was my sandbox, the jobs I took were my toys, and realizing my dream was my process. But even while it was all happening, I would still have this fear. It was the fear that I would be in my rocking chair at eighty and reflect on my life with regret, knowing that if I'd tried harder, I could've made it. I no longer have that fear, because I didn't fuck up, and yet I did fuck up, and I learned from both equally.

My life is exactly what I made it and nothing more. I didn't get lucky, I made what and who I am. And if I dropped dead today, I would have no regrets. My father once said, "Making decisions are easy, living with them is the hard part." I made a lot of decisions along the way, some good, some not so good, but I learned to trust them because I knew that if I made a wrong decision, I'd eventually figure it out. I liked my chances because I was there.

Thank you for letting me do what I have loved since I was a kid, a young lad just trying not to bump the record. It was because of you and your passion for the show that I got the chance to travel my road, and I sincerely cherished the ride.

Image courtesy of Teri Garza

EPILOGUE

66 Being a mama can be tough, but always remember, in the eyes of your child, no one does it better than you.99

—UNKNOWN

Technically, I'm retired, but I don't like the word. It indicates that you don't do anything. I simply don't do what I used to do. But as I'm figuring out what is next for me, I've learned how lucky I am. For some reason I was given the gift of knowing what I wanted in life. I knew it at a very young age, and I thought everyone did, but they don't.

My single goal was major market radio, and it was already inside me to never give up. At times I didn't feel I could continue, but there's always something on the other side, and you won't know that unless you keep going. Once I achieved my goal, it wasn't perfect, but I never thought it would be. Nothing ever is and never will be for anyone.

Whenever I meet someone who tells me they're a perfectionist, the same thought always crosses my mind: You must be the unhappiest person on earth, because perfect doesn't exist in my mind, with the exception of sunsets on Lake Norman, North Carolina, and Mother Nature handles those.

When I did my chores as a kid, I knew my father was going to check my work, and no matter how perfect I felt it was, it was never good enough for him. I realized then that perfection is a personal perception, not a reality. Instead of seeking perfection, we should do the very best we can in the time we have because that's real, that's obtainable, perfection isn't. Nothing that exists is truly perfect, not your job, not your marriage, certainly not life, nothing. And if you seek perfection, you'll find only heartbreak.

So, it shouldn't be the perfect destination you seek. It truly is the road traveled, and it will be bumpy so brace for it, learn from it, but most importantly, enjoy it. My road gave me everything. I was given the journey of a lifetime with career, sorrow with death in the family, joy with new life in the family, but the whole enchilada is ultimately what you make it.

Mistakes are the single greatest gift you can receive. If you play the victim, then you blame someone else and learn nothing. But if you reflect on that mistake, figure out what you did wrong and fix it, then you've been handed a valuable lesson that strengthens you.

Truly, the strong do survive, because they never give up, and they look at both the heartbreak and the joy as the sum of what their life has become. Instead of wishing you had a different life, try changing the one you have.

I had my first "moment" when I was a kid, maybe ten. My mother and I were standing in the area between the kitchen and dining room. I know this because my eyes took a picture of that moment.

My mother was my first love. She alone made my childhood joyous. She was a simple person, not educated, someone who didn't burn with desire to achieve. She was a wife and mother, who suffered much in her life. There were times she endured what most can't, and I feel guilt I wasn't there for her; I just didn't understand. She loved me more than she should have because she saw something in me that I didn't.

She placed her hands on the sides of my face and lifted it so I could see her eyes. This is where my mind took the picture. I had never seen her look at me so deeply, so I knew something was about to happen. She wasn't emotional, she was focused, and whatever was about to happen was intentional.

She stared at me and said, "I get the feeling you were put on this earth for a reason."

This moment taught me about the power of words, how they can endure, how they can affect and make change, lasting change. This was my mother, the only person in the world I truly loved. It was her love for me that taught me what love is, and she spoke thirteen words to me that she desperately wanted me to hear.

My memory is crystal clear on this one; it's exactly what she said, words that found a permanent place within me. I didn't truly understand what she meant at the time, but I believed her.

I packed my Chevrolet Monte Carlo with everything I owned at the age of twenty-one and backed out of my family's driveway for the last time as a resident. I had no idea where my journey would take me and didn't care. I was floating on the edge of a dream, which couldn't be realized by staying home. It wasn't going to come to me, I had to go find it, whatever "it" was. I was leaving everything I'd ever known, seeking experiences I'd never known, and those could only be found by going *out there*.

As my tires left my driveway, they met the cracked black asphalt of my street, and my childhood home, my room, were all in my view. I turned my steering wheel in the opposite direction, and waved goodbye to my mother. Her words were with me, and I've never felt more alone or more exhilarated.

My adventures had only just begun, but I never forgot where I came from.

Remembering a Friend

"Of course, brother.**"**

—LUKE PERRY

When Producer Ted first mentioned him as a possible guest, I didn't know who he was. I had heard of *Beverly Hills 90210* but had never seen it. I was busy, plus, not my thing. Ted told me Luke was big and that we should have him on.

I was surprised by Luke. He didn't act like a star, he acted like a guy, any guy, *every guy*. He had a playful, sarcastic way. After every sarcastic comment from his mouth, he would follow that with this smirkish grin, letting you know he was "funnin' yuh," as he would say. I loved what he was, and who he wasn't.

I don't profess to have been his best friend. I never went to his house, he never came to mine. But we bonded over the *Andy Griffith Show.*

He was raised in Ohio but was a southern boy. I can't explain what that means, exactly, but he was; we had that bond. I called him one afternoon and he was in the "crick" with his kids, pant legs rolled up, catching crawdads.

Luke was deeply private. I once called him at a certain location and he told me, "Don't tell anybody about this place." I never did.

Most of our relationship was by text, where we played a game. One of us would text the other a quote from *Andy Griffith*, and the challenge was to respond with the precise line that came right after that. Tough game, and neither one of us was ever at a loss for the next line.

One of our favorites was "Goober says hey," and the correct response is, "Hey to Goober." It could've been months since I'd heard from him, and out of the blue I would get his text that simply said, "Goober says hey," and that would be his entire text message.

Whenever I needed a celebrity for whatever, I would always call Luke. His response was always the same: "When and where, brother?"

I texted Luke telling him that if his work brought him to the east coast, he should build in a few days to come stay with us and we could have some deeper, richer conversations. He responded, "Of course, brother," his last words to me.

Lynda told me first thing that morning about Luke's passing. We were taking care of our very sick dog, which took my attention throughout the day. But that night I had a moment, and I didn't find it odd at all to do what I did. I pulled out my phone and texted Luke, "Goober says hey," knowing full well he would never text me back.

> **❝** Don't ever forget where you came from.**❞**
>
> —BILL SOMMERS

I was asked by author, Wendy Nelson Pollitzer, to write about my memories of growing up in the south. My essay was included in her book, *South: What it Means to be Here in Heart or in Spirit.*

Hose Pipe Memories

As a kid raised in Alabama I can remember lightning bugs, or fireflies as many call them, filling the night sky in the summer months. And I'm talking hundreds, so many that it could actually light up the backyard.

It never rained all day in the south. It would be a beautiful morning, cloud up in early afternoon, then a pretty raucous thundershower for an hour; clouds would dissipate to reveal a fantastic afternoon. You could smell the rain everywhere, and after the water hit the sun-warmed streets, you could see and feel the heat coming up off the pavement. This thundershower was a welcomed visitor. Nothing could cut through the blazing humidity of a southern summer day like a thundershower.

My mother would jot a few things down on a notepad every night and then hang it on a nail just outside our back door. The next morning, eggs, butter, and fresh milk had replaced the note.

Mid-morning an old, weathered truck would slowly move down our street. It would slow to a stop and a guy in overalls would get out and walk to the back. My mother and several like her would congregate around the truck and survey the selections. Baskets of fresh vegetables hung from the railing of the truck; corn, tomatoes, squash, peas, onions, all pulled from the ground that morning.

Many of the vegetables still had dirt clinging to them from the field, as did the farmer. Each customer would fill her basket and pay the man with crumpled $1 bills, though every now and then a five would make an appearance. There was rarely change. The farmer would round up or down and let it go at that.

My first time seeing the truck I was intrigued as to why there was a rake in the back. After all the mothers had pulled back the husk on the ears of corn to make sure there were no bugs, there was quite a mess on the street. The farmer would rake the mess and load it back in his truck. By the time the truck left our street, the farmer had to head back home for another load.

Since I'm from the south I have never once eaten dinner, I only ate supper. Sweet tea brewed by the summer sun through our living room window was in my glass every night.

Four full seasons of weather were part of southern life. I hated winter. It was nothing more than cold and dead, but it made way for spring, which meant Easter Sunday, wearing white as we drove to church. The flowers exploded with color.

Summer was little league and neighborhood cookouts. We didn't call them barbecues back then, it was a cookout, usually burgers and backyard baseball with kids who were nowhere near as good as me.

Fall was my favorite. The fall colors of the trees lined every street. And fall signified three things: Halloween, Thanksgiving, and Christmas, which meant days out of school.

But there is one thing about the south that no one did in California. After supper we would always go outside, weather permitting. My sister might play on the swings, I would bounce a rubber ball off the brick house and catch it, while my parents sat and sipped a cool beverage. After my sister and I had properly worn ourselves out we would join them. Sometimes we would talk, most times we didn't.

On many occasions you could smell a neighbor five houses down who was cooking out. I became proficient at being able to tell if burgers were on the grill; I could actually smell the pepper on the roasting meat. You could hear dogs bark several neighborhoods over and kids playing with the water hose. We didn't need a pool, a water hose and a creative thumb for intensified spray were all that was required. This is one of the reasons we didn't talk, there was so much to hear.

As an adult with a career in radio broadcasting, I moved all over the south for each job: Knoxville, Birmingham, Savannah, Montgomery, and eventually Los Angeles, CA.

I spent twenty-five years there and enjoyed the many things that California has to offer. As my career wound down, I craved life on a lake, which had been a big part of my childhood in the south.

My wife and I flew into Charlotte, NC, to look at homes. After viewing several we stopped by the grocery store to pick up a few things before heading back to the hotel. As I entered the store, a stranger said, "Hello."

That was something I had not experienced in twenty-five years, and it was surprising how warm it made me feel. A southern memory glossed over and made whole again by the kindness of a southern stranger.

I don't have to tell you where I live now, do I?

Acknowledgments

❝ If the only prayer you ever say in your entire life is thank you, it will be enough.**❞**

—MEISTER ECKHART

know it's unusual for this section of the book, but first I want to thank an inanimate object and the many nameless people who seemed to live inside that object.

As a child, I was frightened of the dark and my father was too cheap to keep the lights on at night, worrying we might burn an extra watt of energy. I found that if I turned on my *radio*, the light from the dial would illuminate the room just enough for me to see the monster about to eat me. It was during these late-night moments that I fell in love with radio. As I laid there trying to sleep, I would listen to the many voices and the crackling sound the needle made as it scraped over the record's vinyl, and the sounds comforted me. I knew I could call the radio station and someone would answer, and that gave me some reassurance, too. After many years of late-night listening, the radio became much more than a number on the dial; it was my friend, and became *my* life, too, so thank you.

My first true job at a radio station was doing janitorial duties for a country station. I would clean up the place after school, but it didn't matter because I was cleaning a radio station. I was hired by the GM there, *Gary Wright*. He saw I was eager and even gave me twenty bucks out of his own pocket to get me through until my first paycheck. Thank you, Gary.

My first on-air job was at the same station I listened to all those sleepless nights, WOWL. The PD who hired me was *Rick Shayne*. He treated me very well and was so proud when I hit the big-time in LA. He felt he was part of that, and he was, so thank you, Rick.

I'm aware that I would've never been in this position were it not for a few people who played a huge part in my career. *Bob Kaghan* shared one small bit of advice and changed my entire life. Kaghan got to see me make it to LA, and I know that made him proud.

Possibly the biggest thank you goes out to *Mark St. John, Randy Lane*, and *Bernie Barker*. If not for these three men, Mark and Brian wouldn't exist. Mark and Randy brought each of us into this project and Bernie decided to give it a try. Thank you, gentlemen.

On September 8, 1987, I walked into the control room of KLOS for our very first show and I saw a guy smiling at me through the glass window of the adjoining studio. *Chuck Moshontz* did news for KLOS and had inherited Mark and Brian as workmates. From day one, Chuck was all-in; he was the third Beatle. I can't possibly explain what a huge part of our early success was due to Chuck's willingness to participate in all the craziness. The listeners must have felt, "If Chuck's in, then I'm in." Thank you, Chuck! You are one of the most original and unusual people I have ever met, and I truly love you, but I think you know that.

Ann Cerussi worked for the creative services department when we first started, and she liked what we were trying to do and offered a helping hand without pay. She would arrive before us each morning and act as our producer. I don't think she had ever been around anything quite like us, which is what I think attracted her. Both Ann and Chuck are in my personal Hall of Fame. They both supported us when we needed it most.

Steve Smith was the head of the creative services department in charge of helping with our very first appearances. Most of my early exposure to Los Angeles landmarks was through Steve, who drove us around the city and showed everything to us. Thank you, Steve.

CW West replaced Steve Smith at KLOS. If you got a lovely parting gift or attended a Disney promotion, that was his work. Thanks, CW.

All the people who worked in creative services and on the KLOS *Community Switchboard*, thank you. It was your job, but the Mark and Brian show was not the job you had been doing. It went from a few hundred listeners at events to thousands very quickly and with no road map. Both inside and outside the station, I appreciate your dedication to us and the listeners.

Arlo Hults was a sales guy who became a friend and family member on the show. His hearty laugh made the audience feel we were funnier than we were.

Todd Donaho was our first and only sports guy. He was with us for the whole run. Todd understood what it meant to be a sports guy on our show. I can truly say that we brought out a side of Todd that even *he* had never seen. Todd and I still talk to this day, great dude. Thank you, Todd.

Our first and only helicopter traffic guy was *Scott Reiff,* the Skylord. He was involved in many stunts on the show and flew us all over the city. The major thing about Scott is that he was and is one of the most dependable people I've ever known. If he told you he would do something, it would be done better than you could've done it yourself. Scott has done extremely well for himself because he's smarter than most and works harder than everybody. Huge muscles, little, tiny pecker. Thank you, Scott.

Rita Wilde was the air personality we replaced at KLOS. She became a life-long friend. The first morning of our first show, she left us a note to wish us luck and thanked us for being there, because now she could sleep later in the mornings. Well, her morning slumbers were short lived. Several months later she returned to the mornings to run our board. Thank you, Rita.

Other than Ann, *Nicole Sandler, Frank Murphy, Johnny Vega, Rosemary Jimenez*, and *Ted Lekas* all served as our producers throughout our twenty-five years. I always referred to the Johnny Vega stint as, "the Vega months," and Ted was with us the longest and proved very dependable. Thank you, all.

I never got tired of hearing security guard *George* describe what he had for breakfast on the show, and never will. We had to pry it out of him like it was a secret. As his wife once told us, "George doesn't have a romantic bone in his body."

Robert Duggins was a switchboarder who became a beloved family member best known as, "The Lucky Butt." There was no place we could find that he wouldn't run his bare ass on.

Ted Prichard ran the control board for us in the early days. We had a ton of fun with the fact that Ted was in the film, *King Kong Lives*, and he had one line: "How did you get the ape from the jungle?" We would play the music from the film and force Ted to say his line and I never got tired of hearing it. In truth, I thought Ted was a star since he was the first person I had ever met who was in a movie.

These people were also key personalities both on and off the air: *Kelli Gates,* custodian *Lynn Mink, Daniel Mizrahi, Mike Sherry, Stew Herrera, Roxane Requio, Mike Olson, John Spence, Rhonda Cherney, Leonard Madrid, Ted Schermerhorn, Peter Tilden, Pam Baker, Sammi Marino, Mary Oppermann, Andy Geller, Security Guard Roger, Nurse Susan, Bob Koontz, Charlie West, Preva Lohla, Bob Buchmann, Carey Curelop, and Nelkane Benton.*

As far as this book project is concerned, I have only a few to thank but they are a passionate group who cared deeply about the quality of the book they helped to produce.

Laura Stringer (Switchboarder Laura) is my strongest supporter, biggest fan, and a very dear friend. There would be no book without Laura and her husband, *Michael Stringer,* who has spent most of his life writing and editing all kinds of stuff. Together, they took my fumbling collection of stories and turned them into a real book by editing, reorganizing, and cleaning up all my choppy writing. If you like the book, you can thank me. If you hate the book, then blame Laura and Michael, but mostly Laura. Thank you, Laura and Michael.

Marc Bonilla has been a dear friend for years who beautifully produced and scored the audiobook. Marc scored both of my films and had it not been for Bonilla, most of our Christmas Shows would never have gotten off the ground. Thank you, Marc.

I needed to make sure my facts about radio's history and current state were correct in the preface of this book. I had a strong base of information to start but I needed professional opinions from folks who know more about the subject than I do. My sincerest gratitude goes to *Kraig Kitchin*, who is the most knowledgeable person I know when it comes to radio. But first and foremost, he is a radio geek, which is what I love most about him. Also, many thanks again to Mark St. John for giving me several reads and solid information for the preface, but mostly for his friendship over these many years. Thank you, guys.

Norm Avery is the man who designed and built the "Building that Mark and Brian Built." Norm is my head engineer to this day. Quiet dude, but a genius.

Simply put, *Lori McCreary* has always been there whenever I needed a professional, and one of the smartest and nicest people I know.

Don, Eliot and *David Ephraim* deserve my sincerest appreciation. The Ephraim family have been my attorneys since 1985. I don't make a move without them knowing about it.

Chase Mellen is my entertainment attorney and the one who chased down any and all material that you saw or heard in this book. Thank you, Chase.

Scott Dahlgren came into the studio with Danny Bonaduce, and they began their friendship in high school. Scott and I became very close friends, along with his sister, *Linda*. This was soon after our move to California, and Lynda and I had a six-month old child with no family anywhere near us. Scott welcomed us into his family's home. In the early years, we spent each Thanksgiving and Christmas with the Dahlgren's, even helping them decorate the tree every year. We felt and were treated like members of the family. Though I told them often, they couldn't have known how important they were to our feeling comfortable in southern California. They became a major piece of the puzzle in our transition to California and adapting so quickly. Scott's mother was named Gwenie (how can you not love that?), and one of the best cooks I've ever encountered. To the *Dahlgren* family, I throw a hearty thank you. You are good, nice people and this life has far too few of folks like you.

Acknowledgments

When I was a kid, I was never interested in hanging out with a group of people. It was always *Keith Irons* and me. There was no leader, there was no follower, we always did exactly as we wanted, and it simply happened to be the same thing at the same time. Keith's father was a sheriff, and he took Keith's level of "street smarts" completely off the charts. Keith had a police scanner in his car, and we would check out the latest crime scenes while it was still happening. Keith would rather follow that fucking scanner than get laid, which is where we parted ways. Keith dated and married *Mary* who became a dear friend as well. If central casting asked me to send over a sweet, sincere southern bell, I would send Mary right over. You couldn't help but smile at her since she was always smiling at you. Their hospitality and friendship cannot be equaled or rivaled. Keith would give you his last few dollars and the keys to his car if you needed them, but if you had ideas of taking advantage of him, he would know it before you did. Keith saved me many times from doing something stupid by saying, "You might wanna hold back onnat." Thank you, Keith and Mary, I love you both.

Clearly, this next person needs no introduction. *Brian*, you taught me about comedy both on the air and on stage, and I simply followed your lead. Without you, the smiles and laughter we brought to millions would've been muted, like someone turning down the volume on their radio dial. Together, we cranked it up full blast, and did it *our* way. It was a joy and pleasure to work alongside you those many years. I'm reminded of a famous line from a famous film, so "sit back, relax *and* enjoy . . . miniature theater." Imagine, Brian, if you will, that I'm Tom Cruise and you're Renee Zellweger. I walk into a living room with you and several of our long-time listeners and say, "You complete me . . . " but you interrupt with, "Stop . . . you had me at Hooty Hoo!!!" Yes, I went there . . .

Finally, to our *listeners*, thank you for tuning in and joining us for all our stupid crap . . . *love you!*

No individual on this earth becomes whoever they are without the help and kindness of the people around them. A gesture of kindness or a helping hand along the way means so much. Thank you, all. You made the ride better for me.

Made in the USA
Las Vegas, NV
17 December 2022

63092253R00160